T0227880

Ethics and the Internal Auditor's Political Dilemma

Tools and Techniques to Evaluate a Company's Ethical Culture

Internal Audit and IT Audit

Series Editor: Dan Swanson

A Guide to the National Initiative for Cybersecurity Education (NICE) Cybersecurity Workforce Framework (2.0)
Dan Shoemaker, Anne Kohnke, and Ken Sigler
ISBN 978-1-4987-3996-2

A Practical Guide to Performing Fraud Risk Assessments
Mary Breslin
ISBN 978-1-4987-4251-1

Corporate Defense and the Value Preservation Imperative: Bulletproof Your Corporate Defense Program
Sean Lyons
ISBN 978-1-4987-4228-3

Data Analytics for Internal Auditors
Richard E. Cascarino
ISBN 978-1-4987-3714-2

Fighting Corruption in a Global Marketplace: How Culture, Geography, Language and Economics Impact Audit and Fraud Investigations around the World
Mary Breslin
ISBN 978-1-4987-3733-3

Investigations and the CAE: The Design and Maintenance of an Investigative Function within Internal Audit
Kevin L. Sisemore
ISBN 978-1-4987-4411-9

Internal Audit Practice from A to Z
Patrick Onwura Nzechukwu
ISBN 978-1-4987-4205-4

Leading the Internal Audit Function
Lynn Fountain
ISBN 978-1-4987-3042-6

Mastering the Five Tiers of Audit Competency: The Essence of Effective Auditing
Ann Butera
ISBN 978-1-4987-3849-1

Operational Assessment of IT
Steve Katzman
ISBN 978-1-4987-3768-5

Operational Auditing: Principles and Techniques for a Changing World
Hernan Murdock
ISBN 978-1-4987-4639-7

Securing an IT Organization through Governance, Risk Management, and Audit
Ken E. Sigler and James L. Rainey, III
ISBN 978-1-4987-3731-9

Security and Auditing of Smart Devices: Managing Proliferation of Confidential Data on Corporate and BYOD Devices
Sajay Rai and Philip Chuckwuma
ISBN 9781498738835

Software Quality Assurance: Integrating Testing, Security, and Audit
Abu Sayed Mahfuz
ISBN 978-1-4987-3553-7

The Complete Guide to Cybersecurity Risks and Controls
Anne Kohnke, Dan Shoemaker, and Ken E. Sigler
ISBN 978-1-4987-4054-8

Tracking the Digital Footprint of Breaches
James Bone
ISBN 978-1-4987-4981-7

Ethics and the Internal Auditor's Political Dilemma

Tools and Techniques to Evaluate a Company's Ethical Culture

Lynn Fountain, CRMA, CGMA

CRC Press
Taylor & Francis Group
Boca Raton London New York

CRC Press is an imprint of the
Taylor & Francis Group, an **informa** business
AN AUERBACH BOOK

CRC Press
Taylor & Francis Group
6000 Broken Sound Parkway NW, Suite 300
Boca Raton, FL 33487-2742

First issued in hardback 2017

Version Date: 20161102

ISBN-13: 978-1-4987-6780-4 (pbk)
ISBN-13: 978-1-138-43681-7 (hbk)

Visit the Taylor & Francis Web site at
http://www.taylorandfrancis.com

and the CRC Press Web site at
http://www.crcpress.com

Contents

PREFACE   xv

AUTHOR   xix

CHAPTER 1   INTRODUCTION   1
            Learning Ethics as a Child   1
            Section 1: How Ethical Are You?   2
                Drawing the Ethical Line   3
                    How Ethical Are You? Scenario One   3
                    How Ethical Are You? Scenario Two   4
                    How Ethical Are You? Scenario Three   4
                    How Ethical Are You? Scenario Four   4
                    How Ethical Are You? Scenario Five   5
                Conclusion   5
            Section 2: Analysis of High Profile Cases   22
                Example 1: Analysis of Adelphia Communications   22
                    Adelphia - Lessons Learned from a Family Business   22
                    Adelphia - Lessons Learned from Lack of Oversight   23
                    Adelphia - Lessons Learned from Lack of Independence   23
                    Adelphia Summary   23
                Example 2: Analysis of Western Resources, David Wittig   24
                    David Wittig - How Could This Happen?   24
                    David Wittig - Lessons Learned from Executive
                    Spending Habits   24
                    David Wittig - Lessons Learned from Responsibility
                    for Reporting   25
                Example 3: Analysis of Bernie Madoff   26

Bernie Madoff - Lessons Learned from Personality   26
Bernie Madoff - Lessons Learned When Things
Appear Too Good to Be True   26
Bernie Madoff - Lessons Learned from Relying on
One Investor   27
Section 3: Why Do Issues Continue to Evolve?   27
Section 4: A Company's Moral Compass, and Who Is Responsible? 33
Establishing a Strong Moral Compass   34
Can Moral Compass Be Audited?   35
Leadership and Moral Compass   36
Section 5: The International Professional Practices
Framework Standards for Ethics for Internal Auditors   38
Integrity   39
Objectivity   40
Confidentiality   41
Competency   41
Rules of Conduct: Integrity   42
Rules of Conduct: Objectivity   43
Rules of Conduct: Confidentiality   44
Rules of Conduct: Competency   45
The Realities of How Internal Auditors Can Work with
Ethical Concepts   46
Summary   48

CHAPTER 2   PRINCIPLES THAT IMPACT ETHICAL BELIEFS
             AND ETHICAL CULTURE   49
Section 1: Psychology of Ethics and Impact on Work Culture 49
Section 2: Theories behind Ethics and Ethical Principles   51
Introduction   51
Ethical Principles and Ethical Theories   52
Philosophy 101: Introduction to Ethics   53
Ethical Theories   53
Meta-Ethics   54
Normative Ethics   55
Business (Virtue Ethics)   57
Business (Deontology Ethics)   59
Business Consequentialist Theories   60
Applied Ethics   66
Everyday Moral/Ethical Judgments   66
Summary   67
Section 3: University Organizational Theory and Behavior
Curriculum   68
Tricks of the Trade Scenario   70
Section 4: Understanding the Internal Auditors Code of
Ethics and Related Principles   72
Introduction   72

Internal Auditors Code of Ethics   72
Objectivity, Independence, and Assurance   73
Partial Definition of Internal Auditing   73
   Professional Skepticism Scenario   74
Internal Audit Definition   76
Partial Definition of Internal Audit   76
Code of Ethics: Principles   76
   Integrity   76
   Objectivity   77
   Confidentiality   77
   Competency   77
   Integrity Scenario   77
   Objectivity Scenario   79
   Confidentiality Scenario   80
   Competency Scenario   81
Section 5: Understanding the Internal Auditors Code of
Ethics and Rules of Conduct   82
   Rules of Conduct: Integrity   83
   Rules of Conduct Illegal Actions   86
   Rules of Conduct Legitimate and Ethical Objectives   86
   Rules of Conduct: Objectivity   86
   Accepting Gifts   87
      Rules of Conduct: Confidentiality   89
      Rules of Conduct: Competency   89
Section 6: Corporate Ethics in the Future—Could There Be
an App for That?   90
   Introduction   90
   Steps for Application   91
Section 7: Global, Diverse, and Expanding Workforce   92
   Introduction   92
   Diverse Workforce Scenario One   92
   Diverse Workforce Scenario Two   94
   Summary   98
Section 8: Internal Auditors Working with Diverse
Cultures and Beliefs   99
   Introduction   99
   Respect Scenario   100
   Summary   102

CHAPTER 3 ESTABLISHING AN ETHICAL CULTURE AND THE
CONNECTION TO COSO 2013   103
Section 1: Committee of Sponsoring Organizations
(COSO) 2013 Control Environment Principles and
Corporate Ethical Culture   103
   Introduction   103
   The Updated COSO Framework   105

Section 2: COSO Principles One and Two: Demonstrates
Commitment to Integrity and Ethical Values and Ensures
the Board Exercises Oversight Authority   107
   Introduction   107
   Scenario One: Board Composition   109
   Scenario Two: Internal Audit Oversight   109
   Scenario Three: Audit Committee Communication   109
   Scenario Four: CAE Selection   110
   Scenario Analysis   111
Section 3: COSO Principle Three—The Organization
Establishes Structures, Reporting Lines, Authorities, and
Responsibilities   113
   Introduction   113
   Downsizing Scenario   114
Section 4: COSO Principle Four—Commitment to
Competence   114
   Introduction   114
   Executing Commitment to Competence   115
Section 5: COSO Principle Five—Individuals Are Held
Accountable for Their Internal Control Responsibilities   116
   Introduction   116
     Scenario One: Internal Control   117
     Scenario Two: The New CFO and CAE   119
     Scenario Three: ABC Consulting Company   121
   Summary   123
Section 6: Organizational Requirements to Align with the
New COSO Framework and Ethical Principles   123
   Introduction   123
   Principle Mapping Process   124
   Considerations When Examining COSO Alignment   125
Section 7: Nontransition to COSO 2013 and Implications
to the Ethical Culture   126
   Introduction   126
   Challenges in Evaluating Ethical Culture   127
Section 8: Internal Audit's Role in the Evolution of Ethics
in the Corporate Culture   128
   Introduction   128
   Internal Audit's Role in Ethics   128
     Scenario One: Internal Audit and Evolution of Ethics   129
Section 9: Dissecting Ethics   132
   Introduction   132
     Everyone Is Responsible   132
     Tone at the Top   133
     Honesty   133
     Integrity   134
     Corporate Social Responsibility   135

    Silence Is Not Acceptable   136
Summary   136

CHAPTER 4   METHODS FOR IDENTIFYING AND MEASURING
    ETHICAL BEHAVIOR   137
Introduction   137
Section 1: Moving Past Surveys, Questionnaires, and
Interviews   139
    Introduction   139
    Critique with Etiquette   139
        Use Your Words   142
        Be Specific   142
        Avoid Personal References   142
        Consider What Information Is Important to Improve
        the Process   143
        Provide Respondents with Instructions   143
        Consider Gathering Demographic Information   144
        Carefully Consider Questions for the Survey   144
        Provide Guidance for Comments   144
Section 2: Assessing Effectiveness of a Survey or Interview   145
    Introduction   145
    Utilizing Questionnaires to Evaluate Ethical Culture   146
        The Company Has a Code of Conduct   146
        The Company's Code of Conduct is Effective   147
    Interviewing   147
Section 3: Effective Survey Techniques   148
    Introduction   148
    Developing Surveys   148
    Step One: Developing Surveys Clarify the Objectives of
    the Survey   148
    Step Two: Communicate Survey Purpose   150
    Step Three: Gather Logistical Information   150
    Step Four: Determine Requirement for Anonymity   150
    Step Five: Survey Distribution   151
        Online Surveys   151
        One-on-One Surveys   152
    Step Six: Test the Survey   152
    Step Seven: Analyze Results   152
Section 4: Effective Interview Techniques   153
    Introduction   153
    Interview Techniques   153
        Step One: Effectively Plan the Interview   154
        Step Two: Building Rapport   154
        Step Three: Control the Interview   154
        Step Four: Don't Overanalyze   155
        Step Five: Listen   155

Section 5: The Impact of Perception on Ethical Culture   156
Introduction   156
Ethical Scenario One Perception   156
Ethical Scenario Two Perception   156
Ethics Examination and Obtaining Management and
Board Acceptance   157
Section 6: Utilizing a Maturity Model Approach   159
Introduction   159
Building the Approach   160
Maturity Model Development   161
Step 1: Identifying Attributes   161
Step 2: Subject Matter Experts   162
Step 3: Defining Stages   162
Step 4: Customizing the Matrix   162
Step 5: Determine the Naming Convention for Stages   163
Step 6: Establish the Assessment Process   166
Step 7: Execute the Assessment Process   168
Step 8: Utilizing the Output   169
Summary   169

CHAPTER 5   ETHICAL SCENARIOS AND POSSIBLE
ALTERNATIVE SOLUTIONS FOR THE INTERNAL
AUDITOR   171
Introduction   171
Section 1: Sports and Ethics   171
Introduction   171
Sporting Scandals   173
The New Orleans Saints "Bounty"   173
Michael Vick Dogfighting Scandal   174
Ray Rice - Physical Abuse   175
Pete Rose Betting Scandal   175
Sports Scandal Analysis   175
Section 2: Internal Auditors and Ethics   176
Introduction   177
Internal Pressure   177
Section 3: Ethical Scenarios   178
Introduction   179
Scenario One: The Audit Assignment Conflict of
Interest   179
Scenario Two: Management Pressure and Influence   180
Scenario Three: Revenue Recognition   183
Scenario Four: Management Incentives   185
Scenario Five: Audit Report Issuance   187
Scenario Six: The Procurement Audit   189
Scenario Seven: The Staff Auditor's Predicament   192
Scenario Eight: The Bank's Loan Review Audit   193

Scenario Nine: You Must Agree with Your Boss   194
Scenario Ten: Is it Legal, or is it Ethical?   196
Summary   197

CHAPTER 6   REPORTING RESULTS OF ETHICAL
              EVALUATIONS: THE TURNING POINT   199
Section 1: Dissecting Corporate Values   199
Introduction   199
Integrity   199
Scenario One: Integrity in Everyday Actions   200
Scenario Two: Integrity in Business   200
Corporate Social Responsibility   202
Scenario One: The Professional Sports Team   202
Scenario Two: The Oil Company   204
Scenario Three: The Food Company   206
Honesty   207
Loyalty and Respect   208
Scenario One: Personal Respect   208
Summary   209
Section 2: Ethics and the Control Environment   209
Introduction   209
Evaluating the Control Environment   209
Measuring Tone at the Top   212
Scenario One: ABC Company Authorization Policy   212
Evaluating Management Philosophy and Operating Style   214
Scenario One: SOX 302 Attestation   214
Evaluating Segregation of Duties   216
Summary   217
Section 3: Corporate Director's Ethical Fiduciary Duty   217
Introduction   217
Evaluating Board Composition   218
How Were Board Members Selected?   218
Have the Composition and Charters of Board
Committee's been Compared to Exchange Listing
Requirements?   219
What Is the Acceptable Practice of Board
Communication with Individuals Outside Senior
Management?   220
Does the Board Have Input into Corporate Strategy?   220
What Is the Board's Role in Understanding Fraud
Investigations, Whistleblower Issues, and Corporate
Misconduct?   221
Does the Board Have Input into Performance
Appraisals of Executives?   222
How Is the Evaluation of the Board of Directors
Conducted?   223

How Does the Board Respond to Identification of
Internal Control Issues?   225
Section 4: Reporting Ethical Issues   226
Introduction   226
Employee Hotlines   226
Lessons Learned   227
Section 5: Protocols for Reporting Ethical Issues—The
Whistleblower Hotline   228
Introduction   228
Whistleblower Procedures   228
Corporate Hotline History and Procedures   229
Company Program Assessment   230
Board Program Assessment   232
Summary   233
Section 6: Communicating with Management and the
Audit Committee   233
Introduction   233
Handling Everyday Ethical Issues   233
Summary   239
Section 7: Developing Action Plans to Address Identified
Ethical Issue Gaps   240
Introduction   240
Framework Action Plan   240
Issue Evaluation   240
Examination and Investigation   241
Issue Reporting   242
Issue Remediation   242
Summary   243

CHAPTER 7   CORPORATE ETHICAL CULTURE IN THE FUTURE   245
Introduction   245
Section 1: Social Media and Technology Advances   246
Ethics and Social Media Policies   249
Internet Usage Policies   251
Social Media Sites and the Hiring Process   252
Using Information on Social Media   253
Section 2: Ethics and the Generations   254
Introduction   254
Baby Boomer I   254
Baby Boomers II   255
Generation X   257
Gen Y (millennials)   258
Gen Z   258
Combination of Generations   258
Scenario One: Work Atmosphere   259
Summary   263
Section 3: Ethics and Business Globalization   263

Scenario One: Globalization of Business and Ethics 264
Scenario One: Alternatives 265
Section 4: Internal Audit's Ethical Role in the Future 266
The Final Word 267

INDEX 269

Preface

Charles Dickens' famous quote sums up many of the issues that have impacted corporate ethics. The quote can be representative of many of the corporate scandals, failures, and ethical incidents that have occurred since 2000.

It was the best of times, it was the worst of times, it was the age of wisdom, it was the age of foolishness, it was the epoch of belief, it was the epoch of incredulity, it was the season of Light, it was the season of Darkness, it was the spring of hope, it was the winter of despair, we had everything before us, we had nothing before us.

Charles Dickens
A Tale of Two Cities

Reflect on the following parts of the quote from Charles Dickens. Consider the corollary drawn at the end of the quote.

It was the best of times, it was the worst of times—The Enron crisis.

It was the age of wisdom; it was the age of foolishness—WorldCom and TyCo debacle.

It was the epoch of belief; it was the epoch of incredulity—Arthur Andersen failure.

It was the season of Light, it was the season of Darkness—Housing and mortgage crisis.

It was the spring of hope; it was the winter of despair—Bernie Madoff Ponzi scheme.

We had everything before us, we had nothing before us—The current standing of today's business economy.

The corollaries drawn with the Charles Dickens quote seem to point to the fact that corporate America continues to struggle with the concept of business ethics. You may be thinking to yourself— not another book on ethics? Haven't we had enough of that topic? What else is there to review, study, or learn? Well, obviously there is a lot, since ethical incidents continue to impact our daily lives. If only things were as simple as when we were children and told,

You better watch out, you better not cry, you better not pout I'm telling you why

Of course, that little jingle was to attempt to convince children to behave so Santa Claus would be sure to gift them with precious toys. What is so different about the behavior traits that we are taught as children and those we end up exhibiting as adults? If there was a magic answer or formula, we would assume someone would be really rich by now!

Ethical issues stretch back as far as the imagination can reach. They relate to issues that have occurred in politics, corporate America, sports, school and even the government. In the early days, ethical scandals may have been considered as instances where a famous figure committed infidelities. But in the new world, ethical concepts stretch far past misdeeds of a personal nature.

In the business world, ethics continues to come to the forefront of corporate, shareholder, stakeholder, and regulatory conversations. Companies continue to look for ways to emphasize the importance of strong ethics, integrity, and proper behavior and find ways to embed processes within their organizational structure. But, as we know, incidents still occur. It is an ever evolving phenomenon. Once we find the answer to address a specific issue, another question or problem arises.

Ethics impacts every professional's job regardless of job status, tenure, or selected profession. For internal auditors, ethics can become a very sensitive issue and political dilemma when attempting to execute their responsibilities and fiduciary duty. This is because auditors are often put in positions where they must make difficult and uncomfortable inquiries. This can appear to management as an attack on personal integrity or on personal morals and ethics.

As a longtime internal auditor and a past chief audit executive (CAE), I have dealt with my own challenges related to ethical questions. The answers are never the same, and I've found that sometimes people revert to their own personal morals when attempting to resolve a situation. This is what makes the topic such a dilemma. Each and every individual may have very different thresholds when it comes to defining where they believe the ethical white line, gray line, or black line stand. The more we learn and understand why individuals do the things they do and how personal beliefs and morals mix into decisions, the better equipped we will be when faced with issues.

Concepts included in this book are taken from a combination of ethical issues submitted by internal auditors and CAEs along with information obtained during the 2012–2014 E-workshop that this author facilitated for the Institute of Internal Auditors (IIA). The workshop was titled "Ethics and The Internal Auditor's Dilemma." During these workshops, guest CAEs discussed their own personal challenges when faced with ethical decisions that could ultimately impact not only the outcome of an audit but their own personal reputation. The book will serve as a guide for auditors when faced with ethical questions where it may seem that there is no single, absolutely correct and political proper answer.

As you read through the various chapters and consider the concepts and alternatives outlined, you may or may not agree with the scenario and information presented. You may feel as if the scenario or information is very simple, and the answer is black and white. Keep in mind, as we will discuss throughout this book, not all individuals think alike. This isn't a simple math problem. One plus one may not always equal two. The examples, alternatives, and concepts are outlined to assist you, as the reader, to take time to peer outside your own moral and ethical box. Take time to examine moral concepts from a different viewpoint and consider how they may mesh into your current organizational culture. The information outlined is meant to help you evaluate how others may be viewing the particular situation. This is what makes the concept of ethics so interesting. There may not always be one correct answer. If you find yourself reading the scenario or the information and disagreeing with the manner in which it is outlined, that is absolutely fine. But challenge yourself to ask "why" you believe the information as outlined is wrong in your own mind. This may help you better understand how other individuals may see the situation.

Author

Lynn Fountain has over 35 years of experience spanning public accounting, corporate accounting and consulting. Twenty years of her experience has been working in the areas of internal and external auditing. She is a subject matter expert in multiple fields including internal audit, ethics, fraud evaluations, Sarbanes–Oxley, enterprise risk management, governance, financial management and compliance and she has held two chief audit executive (CAE) positions for international companies. In one of her roles as CAE, she assisted in the investigation of a multimillion-dollar fraud scheme perpetrated by a vendor that spanned seven years and implicated 20 employees. The fraud was formally investigated by the Federal Bureau of Investigation (FBI) and resulted in five indictments representing a $13 million fraud loss.

Ms. Fountain is currently engaged in her own consulting and training practice. Her consulting extends from enterprise risk management, business efficiency, internal audit, accounting and interim chief financial officer (CFO) services. She has also trained internationally. In addition to her personal training, she also serves as a discussion leader for numerous courses offered by the American Institute of Certified Public Accountants (AICPA). Topics include fraud and forensic courses for both profit and not-for-profit, internal controls for large and small entities, Committee of Sponsoring Organizations of the Treadway Commission (COSO) 2013, ethics, and risk management and various leadership courses.

Ms. Fountain is the author of two separate technical books published in 2015, The first, entitled *Raise the Red Flag – The Internal Auditors Guide to Fraud Evaluations*, was published by the Institute of Internal Auditors Research Foundation and published in April 2015. Her second book, *Leading The Internal Audit Function*, was published in October 2015 by Taylor & Francis. This book serves as the initial launch for a series of leading practice internal audit and information technology publications and is her third formal publication.

Ms. Fountain obtained her BSBA from Pittsburg State University, Pittsburg, Kansas, and her MBA from Washburn University, Topeka, Kansas. She has her CGMA, CRMA credentials and CPA certificate.

1

INTRODUCTION

Learning Ethics as a Child

During my childhood years, my parents instilled the concepts that lying, cheating, stealing, being rude to others, telling untruths to get ahead, and backstabbing were all inappropriate behaviors. Once I reached adulthood and entered the working world in the early 1980s, I was surprised that in some business situations, ethical conduct often seemed questionable. Of course, this was many years ago, and the dynamics of the workforce and how professionals act have dramatically changed.

As a young female professional entering the workforce in 1980, it was difficult not to speak my mind when it came to issues I felt were personally inappropriate. These issues extended from sexual harassment to inappropriate work requests and even inappropriate treatment by superiors. Luckily, the world has changed since then, and many of the difficulties faced in the 1980s are no longer accepted.

Even though times have changed and ethical conduct is now a significant focus, in many aspects of our daily lives it is surprising how often issues continue to occur. During a recent interview with a public accounting firm, one of the lawyers actually inquired when I planned to retire. Do you view that as an inappropriate or potentially unethical question? I was surprised that anyone would make this type of inquiry, let alone a lawyer. My surprise may have been associated with the fact that I am considered a baby boomer and thus classified as an older-generation worker. Age bias appears to be a reality when trying to identify a new position. How do you properly respond to an inquiry such as this? Had I said "It is none of your business!," obviously the interview would have quickly come to an end. Had I responded "I had not considered when I might retire," again, the interview may have come to a stop. So, my response was that I enjoyed working and had no immediate thoughts of retirement. That may have been the most

Children and ethics

politically correct answer, but I left the interview questioning whether the firm was one that I would even wish to work for. To me, the gentleman had crossed a very sensitive personal and politically ethical line. It was like asking "How old are you?" rather than "What can you contribute to our organization?"

Ethical conduct is correlated to an individual's personal morals, values, and how he or she thinks. With all the people in the world and the varying personalities, the topic of proper ethical conduct will always be one that is debated and discussed. Think about this concept and reflect on the people you work or associate with in a professional organization. You most likely grew up in a different family environment, you may have been reared in a different town, you probably have varying religious beliefs, you may likely come from different generations (which also have their individual idiosyncrasies), and you may vary in gender. Each of these factors shape our personal moral and value system.

Section 1: How Ethical Are You?

Got ethics?

There is a quote by Sallie Krawcheck from Corporate Bytes that states,

> When it comes down to ethics versus a job, choose ethics. You can always find another job.

I agree with this statement. I also believe individuals should be prepared for what may come when they stand by their ethics and morals, but others don't follow the company line or the expected approach. The part of the quote indicating "You can always find another job" may be questionable in today's economy. Professionals must be prepared to understand that the "other job" may be in a different field or require different talents. You cannot assume that you will be able to easily replace your current job from the aspects of income, responsibility, and satisfaction.

Internal auditors are faced with this dilemma all the time. The most recent studies continue to indicate that auditors are always under pressure by management to reword findings or eliminate observations. In some cases, the issue may not breach any ethical concepts. In other cases, it may. Until internal auditors can stand true to their ethics and morals and stand up to management with regard to the issues at hand, auditors will continue to face difficulties in the ethical arena.

The lesson learned by some individuals who may take the leap and stand their ground when it comes to a difficult ethical decision may sometimes be hard to swallow. They may find themselves in a predicament where they cannot find another job in the same field. But, what would you rather do—compromise your ethics, or work for a company who forced you to compromise your ethics?

Drawing the Ethical Line

Where do you draw your own ethical line? Does it depend on the circumstance of the issue or possibly the individuals involved in the particular issue? Does it depend on your perception of whether you will get caught in a lie? The following narrative outlines a few typical ethical scenarios. As you read each scenario, ask yourself how you would react in the situation. This will begin to help you understand your own personal moral compass.

How Ethical Are You? Scenario One You are in the checkout line at a grocery store. The gentleman in front of you has been arguing with the clerk about various items. The discussions further delay the checkout process. The man finally reaches into his wallet to pay the clerk in cash. As he pulls out his wallet, a $50 bill drops directly into your cart. No one else notices. What would you do?

How Ethical Are You? Scenario Two   Again, you are at a grocery store, and the clerk is extremely slow. You are in a hurry. When you finally reach the front of the checkout line, you pay your bill with cash. The clerk has been very talkative and mistakenly hands you change for a $50 bill rather than the $20 bill you gave him. Would you say or do anything to alert the clerk of his error?

These are minor everyday events, so let's try a few scenarios that an internal auditor may face.

How Ethical Are You? Scenario Three   You are a senior auditor in your department. You have developed a very close relationship with several of the staff auditors. You have favorite staff you prefer to work with. Your chief audit executive (CAE) assigns you a new audit. He assigns a young senior male auditor and a young senior female auditor to assist. The review will require significant travel. Both you and the male auditor like to spend evenings at bars. The female auditor prefers not to engage in this activity. As such, you feel she would not be a good fit for the audit team. You tell the CAE you do not believe she has the right background and training beneficial to the assigned audit (even though she does). The CAE questions your judgment, but you continually press for someone else to be assigned. In the meantime, the female auditor has become aware of the issue. She would like to participate on the audit due to the recognition and experience it may provide her. She feels the comments made by the senior auditor to the CAE are disrespectful. As the CAE, what should you do? As the female senior auditor, what should you do? Does the senior auditor's actions represent any type of discrimination?

How Ethical Are You? Scenario Four   You are the CAE and report directly to the chief financial officer (CFO). You work for a nonpublicly traded company. The CFO informs you it is not acceptable to issue internal audit reports unless he has reviewed and approved the report and its content. In addition, you have been informed that you are not allowed to speak to the audit committee unless the communication is preapproved by the CFO. You explain the Institute of Internal Auditors

(IAA) *Standards* to the CFO, but the response you receive is that the company believes the *Standards* are simply guidelines and not requirements of the profession. You are fully aware that if you ignore the CFO's direction, you will be fired. Although you understand your fiduciary obligations to the audit committee, because of several personal financial obligations and the need to keep your job, you choose to abide by the CFO's demands. Have you compromised your ethics?

How Ethical Are You? Scenario Five You are the CAE of a publicly traded company. The company has a trusted long-term joint-venture partner. One of the senior executives of the joint-venture partner is a distant relative. This relationship has not been previously disclosed because your company does not execute regular conflict of interest statements.

The company receives a complaint about the joint-venture partner, and your department is asked to perform a review. Since your personal relationship is long distance and you have infrequent contact with your relative, you conclude it is not a conflict of interest to work on the review. You do not inform anyone of your relationship with the senior executive of the joint-venture partner.

The audit reveals many abnormalities that should be reported to your company's management. Prior to issuance of the report, you receive a call from "Aunt Jane" (who is the mother of the relative). She provides several reasons why issues identified during the audit occurred. She asks you not to disclose the issues. You listen to her comments, perform some independent follow-up and personally determine that the issues are not reportable. Were there any ethical breaches in this scenario?

Conclusion

For many individuals reading these scenarios, you may feel the answers are obvious. However, remember you are not the person actually in the situation. Each scenario is true, and in each case the person did what most of us would categorize as the unethical choice. Why would this happen? There are a multitude of reasons including personal opinion, a person's stature within the company, personal financial considerations, rationalization, and personal tolerance related to the issue. These scenarios are good examples of why professionals should study and understand the dynamics involved in corporate culture and ethical decision making.

The next section of this chapter will review a time line associated with certain high profile corporate ethical issues that have occurred since 2000 (Exhibit 1.1). This time line and the related incidents will assist in understanding how ethics continues to evolve and how it is affected by many variables associated with corporate America.

To effectively understand the impact of ethics on business and to identify methods to mitigate future ethical issues, it is helpful to analyze and evaluate incidents of the past and determine why they

2000–2005	2005–2010	2011–2015
Corporate scandals	**Corporate scandals**	**Corporate scandals**
• Enron (2000–2002)	• Deutche Bank Spying (2006)	• Southwest Airlines (2011)
• SwissAir (2001)	• HP Spying (2006)	• Volkswagen 2008–2015
• HIH Insurance (2001)	• Bristol Myers Squibb (2006)	• Barclays Libor (2012)
• Arthur Andersen (2002)	• Options Backdating (2006)	• Wal-Mart (2012)
• WorldCom (2002)	• British Petroleum CEO (2007)	• Dynegy (2012)
• Tyco (2002)	• Quest (2007)	• Capital One (2012)
• RiteAide (2002)	• Starwood Hotels, CEO (2007)	• Peregrine Financial Group
• Aldelphia (2002)	• Lehman Brothers (2008)	• Glaxo Smith Kline bribery (2013)
• Martha Stewart (2002)	• Bernie Madoff (2008)	• Tesco Accounting (2014)
• HealthSouth (2003)	• Bear Sterns (2008)	• Olympus (2014)
• Conrad Black/Hollinger Enterprises (2003)	• Siemens (2008)	• Penn West accounting irregularities (2014)
• David Wittig (2003)	• Satyam (2009)	• The Snappening (2014)
• Wal-Mart (2004)	• Hewlett-Packard (2010)	• American Apparel CEO (2014)
• AIG (2005)	• Lehman Brothers Repo (105–2010)	• Sony Hack (2014)
	• BP Oil Spill (2010)	• Vatican Bank Scandal (2014)
Government scandals	• Foreclosure Gate	
• Freddie Mac (2003)		**Government scandals**
• Fannie May (2003)	**Government scandals**	• Edward Snowden and NSA leaks (2013)
• Parmalat (2003)	• Jack Abramoff (2006)	• Healthcare.gov (2013)
	• WalterReed Medical Neglect (2007)	• Representative Dennis Hastert
Sport scandals	• Representative W. Jefferson (2007)	
• MN Vikings Party Boat (2005)		
	Sport scandals	
	• NFL Player conduct controversy (2007-present)	
	• Duke LaCrosse rape allegations (2006)	
	• NE Patriots Spy Gate (2007)	
	• Penn State child sex scandal (2011)	
	• Lance Armstrong doping (2012)	
	• New Orleans Saints bounty scandal (2012)	
	• Deflate Gate (2015)	
	• FIFA corruption case (2015)	

Exhibit 1.1   Timeline of ethical issues and reaction by corporate America.

may have occurred. Just like studying history in school, lessons of the past may teach us actions for the future (as long as we listen). Any action that involves more than two individuals will create dynamics that may not always be easily controlled. Yet, it is still important to evaluate past ethical incidents to attempt to identify procedures, processes, or actions organizations can take to minimize incidents in the future.

The most famous ethical and fraudulent incident that has occurred in recent years is the Enron scandal. The issues faced by Enron were revealed in October 2001 and eventually led to the company's bankruptcy and the de facto dissolution of the public accounting firm Arthur Andersen. The incident along with other high-profile corporate scandals perpetuated the passing of the Sarbanes–Oxley (SOX) legislation in 2002. From a business perspective, the ensuing impact on corporate America to comply with the many aspects of the SOX legislation should, in theory, have resulted in a strong decline in the ethical and fraudulent issues that later would occur in business. However, reviewing our time line of ethical issues outlined in Exhibit 1.1, you may come to the conclusion that the legislation did not have as great an impact as intended.

Although there are many advantages that have resulted from the work attributed to SOX compliance, ethical incidents continue to occur. It is clear even with all the work companies have dedicated to transparent financial reporting, ethical issues continue on various levels. Take a minute and review the information presented in Exhibit 1.1. You may find it surprising the number of issues that continue to impact our business culture. The question is, why? It is not as if the issues have passed by without some type of recognition by the public. In addition, many of the issues have resulted in additional legislation or guidelines targeted at the industries the issue may have impacted. Some of the major corporate ethical or fraudulent scandals since 2000 are further detailed in Exhibit 1.2. This illustration outlines the facts behind the particular incident as well as outcomes and ramifications. Also listed is the impetus of any legislation the issue caused. It can be exhausting to review this list and relive the many issues that have occurred because of unethical individuals.

As you review the illustration, you may ask:

How can corporate America possibly continue to experience this level of unethical behavior and the subsequent consequences? Have we not learned that if we do not regulate our own actions, Congress will legislate some new mandate in an attempt to bring the 'heavens' back to alignment?

Prior to continuing with this chapter's readings, take a moment to review and understand Exhibit 1.2. The information presented in this exhibit is detailed. The purpose for careful review is to provide you as the reader a sense of the psychology behind why many issues have occurred. After you have reviewed Exhibit 1.2 in detail, come back to this section, and we will take a few of the publicized incidents and analyze some of the facts behind the issues that allowed the scandal to reach the level of concern publicized.

Scandal Explanations

Enron Scandal (2000–2002)

Company: Houston-based commodities, energy and service corporation.

What happened: Shareholders lost $74 billion, thousands of employees and investors lost their retirement accounts, and many employees lost their jobs.

Main players: CEO Jeffrey Skilling, former CEO Ken Lay, CFO Andy Fastow.

How they did it: Special purpose entities and keeping huge debts off balance sheets.

How they got caught: Initially turned in by internal whistleblower Sherron Watkins; high stock prices fueled external suspicions.

- Between 1998 and 2001, Lay received $300 million from the sale of Enron stock options and restricted stock, netting a profit of more than $217 million. He was also paid $19 million in salary and bonuses.
- Skilling, denied any wrongdoing. He was charged with 42 counts that included insider trading and securities fraud. The deals netted him $62.6 million from stock sold between April 2000 and September 2001.
- The company filed for bankruptcy.

Interesting fact: *Fortune Magazine* named Enron "America's Most Innovative Company" six years in a row prior to the scandal.

Outcome: The scandal and its outcomes were a major impetus for the Sarbanes–Oxley legislation.

- Jeffrey Skilling was sentenced to 24 years in prison. In 2013 his sentence was reduced to 13 years and he will leave prison in 2020.
- Ken Lay died before serving time.

Exhibit 1.2   Scandal explanations.

- Andy Fastow spent five years in prison and was released. He is now working as a document review clerk for the Houston law firm that represented him in civil cases over the last decade.
- Richard Causey, Enron's chief accounting officer, was released in 2011 after serving more than five years in prison following a guilty plea.
- Arthur Andersen was found guilty of fudging Enron's accounts and was later dissolved as an organization.

SwissAir Scandal 2001

Company: SwissAir (2001) (the national airline for Switzerland for many years).

What happened: Overexpansion in the 1990s and the economic downturn following the September 11 terrorist attacks contributed to SwissAir's lost asset value. The airline was grounded in October 2000. It was kept alive until March 2002 by the Swiss Federal government. On October 2, 2001, Switzerland's national carrier SwissAir halted all its flights due to a severe cash shortage.

How they got caught: Intensive negotiations took place with SwissAir's main creditor banks regarding further credits and the reorganizations of SwissAir.

- The airline was almost bankrupt on September 26, 2001, after several smaller banks cut their lines of credit, leaving only $61 to $122 million in liquid assets.
- Through negotiations it was agreed the banks would purchase a $160 million share in Crossair and give SwissAir an interim credit of $154 million to guarantee flights until October 3, 2001.

Outcome: The contract signing and the transfer of funds was delayed. The delay caused SwissAir to ground all its flights.

- The company did not have the money to pay for fuel and airport taxes. It had to declare bankruptcy.
- In 2007, several SwissAir board members and executives were charged over the airline's bankruptcy. There were 19 defendants including: three former chief executives; leading bankers and consultants; current and former directors of national groups such as Credit Suisse, Nestle, UBS and Holcimare. Management realized the reductions in wages and layoffs necessary to restructure SwissAir could not be implemented without meeting considerable resistance.
- Government representatives made it clear their main concern was above all to "limit the damage to the country's image". Swiss ruling circles came to the conclusion they should follow the policy of cuts in social spending and wages long the norm in the United States.

WorldCom (2002)

Company: Telecommunications company; now MCI, Inc. WorldCom was the second largest U.S.-based telecommunications company until its downfall.

What happened: The company suffered a massive accounting scandal that led to filing for bankruptcy protection in 2002. The scandal included inflated assets by as much as $11 billion, leading to 30,000 lost jobs and $180 billion in losses for investors.

Exhibit 1.2 (Continued)

Main player: CEO Bernie Ebbers; CFO Scott Sullivan; Controller David Myers; Former Director of Accounting Buddy Yates; Former Director of Corporate Accounting Betty Vinson; Former Accountant Troy Norman; Arthur Andersen LLP.

How they did it: WorldCom made major accounting misstatements hiding the company's deteriorating financial condition. During the first quarter of 2002, the company counted as capital investments $3.8 billion that it spent on everyday expenses.

- More than $9 billion in false or unsupported accounting entries were made in WorldCom's financial systems in order to achieve desired reported financial results.

How they got caught: Through efforts of the internal audit department, WorldCom admitted to $3.85 billion in accounting misstatements (the figure eventually grew to $11 billion). The fraud involved claims that money spent on operating expenses was really spent on investments. The WorldCom issue pushed the need for Congress to escalate the Sarbanes-Oxley bill quickly through the house and the senate.

Interesting fact: The driving factor behind this fraud was the business strategy of WorldCom's CEO. In the 1990s, Ebbers was focused on achieving impressive growth through acquisitions.

Outcome: The instance helped inspire the most significant portions of the SOX legislation – Section 404. Sarbanes-Oxley is considered by far the most dramatic piece of legislation to impact Securities law since the Great Depression.

- Bernie Ebbers was charged with securities fraud and conspiracy and sentenced to serve 25 years at the Oakdale Federal Correctional Institution in Louisiana.
- Scott Sullivan was a star witness for the prosecution in the trial of Bernie Ebbers. He received five years in prison for his role in the scandal.
- David Myers and Buddy Yates were sentenced to one year and one day in prison. Betty Vinson was sentenced to five months in prison.
- Troy Normand received three years probation.
- The primary auditors Kenneth Avery and Melvin Dick of Arthur Andersen were accused of not exercising professional skepticism and due care in their 2001 audits of the company. Dick was barred from practicing accounting for four years and Avery was barred for three years.

Tyco Scandal (2002)

Company: New Jersey-based blue-chip Swiss security systems company.

What happened: CEO and CFO stole $150 million and inflated company income by $500 million. SEC and Manhattan district attorney investigations uncovered questionable accounting practices, including large loans made to the CEO that were then forgiven.

Main players: CEO Dennis Kozlowski and former CFO Mark Swartz.

How they did it: Siphoned money through unapproved loans and fraudulent stock sales. Money was smuggled out of company disguised as executive bonuses or benefits.

Exhibit 1.2 (Continued)

Interesting fact: Some contend that Kozlowski and Swartz should not have been convicted of the unauthorized compensation charges.

- The claim is based on the legal premise of *mens rea* referring to a person's state of mind. The principle indicates that in order for an individual to be convicted of a crime, the prosecution must provide, beyond a reasonable doubt, that the accused acted with some degree of criminal intent.
- The compensation went through proper channels of the organization's processes and the board and company was fully aware, it is believed Kozlowski and Swartz felt the compensation was appropriate.

Outcome: CEO Dennis Kozlowski and CFO Mark Swartz were convicted of a number of felony charges related to unauthorized compensation during the decade they led Tyco.

- In 2004, the State of New York paroled both after serving eight years and four months in prison.

Rite Aid (2002)

Company: A drugstore chain in the United States and a Fortune 500 company headquartered in Pennsylvania.

What happened: The SEC charged former CEO Martin Grass, former CFO Frank Bergonzi and former Vice Chairman Franklin Brown with conducting a wide-ranging accounting fraud scheme. The complaint alleged Rite Aid overstated income in every quarter from May 1997 to May 1999, by massive amounts. In March 1999, two weeks after the close of the fiscal year, Bergonzi directed that the books be re-opened to record an additional $33 million in credits.

Main players: CEO Martin Grass and former CFO Frank Bergonzi.

How it was discovered: Former President, Timothy Noonan, wore a hidden tape recorder for the FBI during a meeting with the CEO of Rite Aid. Noonan recorded Mr. Grass stating investigators would not find a machine suspected of being used to generate backdated letters. When the wrongdoing was discovered, Rite Aid was forced to restate its pre-tax income by $2.3 billion and net income by $1.6 billion, the largest restatement ever recorded. Accounting charges included:

- **Upcharges** – Company inflated deductions to vendors for damaged and outdated products;
- **Stock Appreciation Rights** – failed to record accrued expense for stock appreciation rights it granted to employees;
- **Reversals of Actual Expenses** – Bergonzi directed that Rite Aid's accounting staff reverse amounts that had been recorded for various expenses incurred and already paid;
- **Gross Profit Entries** – Improper adjusting entries to reduce cost of goods sold and accounts payable;
- **Undisclosed Markdowns** – Overstated net income by overcharging vendors for undisclosed markdowns on products;
- **Vendor Rebates** – In 1999, Bergonzi directed that Rite Aid record entries to reduce accounts payable and Cost of Goods Sold by $42 million to reflect rebates purportedly due from two vendors;

Exhibit 1.2 (Continued)

- **Dead Deal Expense** – The company routinely incurred expenses for services relating to sites considered but later rejected for new stores and capitalized these costs at the time they were incurred;
- **Will Call Payable**s – Received payment from insurance carriers for prescription orders phoned in by customers but never picked up from the store;
- **Related Party Transactions** – Grass's personal interest in three store locations leased as Rite Aid properties was not disclosed. Grass never disclosed an additional series of transactions in which he funneled $2.6 million from Rite Aid to a partnership he controlled.

Outcome: Q4 1999, Grass, Bergonzi, Brown caused Rite Aid to recognize $17 million litigation settlement. The recognition was improper because the settlement had not yet been consummated. Former CEO Grass was sentenced to eight years in prison, fined $500,000 and given three years' probation. A total of six former Rite Aid executives were convicted on charges.

Adelphia Communications (2002)

Company: In 1952, John Rigas and his brother Gus, founded Adelphia with the purchase of their first cable franchise in Coudersport, Pennsylvania. In 1986 the Rigas family took the company public and consolidated cable properties under Adelphia. In 1991, Adelphia Business solutions was established. In 1998 the company reached a customer base of over two million subscribers.

The players: In July 2002, The SEC filed charges against Adelphia Communications Corp.; its founder John Rigas; his three sons, and two senior executives at Adelphia.

What happened: SEC charged Adelphia fraudulently excluded billions of dollars in liabilities from its consolidated financial statements by hiding them on the books of off-balance sheet affiliates; falsified operations statistics and inflated earnings to meet Wall Street expectations; concealed rampant self-dealing by the Rigas Family, including the undisclosed use of corporate funds for Rigas Family stock purchases.

In addition, records showed:

- The Rigas family used Adelphia as collateral for private loans in 1996, kept hidden from investors.
- The family instructed accountants to inflate cable TV subscriptions to mislead investors.
- Subscriptions from customers coming from non-Adelphia transactions were counted as part of Adelphia's cable TV revenues, including those who placed orders for home security systems.
- The family splurged on expenses, including ventures into film making, estimated to reach $3 billion.
- Adelphia's funds were used to pay for timber rights allegedly worth $25 million, which the cable TV company later sold to the Rigas family for only $500,000. Cable TV funds were used to build a golf course for the Rigas family.

Exhibit 1.2 (Continued)

In its lawsuit the Commission alleged the defendants violated the antifraud, periodic reporting, record keeping, and internal controls provisions of the federal securities laws. In a related move, Adelphia itself was accused of fraud in a similar complaint filed by the SEC.

Outcome: The lack of independent oversight gave the family carte blanche to rob the company blind. They used company funds to buy back Adelphia stock and fund other family enterprises. Everything was off the books. At sentencing in 2005, John said, "In my heart and in my conscience, I'll go to my grave really and truly believing that I did nothing but try to improve the conditions of my employees."

HealthSouth (2003)

Company: At the time, largest publicly traded health care company in the United States.

What happened: Earnings numbers were allegedly inflated $1.4 billion to meet stockholder expectations.

Main player: CEO Richard Scrushy.

How he did it: Richard Scrushy allegedly told subordinates to make up numbers and transactions from 1996–2003.

How he got caught: Sold $75 million stock one day before posting a huge loss, triggering SEC suspicions.

- June 28, 2005 a jury found former HealthSouth CEO Richard Scrushy not guilty on all counts.
- The acquittal marked a major setback for federal prosecutors and a failure in the effort to hold a CEO accountable under the corporate accountability laws.

Interesting fact: Scrushy faced 85 charges of mail fraud, conspiracy, making false statements, money laundering, securities fraud and wire fraud resulting in a $2.7 billion inflation of HealthSouth's profit.

Outcome: Only 36 charges ultimately went to the jury. Many observers considered this the first real legal test of the provisions of Sarbanes-Oxley Act relating to a CEO's certification of misleading or inaccurate financial statements.

- Scrushy was terminated as Chairman and CEO, and Bill Owens was terminated as CFO.
- The board addressed obtaining cash for interest payments of senior bonds and principal payments due on a $344 million convertible bond.
- The company hired restructuring firm Alvarez and Marsal to bring its finances in order and immediately appointed Bryan Marsal Chief Restructuring Officer. By the end of 2003, the company had most of its finances reorganized and was able to avoid Chapter 11 bankruptcy.
- By mid to late 2006, HealthSouth, which never had to file for Chapter 11 bankruptcy protection, completed its recovery and relisted its stock on the New York Stock Exchange HLS.

Exhibit 1.2 (Continued)

Freddie Mac (2003)

Company: Freddie Mac was chartered by Congress in 1970 to keep money flowing to mortgage lenders in support of homeownership and rental housing.

What happened: An accounting scandal occurred at the company in June 2003 when it disclosed it had misstated earnings by approximately $5 billion. Most of the earnings were underreported for 2000–2002 to smooth quarterly volatility in earnings and meet Wall Street expectations.

Main players: President/COO David Glenn, Chairman/CEO Leland Brendsel, ex-CFO Vaughn Clarke, former senior VPs Robert Dean and Nazir Dossani.

How they did it: Intentionally misstated and understated earnings on the books.

How they got caught: In an SEC investigation, the SEC said Freddie Mac "engaged in a fraudulent scheme that deceived investors about its true performance, profitability and growth trends."

Outcome: Freddie Mac paid a then-record $125 million civil fine in 2003 in a settlement with the Office of Federal Housing Enterprise Oversight. The company's top executives, Glenn, Clarke, and Brendsel, were ousted.

Fannie May (2003)

Company: The Federal National Mortgage association (FNMA) was founded in 1938. It is government-sponsored and has been a publicly traded company since 1968.

What happened: After accounting issues arose at its smaller sibling, Freddie Mac, the Office of Federal Housing Enterprise Oversight (OFHEO) began to examine Fannie Mae's accounting practices. The result of the probe, detailed in a 211-page report, paints Fannie Mae as an Enron-in-the-making. OFHEO found a "pervasive" misapplication of accounting standards, poor internal controls, and pay structure that rewarded executives for meeting earnings goals. This encouraged executives to manipulate earnings. Fannie Mae engaged in "extensive financial fraud" over six years by doctoring earnings so executives could collect hundreds of millions of dollars in bonuses.

Outcome: In December 2006, Fannie Mae said it would reduce its earnings by $6.3 billion to correct several years of accounting problems.

- In 2008 Fannie and Freddie lost a combined $47 billion forcing the companies to dig deep into their capital reserves.
- Nearly half of those losses came from Alt-A loans, despite those loans accounting for just 11 percent of the companies' total business.
- Between January 2008 and March 2012, Fannie and Freddie would lose a combined $265 billion, more than 60 percent of which was attributable to risky products purchased in 2006 and 2007. By late summer in 2008, Wall Street firms had, for the most part, abandoned the U.S. mortgage market. Pension funds and other major investors throughout the world continued to hold large amounts of Fannie and Freddie securities.
- The Bush administration in September 2008 responded by placing Fannie Mae and Freddie Mac into government conservatorship, where they remain as of 2016.

Exhibit 1.2 (Continued)

Parmalat (2003)

Company: Entrepreneur Calisto Tanzi converted his father's ham establishment in the city of Parma into a global dairy and food giant largely on the basis of long-life milk.

The players: Owner Calisto Tanzi, CFO Fausto Tonna, chief accounting officer Luciano Del Soldato.

What happened: Parmalat defaulted on a $185 million bond payment that prompted auditors and banks to scrutinize company accounts. Thirty-eight percent of Parmalat's assets were supposedly held in a Bank of America account of a Parmalat subsidiary in the Cayman Islands. In December 2003, Bank of America reported that no such account existed.

Later, investigators said they discovered management invented assets to offset as much as $16.2 billion in liabilities and falsified accounts over a 15-year period.

- Trading in Parmalat shares were frozen.
- Tanzi, family members, and several executives were arrested, including CFO Fausto Tonna.
- In 2004, Parmalat's debts were fixed at eight times what the firm admitted. After initial denials, Bank of America's former chief of corporate finances in Italy admitted to participating in a kickback scheme.
- U.S. creditors filed a $10 billion class action suit against Parmalat's former auditors and bankers while Parmalat's administrators separately sued Bank of America, Citigroup, Deloitte & Touche, and Grant Thornton for $10 billion each.
- The U.S. SEC called the affair a "brazen corporate financial fraud."
- In 2005, a reconstructed Parmalat was relisted on the Milan exchange.

Outcome: In 2008, Fausto Tonna was given a two and a half year jail sentence as the mastermind of a complex web of offshore subsidiaries to disguise the company's position. Five banks – Bank of America, Citigroup, Morgan Stanley, Deutsche Bank and UBS – stood trial in Milan on charges of market-rigging.

Conrad Black – Hollinger Enterprises (2003)

Company: Hollinger Enterprises. A large publisher of English-language newspapers, including the *Chicago Sun-Times*, the U.K.'s *Daily Telegraph*, and Canada's *National Post*.

What happened: CEO accused of looting the corporation and the expenses of the shareholders.

The player: Lord Conrad Black

How it occurred: Black packed the board of directors with his own nominees. The board turned a blind eye while he robbed the company of more than $400 million. This sum was equal to 95% of the net profits for the period between 1997–2003.

Interesting fact: A Breeden report blamed the directors, notably Richard Perle, the former U.S. defence advisor, and other well-known financial and political figures, who failed to stop the alleged looting. It criticized the auditors, KPMG,

Exhibit 1.2 (Continued)

and the Canadian law firm, which acted for both Hollinger International and Lord Black's personal equity company, saying that they should have warned Hollinger International but failed to do so.

Outcome: Black was forced to step down as CEO of Hollinger International (although he remained as chairman). He was required to repay the $32 million in identified unauthorized payments and conceded to the demand for a fuller investigation by Richard Breeden.

- In 2004, Black was prosecuted in the United States. Black was charged of allegedly improperly taking or spending over $80 million in assets. He was convicted of three counts of fraud and one count of obstruction of justice in 2007. He was sentenced to six and a half years' imprisonment.
- In 2011, two of the charges were overturned on appeal and Black was re-sentenced to 42 months in prison on one count of mail fraud and one count of obstruction of justice. He was released in May 2012, after serving a total of 37 months in prison.

David Wittig (2003)

Company: Western Resources, Topeka, KS

What happened: David Wittig was named President in 1998 and Chairman and CEO in January 1999. He became one of Topeka's most prominent citizens. He would be later accused of looting the company for personal gain.

The players: CEO, David Wittig and Corporate Strategy Vice President, Douglas Lake

What he did: Witting and Lake were accused of looting the company through the use of corporate jets and funds for personal purposes.

Outcome: The two men were tried on 39 charges in the fall of 2004.

- On September 12, 2005, Wittig was convicted of 39 counts and Lake was convicted of 30. On April 4, 2006, US District Judge sentenced Wittig to 18 years and ordered him to pay a $5 million fine in addition to $14.5 million in restitution. Wittig faced a maximum of 45 years behind bars and intended to appeal.
- He was scheduled to be retried for the third time for looting Westar in September 2008. The new trial was set to begin September 20. However, before the trial could commence the trial judge had to consider whether a Supreme Court ruling on the conviction of former Enron executive Jeffry Skilling was applicable to Wittig's case. The Supreme Court ruling appeared to limit the government's use of the so called hones service statue to seek convictions in corruption cases.
- In 2010 all charges against Wittig were dismissed.
- In July, 2011, Wittig settled a dispute with the company for back compensation owed him. The settlement amount received by Wittig was $36 million in cash, $3.1 million, in legal fees incurred by Wittig and an additional $2.7 million.

Exhibit 1.2 (Continued)

AIG (2005)

Company: World's largest insurance and financial services company employing 93,000 professionals doing business in 130 countries.

Main player: CEO Hank Greenberg.

How he did it: Allegedly booked loans as revenue, steered clients to insurers with whom AIG had payoff agreements, and told traders to inflate AIG stock price.

What happened: Massive accounting fraud approximating $3.9 billion was alleged, along with bid-rigging and stock price manipulation.

How did it happen: In 2001 the SEC learned AIG assisted a client company in bolstering its balance sheet through a bogus insurance transaction. The SEC initiated and investigation and settled with AIG in 2003 for a $10 million civil penalty. In 2004 a Federal Grand Jury began investigation of AIG on income smoothing products. In 2004 claims of bid rigging were filed against AIG. May 2005 AIG disclosed that a reinsurance deal with GenRe should have been accounted for as a deposit. In May 2005 the restatement resulted in a reduction in 2004 net income of $1.3 billion.

In May 2005, Eliot Spitzer, former governor of New York, filed civil suit against AIG alleging misleading accounting and financial reporting.

In February 2006 the SEC filed a complaint against AIG. The complaint indicated: "This case is not about the violation of technical accounting rules. It involves the deliberate or extremely reckless efforts by senior corporate officers of a facilitator company (Gen Re) to aid and abet senior management of an issuer (AIG) in structuring transactions having no economic substance, that were designed solely for the unlawful purpose of achieving a specific, and false, accounting effect on the issuer's financial statements."

Outcome: In February 2006, the SEC and Justice department settled with AIG. The settlement was in excess of $1.6 billion and related to the alleged improper accounting and bid rigging. The CEO and CFO were replaced. Federal criminal charges were filed against certain executives.

John Browne CEO British Petroleum (2007)

Company: British Petroleum, one of the world's seven major oil and gas companies.

- An oil spill caused by the failure of eight different safety systems mean to prevent this kind of incident.

What happened: The incident resulted in more than 200 million gallons of crude oil being pumped into the Gulf of Mexico for a total of 87 days. The spill is considered the larges oil spill in U.S. history.

- 16,000 total miles of coastline were affected, including the coasts of Texas, Louisiana, Mississippi, Alabama, and Florida.
- Even though the gushing well was capped in July 2010, oil continued to wash up on.
- The initial oil rig explosion killed 11 people and injured 17 others.
- President Obama announced his administration would create a $20 billion spill response fund.

Exhibit 1.2 (Continued)

- Responders used 5.5 million feet of boom, a barrier placed in water, to collect and absorb oil.
- Of the 400 miles of Louisiana coast, approximately 125 miles were polluted by the oil spill. Over 8,000 animals (birds, turtles, mammals) were reported dead just 6 months after the spill, including many that were already on the endangered species list.

Outcome: BP is responsible for close to $40 billion in fines, clean up costs, and settlements as a result of the oil spill in 2010, with an additional $16 billion due to the Clean Water Act. On July 15 2010, after several failed attempts, the oil gusher was finally capped.

- In 2012, three employees were indicted on manslaughter charges in connection with the deaths associated with the spill.
- BP CEO Heyward was released.

Stephen Heyer, CEO Starwood Hotels (2007)

Company: Starwood is a fully integrated owner, operator, and franchisor of hotels, resorts, and residences under the brands St. Regis, The Luxury Collection, The Westin, Le Méridien, Sheraton, Tribute Portfolio, Four Pointts by Sheraton, Aloft, and Element along with an expanded partnership with Design Hotels.

Main players: CEO, Stephen Heyer and board of directors

What happened: CEO resigned after disagreements with the hotel company's board.

- Allegations were made that he had sent inappropriate and suggestive e-mails and text messages to a female employee.
- Heyer was questioned by board members related to a number of anonymous emails and test messages to and from female employees off hours. He was also questioned about his employment and hiring practices. A complaint letter received by board members contained 10 specific instances that allegedly showed Mr. Heyer had created a hostile work environment. It alleged, that on at least one occasion Mr. Heyer made inappropriate physical contact with a female employee outside a restaurant bathroom. Mr. Heyer denied to the board that this incident ever occurred.

Outcome: The board was unhappy with his leadership style and under the terms of his contract, his conduct made him ineligible for $35 million in severance compensation. Heyer chose to resign.

Lehman Brothers (2008)

Company: As a global financial services firm Lehman was the fourth largest U.S. investment bank at the time of its collapse. It employed 25,000 professionals worldwide.

What happened: The firm hid over $50 billion in loans disguised as sales.

Main players: Lehman executives and the company's auditors, Ernst & Young.

How they did it: In 2003/2004, Lehman acquired five mortgage lenders which specialized in sub-prime lending and Alt-A loans (made to borrowers without full documentation.)

Exhibit 1.2 (Continued)

- The company reported profits every year from 2005 – 2007. In 2007, the firm reported net income of a record $4.2 billion on revenue of $19.3 billion.
- In 2007, cracks in the housing market became apparent and sub-prime mortgages rose to a 7-year high.
- In March 2008 after the near collapse of Bear Stearns, Lehman's stock dropped sharply by 48%. Hedge fund managers began questioning the valuation of Lehman's portfolio.
- Lehman attempted to entice partners but with no success. On September 10, 2008, Lehman reported dismal third quarter results which making its fragile position apparent.

Outcome: Lehman's bankruptcy led to more than $46 billion of its market value being wiped out. The collapse served as the catalyst for the purchase of Merrill Lynch by Bank of America.

Bernie Madoff (2008)

Company: Bernard L. Madoff Investment Securities LLC was a Wall Street investment firm founded by Madoff.

What happened: Bernie Madoff scammed investors out of $64.8 billion through the largest/ longest Ponzi scheme in history. Madoff's Ponzi Scheme lured investors in by guaranteeing unusually high returns. To avoid having too many investors reclaim their profits, Ponzi schemes encourage investors to stay in the game and earn even more money. The scheme began to unravel after clients requested a total of $7 billion back in returns. Madoff only had $200 - $300 million left.

Main players: Bernie Madoff, his accountant David Friehling, and Frank DiPascalli.

How they did it: Investors were paid returns out of their own money or that of other investors rather than from profits.

Interesting fact: It is thought that one of the reasons Madoff was able to fly under the radar for so long was because he was a well-versed and active member of the financial industry. He started his own market maker firm in 1960 and helped launch the NASDAQ stock market. He sat on the board of the National Association of Securities Dealers and advised the SEC on trading securities.

How they got caught: Madoff told his sons about his scheme and they reported him to the SEC. He was arrested the next day.

- Madoff really only made off with $20 billion, even though on paper he cheated his clients out of $65 billion.
- Madoff was sentenced to 150 years in prison, the maximum for his crimes.

Satyam Scandal (2009)

Company: An information technology services and back-office accounting firm.

What happened: The scandal occurred in India in 2009. Chairman Ramalinga Raju confessed the company's accounts had been falsified. He resigned on January 7, 2009 and confessed that he had manipulated the accounts by $1.47 billion. In February

Exhibit 1.2 (Continued)

2009, the Central Bureau of Investigation (central agency in India) took over the investigation. In April 2015, Ramalinga Raju was convicted with 10 other members for falsely boosting boosted revenue by $1.5 billion.

Main player: Founder/Chairman Ramalinga Raju.

How he did it: Falsified revenues, margins and cash balances of 50 billion rupees.

How he got caught: Admitted the fraud in a letter to the company's board of directors.

Interesting fact: The case is also called the Enron of India. In 2009, Raju wrote a letter to the Securities and Exchange Board of India (SEBI) and his company's shareholders, admitting that he had manipulated the company's earnings, and fooled investors. Nearly $1 billion (94% of the cash) on the books was fictitious.

Outcome: A special court under India's Central Bureau of Investigation (CBI) in April 2015 held the founders and former officials of outsourcing firm, Satyam Computer Services, guilty in an accounting scam. B Ramalinga Raju, the company's former chairman, was sentenced to seven years in jail.

Hewlett Packard Perma (2010)

Company: Hewlett Packard, a multi-national information technology company that sells hardware, software, and related business services.

The players: Mark Hurad, CEO

What happened: A letter describing allegations of sexual harassment by Hewlett-Packard CEO Mark Hurd surfaced, claiming that Hurd repeatedly pressured a female contractor for sex and bragged about his popularity with "many" women.

Outcome: Hurd resigned in 2007. HP said Hurd didn't violate the company's policy regarding sexual-harassment but submitted inaccurate expense reports that were intended to conceal what the company said was a "close personal relationship" with a woman.

Southwest Airlines 2008 – 2011

Company: Southwest Airlines, headquartered in Dallas, Texas, claims to be America's largest low-fare airline carrier.

What happened: From 2008 – 2011 several safety incidents occurred with various flights that brought into question the safety of Southwest's fleet. In 2015 the airline grounded 128 planes after failing to inspect backup hydraulic systems used to control the rudder if the main system fails.

Outcome: In 2014 the Federal Aviation Authority (FAA) proposed a $12 million fine Southwest for failing to comply with safety related repairs to its fleet of 737 planes.

In 2009 the airline was fined for failing to inspect dozens of planes for cracks in the fuselage. Southwest agreed to pay $7.5 million to settle with the FAA, which had sought a $10.2 million penalty.

Exhibit 1.2 (Continued)

Wal-Mart Scandal 2012

Company: Walmart, retail chain headquartered in Bentonville, AR.

The players: Wal-Mart corporate executives, Wal-Mart Mexico executives, the NY Times.

What happened: A *New York Times* exposé revealed Walmart de Mexico made payments to Mexican government officials in order to facilitate opening new stores.

- Payments totalling more than $24 million were allegedly made win permission to open new stores more quickly than would have been possible had the company adhered to Mexican laws.
- The payments were hidden from Wal-Mart's global headquarters by disguising them as normal legal bills. Payments were characterized as bribes.
- The executive in charge of the payments quit in 2005 after being passed over for promotion. He detailed his behavior to Wal-Mart's lawyers, implicating many senior Wal-Mart executives in the process.
- Wal-Mart's global headquarters launched an investigation. Despite evidence of at least suspicious behavior, Wal-Mart shut the investigation down.
- The CEO of Wal-Mart de Mexico purportedly approved the payments. Wal-Mart assigned the investigation to Wal-Mart de Mexico and then quickly discontinued it.
- Following the article's publication, Wal-Mart said it conducted an "extensive investigation" into its compliance with the Foreign Corrupt Practices Act. In November Wal-Mart broadened its investigation into bribery allegations to include India, China and Brazil.

Outcome: As of June 2014 the retail giant has reported spending $439 million on investigations.

- The piece won a Pulitzer Prize written by the *New York Times* reporter.
- It also raised a host of personal accountability and corporate governance issues.

PennWest Petroleum Accounting Scandal 2014

Company: PennWest Petroleumn operates in the segment of exploring for, developing, and holding interests in oil and natural gas properties.

The players: CEO David Roberts; David Dyck, CFO, accounting staff.

How it happened: David Dyck was hired as the new CFO in 2013. After the hiring of the CEO, David Roberts he informed Mr. Roberts that frank discussions with members of his team expressed concerns about accounting practices going back several years. The company, which has a large number of retail investors had been claiming operating expenses as capital expenses and boosting its cash flow. Cash flow was a key metric that influenced its stock price.

Roberts informed his board. After markets closed on July 29, 2014 the company disclosed it had discovered significant accounting irregularities and the individuals responsible were fired. The statement released at that time indicated Penn West's audit committee and independent advisors were re-examining financial reporting for 2014 and 4 previous fiscal years. It was explained this could delay the release of

---

Exhibit 1.2 (Continued)

second-quarter financial results and impact capital spending, royalty expenses and cash flow.

Outcome: Investors came down strong on stock price. Class action lawsuits were filed in both Canada and the U.S. Activist investors demanded a change in management.

Penn West discovered $300 million in expenses misclassified. They restated results.

Penn West made payouts to investors of $53 million, according to the American lawyers co-leading a New York class-action lawsuit.

Volkswagen 2015

Company: Volkswagen, a car manufacturer, was established in 1937 by the government of Germany, then under the control of Adolf Hitler.

What happened: The Environmental Protection Agency (EPA) charged that many VW cars being sold in America had a "defeat device" - or software - in diesel engines that could detect when they were being tested and would change the testing performance to improve results. When the cars were operating under controlled laboratory conditions the device appears to have put the vehicle into a safety mode in which the engine ran below normal power and performance. Once on the road, the engines switched out of this test mode. The engines emitted nitrogen oxide pollutants up to 40 times above what is allowed. Volkswagen has since admitted cheating emissions tests in the United States.

Outcome: Volkswagen is recalling millions of cars and put aside billions of dollars to cover the costs. In October of 2015, the company reported its first quarterly loss in 15 years.

Exhibit 1.2 (Continued)

Section 2: Analysis of High Profile Cases

Example 1: Analysis of Adelphia Communications

Adelphia Communications was founded in 1952 by John Rigas and his brother Gus. The franchise grew over the succeeding years and was largely uncontrolled from a financial reporting perspective. (Red Flag!)

Adelphia - Lessons Learned from a Family Business The primary senior executives were family members. These facts may lead a skeptical person to ponder the potential for inappropriate, unethical, or fraudulent actions. The dynamics of closely held family-owned businesses can result in difficulties when managing and executing stringent internal controls. Collusion may become rampant and difficult to detect. The facts of this case speak to how the family concealed several self-dealing issues.

Adelphia - Lessons Learned from Lack of Oversight The Securities and Exchange Commission (SEC) alleged that the lack of independent oversight at Adelphia gave the family carte blanche to rob the company blind. Many of the improprieties were off the books and difficult to identify. In addition, research indicates the Rigas family did not play by the rules on the accounting or control side. The family ran the company as their own private cash machine. They were accused of comingling the accounts of Adelphia with their other businesses and borrowing, and allegedly stealing to pay for lavish homes and other personal expenses, including a private jet and the construction of a golf course. (Red Flag!)

Transactions that involved questionable behavior were often initiated, approved, and recorded by family members who had access to make or alter records. Internal controls were nearly nonexistent, which perpetuated the ability for the family to conceal their actions. (Red Flag!)

Adelphia - Lessons Learned from Lack of Independence CFO Timothy Rigas was chairman of the board's audit committee. (Red Flag!) Other details arose about whether the company's accountants, Deloitte & Touche, or its audit committee knew about and ignored the conflicts that were created by the transactions related to utilization of the company's line of credit. (Red Flag!)

Since Timothy Rigas is a graduate of the Wharton School of Business, it should be assumed that he understood his presence as chairman of the board's audit committee represented a conflict of interest. Even if he was unaware, logic would indicate the position should have been questioned by the company's accountants.

Later articles and research indicated the external accountants did not inform Adelphia's audit committee that the family was using the company's credit lines to buy Adelphia stock (Red Flag!). In addition, it is unclear as to whether an internal audit function existed at Adelphia. (Red Flag!) When Adelphia replaced their CFO, she found that many of the company's personnel were truly unaware of the issues that had occurred. (Red Flag!)

Adelphia Summary The issues that occurred with Adelphia were centered on the actions of the company's management and primary owners. It is difficult to understand how the lavish actions of the family were not identified earlier. Were employees and customers not aware of the activities occurring around them? Did they not care, or did they fear repercussions if they said anything? Why did the external accountants not recognize the issues? The truth is, we don't know. The lavish actions of the family could be representative of management's feeling their actions were appropriate in the "normal" course of business. As we will discuss in Chapter 2, there was obviously a form of psychology behind the perpetrators' actions which caused them to believe their actions and business dealings were appropriate.

Example 2: Analysis of Western Resources, David Wittig

The golden boy of Wall Street arrived in the small Kansas town of Topeka in 1998 at the request of the chief executive officer (CEO) of Western Resources, John Hayes. David Wittig was born in Kansas City, Missouri, and by 1995 had earned millions on Wall Street. He was a charming and charismatic individual and accepted the invitation to return to Kansas. In 1999, Mr. Witting was named chairman and CEO of the small utility based in Topeka, Kansas. David Wittig was considered a prominent member of the community and often donated to local charities. Yet, during the period 1998–2003, Mr. Wittig was accused of looting the company for millions of dollars and utilizing company assets for personal purposes. Did the board not see what was happening? Did the internal or external auditors not report any observations of lavish spending? Did management not recognize the liberties the CEO was taking with company assets?

David Wittig - How Could This Happen?   Consider the corporate atmosphere in the late 1990s and early 2000s. SOX was not yet legislation. During those years, many organizations and their executives regularly utilized company assets for personal purposes. It was often considered a "benefit" of serving as an executive. In addition, many internal and external audit functions did not focus their efforts on evaluations of executive spending. Even with these considerations, it is difficult to understand how some of the lavish spending and actions of Mr. Wittig were permissible by the organization and the board. It is reported Mr. Wittig often used the corporate fleet for personal trips for his family.

David Wittig - Lessons Learned from Executive Spending Habits   Mr. Wittig was considered a brilliant and resourceful executive who would launch the small utility into a new era. He was brought into the company at a time when various utility mergers and acquisitions were being evaluated. Reports relay stories of extravagant personal and business spending by Mr. Wittig. He had purchased one of Topeka's landmark mansions, the 17,000-square-foot home built by Alfred M. Landon, the Republican who ran unsuccessfully for president in 1936. Mr. Wittig spent several million dollars remodeling the mansion, knowing that his change of control contract with Western Resources would require the utility to repay him for the remodeling. He also drove a Model 550 Ferrari purchased for $230,000. Mr. Wittig's salary totaled over $25 million and included other compensation paid over 7 years, including $2 million from a life insurance policy while he was still alive. Through all of this, you have to wonder what insiders of the utility or the Kansas utility regulatory commission were thinking. It wasn't until 2002, when Western Resource's issues came into the limelight, that the utility became caught up in a scandal surrounding corporate efforts related to a favor with Tom DeLay, the House majority leader. In September, a Texas grand jury indicted the company on charges of illegally contributing money during 2002 to a political action committee created by Mr. DeLay.

In reality, who should have questioned the activities observed by both employees and community residents? Was it the responsibility of other senior executives, internal audit, or external audit to bring the concerns to the board? In Mr. Wittig's case, the actions were not those of "cloak and dagger." Many of his spending habits occurred in plain sight.

David Wittig - Lessons Learned from Responsibility for Reporting Mr. Wittig resigned in 2002. The company's board commissioned an independent report into his spending habits. The report describes a pattern of excess spending in the late 1990s. Mr. Wittig had pushed for the creation of an entire flight department at Western Resources, with the purchase of two top-of-the-line corporate jets and the hiring of six pilots. He was accused of utilizing the jets for personal trips, including a 10-day family vacation in France and England, which he described as business. During Mr. Wittig's trial, there was testimony of a paranoid corporate atmosphere of code-named projects. It was mentioned that Mr. Wittig hired an investigations firm to look into the finances and legal history of state regulators, senior Western Resources executives, and a local journalist who wrote articles criticizing the company.

Understanding that these events transpired prior to the Enron scandal of 2001, many aspects of Mr. Wittig's behavior appeared to be silently accepted because the utility and senior executives had put their faith in his experience to take the utility to new heights.

The question must be asked again, where was the board? What did the external auditors think? Did the internal auditors notice anything, and even if they did, could they report the issues? What about the employees—were any complaints ever made? It is easy to ask these questions looking in the rearview mirror. Many of the issues that occurred in this scenario may have been considered perfectly acceptable at that time. However, once the Enron scandal broke, issues such as this became high profile.

Example 3: Analysis of Bernie Madoff

Everyone loves a fairy tale. Bernie Madoff's Ponzi scam had all the makings of a fairy tale. Except it didn't end happily for Bernie, his family, or any of his investors. How could these actions have gone on for so long without being noticed?

Bernie Madoff - Lessons Learned from Personality   Bernie was another charismatic and ingenious individual who had strong ties to the financial industry. Bernie could sometimes be described as an egotistical personality. He believed his actions were proper and on the up and up. His ability to believe and rationalize his own actions enabled him to convince and deceive others. He was a master at gaining new and lucrative investors and then convincing those investors to continue their investments. It is also reported that Bernie kept his two sons at bay when it came to understanding the true company business. It is thought that one of the reasons Madoff was able to fly under the radar for so long was because he was a well-versed and an active member of the financial industry. He started his own market maker firm in 1960 and helped launch the NASDAQ stock market. He sat on the board of the National Association of Securities Dealers and advised the SEC on trading securities.

Bernie Madoff - Lessons Learned When Things Appear Too Good to Be True   You may have heard the saying "anything that sounds too good to be true probably is." This statement is certainly true in the case of many of Bernie Madoff's transactions. Low-risk, high-gain outcomes are an extremely low probability. Bernie's investors were lulled into a false sense of security from the promise of large profits and returns. The investors rarely questioned Bernie's tactics. A savvy investor would have asked who profited from the investments; what interests and conflicts could be involved? They would have used a strong level of professional skepticism when investing. If something seems questionable, improbable, or hard to believe, walk away. In today's world, a handshake and a promise isn't good enough.

Bernie Madoff – Lessons Learned from Relying on One Investor Savvy investors know it is important to divest a portfolio. Don't put all eggs in one basket, and don't rely on one investment manager to handle all funds. Remember, it is YOUR money. You are the person who ultimately has responsibility for what occurs. Just like choosing a doctor or health-care provider, you must ensure your personal best interests are appropriately managed.

The collapse of Bernie Madoff's business came with the falling markets. He actually confessed to his two sons about his crimes a few days prior to his arrest. His sons turned Bernie in to the authorities.

Bernie's story affected many investors as well as his own family. One of his sons committed suicide on the anniversary of Bernie's arrest. The wife of that son has changed her name and relocated to another area. Bernie's wife lives in seclusion and rarely speaks to individuals.

Section 3: Why Do Issues Continue to Evolve?

As internal auditors or compliance professionals, we would like to believe there is some "cure" to unethical or inappropriate behavior. But, as observed by reviewing issues that have occurred since 2000, the corporate world continues to evolve. People and cultures continue to evolve, and individuals who comprise organization continue to evolve. All of these dynamics will result in ongoing challenges to properly and effectively manage ethical issues. This is another reason to continue to learn and understand why issues have occurred or why issues continue to occur. In Chapter 2, we will further evaluate the psychological impacts of individual thinking on the aspect of ethics. This may help shed light on why certain incidents occur.

Many laws have been enacted since the Enron incident. Most notably, the SOX Act of 2002. The Act was focused on regaining investor confidence in financial reporting. It was passed as a direct result of the Enron, WorldCom and Tyco scandals and continues to be one of the most significant pieces of legislation ever enacted by Congress. Because of the work requirements associated with the Act, the external and internal audit profession has experienced a surge in growth and attention.

However, most individuals realize the incidents which plagued Enron, WorldCom and Tyco did not occur because an accountant failed to document the accounts payable process from beginning to end. The incidents occurred because of aggressive management behavior, unethical acts, and questionable decisions of individuals in positions of authority. Yet, in the early years of implementation of the Act, companies focused on the tactics around documenting and testing controls. No one wanted to be the next Enron or Arthur Andersen. Auditors, both internal and external, as well as companies were extremely concerned about many of the tactical requirements of the legislation. Many of the larger accounting firms developed standard documents that were an attempt to assess the control environment and ethical behavior of organizations. These documents often fell short of providing adequate assurance of the ethical processes employed by businesses. The tools became mere surveys and checklists that someone in the organization had to complete. They weren't always viewed as a true input into the determination of a proper control environment.

It is important to note that although most individuals associate the SOX legislation with Section 404 requirements, the Act actually includes 18 separate sections (Exhibit 1.3). Examination of these sections reveals evidence the intent of the Act went far beyond the mechanical processes required by Section 404. In fact, in many ways, each section has its own corollaries to addressing ethical behavior. Refer to Exhibit 1.3, which lists each section of the Act. Exhibit 1.3 provides a brief description of the requirements of the particular section and an analysis of the section's link to ethical behavior.

You may draw different corollaries from those listed in Exhibit 1.3. Regardless, take time to evaluate your interpretation of the section and how it has or has not impacted the manner in which organizations have evolved their ethical cultures.

Description	Analysis
Title I – Established the Public Company Accounting and Oversight Board	
Purpose: To provide independent oversight of public accounting firms providing audit services. Includes: • Section 101 – Establishment; administrative provisions • Section 102 – Registration with the Board • Section 103 – Auditing, quality control and independence standards and rules • Section 104 – Inspection of registered public accounting firms • Section 105 – Investigations and disciplinary proceedings • Section 106 - Foreign public accounting firms • Section 107 – Commission oversight of the Board • Section 108 – Accounting standards • Section 109 – Funding	Previous to SOX, public accounting firms were self-regulating bodies. The creation of the PCAOB established a standard oversight over the activities of public accounting firms, the quality of their audits and inspections. Initial requirements to assign members to the PCAOB were contentious with two board members resigning shortly after assignment. This problem further delayed implementation of the Act.
Title II Auditor Independence	
Establishes standards for external auditor independence to limit conflicts of interest. Includes: • Section 201 – Services outside the scope of practice of auditors • Section 202 – Preapproval requirements • Section 203 – Audit partner rotation • Section 204 – Auditor reports to audit committees • Section 205 – Conforming amendments • Section 206 – Conflicts of interest • Section 207 – Study of mandatory rotation of registered public accounting firm • Section 208 – Commission authority • Section 209 – Considerations by appropriate state regulatory authorities	Prior to SOX, auditing firms performed many non-audit and consulting work for clients. These agreements became far more lucrative than the auditing engagement. This created the appearance of a conflict of interest. In addition, public firms had no requirements to rotate partners which further contributed to potential conflict of interests.
Title III – Mandates senior executives take individual responsibility for the accuracy and completeness of corporate financial reports	
Defines the interaction of external auditors and corporate audit committees. Includes: • Section 301- Public company audit committees • Section 302 – Corporate responsibility for financial reports • Section 303 – Improper influence on conduct of audits • Section 304 – Forfeiture of certain bonuses and profits • Section 305 – Officer and director bars and penalties • Section 306 – Insider trades during pension fund blackout periods • Section 307 – Rules of professional responsibility • Section 308 – Fair funds for investors	Section 302 was implemented prior to Section 404. Section 302 required the CEO and CFO or primary financial officer to certify to adequate disclosure controls and procedures over the financial statements. Important to note that in the SEC's final rule they define the term "disclosure controls and procedures" distinct from "internal controls over financial reporting." Most companies established elaborate processes for sub-certification of financial controls by other members of management. CEO's and CFO's were not comfortable signing off on control internal without some assurances from their management.
Title IV – Enhanced Financial Disclosures	
Describes enhanced reporting requirements for financial transactions including off balance sheet transactions, pro-forma figures and stock transactions of corporate officers. Includes: • Section 401 – Disclosures in periodic reports	

Exhibit 1.3   Sections of the Sarbanes–Oxley legislation.

Description	Analysis
• Section 402 – Enhanced conflict of interest provisions • Section 403 – Disclosures of transactions involving management and principal stockholders • Section 404 – Management assessment of internal controls • Section 405 – Exemption • Section 406 – Code of Ethics for senior financial officers • Section 407 – Disclosure of audit committee financial expert • Section 408 – Enhanced review of periodic disclosures by issuers • Section 409 – Real time issuer disclosures	Section 404 was by far the most contentious and difficult section of Sarbanes–Oxley. Companies became embedded in documenting procedures, processes and controls when in reality, many of the important reasons the scandals occurred was because of fraud and misdeeds of executives. However, in the early years, companies did not place significant focus on evaluation of elements such as the control environment. Recent studies by Finance Executives International show SOX 404 costs have continued to decline relative to revenues since 2004. However, when asked in 2006 whether the benefits of compliance with section 404 have exceeded costs in 2006, only 22% agreed.
Title V – Analyst Conflicts of Interest	
Section 501-Includes measures designed to help restore investor confidence in the reporting of securities analysts. • Defines the codes of conduct for securities analysts and requires disclosure of knowable conflicts	This section of the Act clarifies the role of securities analysts who make buy and sell recommendation on company stocks and bonds. It also applies to investment bankers, who help companies with loans or handle mergers and acquisition which could provide opportunities for conflicts of interest.
Title VI – Commission Resources and Authority	
Defines practices to restore investor confidence in securities analysts. • Defines the SEC's authority to censure or bar securities professionals from practice • Defines conditions under which a person can be barred from practicing as a broker, advisor or dealer	
Title VII – Studies and Reports	
Requires the Comptroller General and the SEC to perform various studies and report their findings. • Section 701 – GAO study and report regarding consolidation of public accounting firms • Section 702 – Commission study and report regarding credit rating agencies • Section 703 – Study and report on violators and violations • Section 704 – Study of enforcement actions • Section 705 – Study of investment banks	This section provides information on the various studies and reports that would be issued by the oversight agencies.
Title VIII – Corporate and Criminal Fraud Accountability	
Describes specific criminal penalties for manipulation, destruction or alteration of financial records or other interference with investigations. • Also provides protections for whistle-blowers	Fines include not more than $1M or imprisonment not more than 10 years for criminal penalties. In the event of willful certification knowing the reports do not comport with all the requirements, this section shall assess fines of not more than $5M or 20 years or both.

Exhibit 1.3 (Continued)

Description	Analysis
Title VIX – White-Collar Crime Penalty Enhancement	
Increases the criminal penalties associated with white-collar crimes. • Recommends stronger sentencing guidelines and specifically adds failure to certify corporate financial reports as a criminal offense.	This section specifically outlined criminal penalties for influencing a U.S. Agency investigation. Includes fines and imprisonment of not more than 20 years.
Title X – Corporate Tax Returns	
Requires the CEO to sign the company tax return.	Prior to Sarbanes-Oxley, company CEOs were not necessarily required to sign the corporate tax return. This title was initiated in a further attempt to hold CEOs accountable for financial processes.
Title XI – Corporate Fraud Accountability	
Identifies corporate fraud and records tampering as a criminal offense and adjoins those offenses to specific penalties. • Revises sentencing guidelines and strengthens penalties • Allows SEC to temporarily freeze transactions or payments deemed large or unusual	This section strengthened penalties for the criminal offence related to records tampering.

Exhibit 1.3 (Continued)

Although the SOX Act was released in October of 2002, the auditing standard that assisted in outlining requirements to comply with components of the Act was not released until June 2003. Auditing Standard 2 set out certain criteria by which public accounting firms were required to report the results of their testing on internal controls over financial reporting. One of the requirements included the need for the accounting firm to provide an opinion on the sufficiency of management's evaluation of internal control over financial reporting. This requirement may have exacerbated the focus and level of tactical work attached to Section 404. Companies were concerned about the opinion they would receive from their external auditors. Greater focus was placed on the tactical transaction testing of financial reporting rather than on evaluations of the control environment. Deep evaluation of ethical principles fell to the side. It is much easier to test a process where transactions can be selected, examined, and analyzed rather than trying to evaluate soft control environment elements. This left companies struggling to determine the best process to truly evaluate a company's ethical culture. Many of the areas required to be evaluated were based on attitudes, rationalizations, behaviors, and culture. Auditors and companies alike were being asked to examine areas that typically were not part of the purview of an external or internal audit function. In addition, companies inherently resisted the thought they could have unethical actions occurring under their corporate umbrella. Efforts to apply detailed levels of evaluation were often thwarted by management who believed the manner in which they operated a company or treated employees and customers was up to them.

When Auditing Standard 5 was released in 2007, the importance of a strong control environment and adequate evaluation of a company's ethical tone was reinforced. The Public Companies Accounting and Oversight Board (PCAOB) reminded us that transparent and effective financial reporting starts with a company's control environment and, ultimately, its ethical standards. Auditors and companies began focusing deeper on the true meaning of control environment and how ethical conduct can impact many aspects of an organization's operations. Yet, incidents of ethical misconduct have continued to occur. So, we again must ask ourselves whether our efforts in this area are sufficient.

Undoubtedly, there has been an increased focus on the need for certain elements that contribute to a strong ethical culture. Most organizations understand the need for a code of conduct and conflict of interest policy. In addition, there is far greater focus placed in today's workforce on tone at the top, management philosophy and operating style, integrity, respect, and honesty. These are all positive steps in the battle against inappropriate and unethical behavior. However, just because the "words" are placed in a policy or on a company website, does not guarantee that actions will follow expectations.

Organizations must work to understand the many aspects that impact and comprise ethical decision making. Our world and workforce is a dynamic environment composed of individuals whose own personal morals and decision making processes are impacted by many factors. These factors include religion, ethnicity, generation, gender, family dynamics, peer influence, and emotional and physical characteristics as well as a multitude of internal and external pressures faced in day-to-day living. Not every person's view of black or white, right or wrong, virtue or vice is the same. The simple act of developing a policy on ethical code is not sufficient to ensure employees will behave in accordance with that code. Organizations must continue to understand and evaluate their individual cultures and what comprises the makeup of their business. They must learn how to properly communicate expectations to a wide variety of personnel who may individually have separate or opposite points of view regarding ethical topics and ethical decision making. As easy as it is to assert this fact, it is much harder to implement.

Section 4: A Company's Moral Compass, and Who Is Responsible?

Moral compass

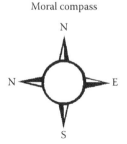

A few years ago, I facilitated a series of e-workshops for the IIA on ethics and the internal auditor. We invited guest CAEs to be part of a panel to field questions from participants on ethical issues and ethical dilemmas encountered during their career. During one session, a panel member indicated she had recently been having difficulties with a multitude of changes within her organization. Some of those changes were impacting the effectiveness of the internal audit department. In a private session with the CEO, the CAE was told she was expected to be the moral compass of the organization. She was curious as to how others would have handled the situation. The following is a sample of the responses provided during the sessions.

Respondent one: "Well thank you Mr. CEO. I'm glad you think highly of my capabilities. However, in my position, I cannot be the sole moral compass of the organization and I would hope management and the board can lead the way in that effort."

Respondent two: "Frankly Mr. CEO I'm a bit surprised to hear you indicate this. I have always been told it is not within my authority to speak directly or privately to the audit committee. In addition, all of my internal audit reports must pass thorough yourself and the CFO prior to being released to the audit committee. They are frequently altered in content and intent. I'm not sure how I can be the moral compass when it appears management is not on the same page in regards to internal audit authority and responsibility."

Respondent three: "Thank you Mr. CEO. Does this mean you will be promoting me to a member of your leadership team? This action would display to the organization that I have the relevant and appropriate authority to execute upon actions which may relate to the moral compass of the organization?"

Respondent four: "I'm a bit confused Mr. CEO, I agree that my actions impact the moral compass of the organization but I also feel all of senior management comprises a portion of the moral compass of the organization. Do you agree with this assessment?"

Whether any of these responses are appropriate for the circumstances, ask yourself how you may have responded if the question were posed to you. It may have depended on your relationship with the CEO, who else was in the room at the time, the type and size of your company, and your overall organizational positioning. The important aspect to understand is that if management views internal audit as the sole owner of the organization's moral compass, you may have a steep road to climb. Management owns the culture of the organization, and that culture will often set the moral compass. They must buy into the direction of the organization and exhibit it during daily actions and events.

Establishing a Strong Moral Compass

Values, mission, and vision statements are widely used and a common practice in today's corporate world. Their creation can be a painful process. It often involves significant discussion and debate among senior leaders of the organization. It is hard for executives to agree on the exact wording and priorities. When the phrase moral compass is used, it typically depicts the organization's consolidated view of how they will do business. The company's moral compass must be agreed on and supported by not only the board but also senior management.

In order to understand moral compass, it is important to distinguish between values, mission, and vision. Vision points a direction, and mission communicates the higher aspirations an organization may seek. It is the values that guide the day-to-day actions and behaviors of an organization. Thus, the organization's moral compass is most closely tied to the organization's values. To determine whether employees buy into or follow the moral compass of the organization, performance reviews should link to company values. How well does an employee demonstrate the organization's values in his or her work?

Some individuals believe that focusing on values, vision, and mission is essentially meaningless. Ask yourself, how could long-term goals be attained if the day-to-day actions that define the organization aren't regularly practiced? As individuals, we must always remember we can fall prey to others' reactions to a situation. This is part of what makes us human. Every employee must be mindful of what they do and how that aligns with the objectives of the company. Individuals must buy into the moral values of the company. If those values go against their own personal moral values, employees will be hard-pressed to follow the directions of their supervisors.

Can Moral Compass Be Audited?

This question is a bit like asking whether corporate culture can be audited. Moral compass is made up of values, mission, and beliefs and vision. In an article authored by Anthony Howard in November 2013, he explains

> A moral leader doesn't worry about being able to tell customers that they have done the right thing by them, but on being able to look at themselves in the mirror and saying they've done the right thing. Moral risk is best managed by focusing not on compliance and what is permissible, but on what is proper. The theory is we learn from the example of good people who operate according to a moral compass. Their decisions and actions demonstrate a sound set of deeply held principles and values that would align with timeless human values. Where decisions impact the life and wellbeing of stakeholders—whether staff, customers, suppliers, shareholders, or the wider community—they have a moral dimension, a sense in which there could be a "right" or "wrong" way to act. The self-evident conclusion is that most decisions have a moral aspect.

> **Anthony Howard**
> *Founder of The Confidere Group. His paper "It's Time for Moral Leadership" received international attention with its call for leaders to do what is proper, not just what is permissible.*

As we all know, leaders, as well as others, frequently experience real moral challenges involving difficult choices. When faced with these challenges, people tend to rely on a moral code. Mr. Howard's research indicates that often what people call a moral code is actually a business or industry code of ethics, rather than a deep personal moral code that directs their actions. These are good people who tend to judge actions on the basis of regulation or law. However, as we have readily seen, focusing on compliance alone can cause difficult issues.

Andrew Fastow, the former CFO at Enron who was jailed for his role in the failed firm, has been quoted as saying:

> The question I should have asked is not what is the rule, but what is the principle.
>
> **Andrew Fastow**
> *Former CFO Enron*

Leadership and Moral Compass

Although different words can be used, the majority of conversations about leadership and success often turn to the absence of leadership, and the shortage of character among leaders. In essence, the type of leader being sought is a leader of stature and vision but, more fundamentally, a leader of character and courage, a leader who brings out the best in others. Ultimately, we want someone we can call a moral leader.

How does someone become a moral leader in today's world amid all the pressures of personal and professional lives? We must first recognize the foundation of moral leadership is one's moral compass, a set of moral principles, informed by a sound conscience, reinforced by repeatedly acting in accord with those principles. Our moral compass needs to be grounded in some reality against which it can be measured or checked.

A sound starting point is an understanding of what it means to be human, and what promotes the good of the human person. This may mean taking an inside look at your own personal life as well as your organization and the individuals who comprise the organization. Many people will suggest

- Treat others the way you wish to be treated.
- Act in a way that promotes good and avoids evil.
- Understand what you view as hateful, and do not do those things to others.

Living by these concepts, and taking time to evaluate personal actions in light of them, will assist individuals in identifying their own moral compass. This tactic will assist in building self-awareness and a better understanding of your own moral compass or true north. Evaluate whether you truly act in a way that is the best for the organization. All individuals must continually evaluate their own skills and actions. Professionals must work on their basic skills to maintain lifelong good habits. Ensure you understand the meaning of justice. This will help you appreciate that everyone is a member of the human community, and it will balance your needs with those of others.

Experts will say by cultivating virtue, we build a character based on principles. This will give us strength to continue to act for the greater good. As we abide by our principles, we exercise moral leadership. Individuals around us will begin to take notice and may mimic our actions.

Anthony Howard indicates,

> Moral leadership is not about being able to look stakeholders in the eye and tell them you have delivered the best results and are fully compliant with regulations. It is about looking at yourself in the mirror and being able to tell yourself you have done the right and proper thing. It is about being able to live with your choices when these are tested against timeless values, not when tested against quarterly results or the hurdle of regulatory compliance.

Anthony Howard

Leaders in today's business require considerable intellectual, emotional, and interpersonal capabilities to succeed. By accepting these moral dimensions of business, it becomes clear the biggest risk businesses face today is moral risk. Moral risk can be defined as

> The risk that an individual, who appears to ascribe to the corporate values, operates in such a way that their actions could damage the strategy, the financial results, or the stability of the entire firm.

Researchers believe the greater leadership need is for moral leadership, demonstrated by people with outstanding moral competence. These leaders consistently focus on what is proper. Their moral outlook, moral commitment, and moral courage, encourages others to find and live by a moral compass.

Section 5: The International Professional Practices Framework Standards for Ethics for Internal Auditors

Most major professions establish individual codes of ethics. Organizations may also prescribe their own individual code of ethics. Sometimes, reconciling these codes can become a difficult task. The IIA Code of Ethics states the principles and expectations governing the behavior of individuals in the conduct of internal auditing. It describes the minimum requirements for conduct, and behavioral expectations rather than specific activities. The purpose of the institute's Code of Ethics is to promote an ethical culture in the profession of internal auditing. Part of the Code of Ethics for internal auditors incorporates the definition of internal auditing.

> The term internal auditing is an independent, objective assurance and consulting activity designed to add value and improve an organization's operations. It helps an organization accomplish its objectives by bringing a systematic, disciplined approach to evaluate and improve the effectiveness of risk management, control, and governance processes.

Institute of Internal Auditors
Code of Ethics

A Code of Ethics is necessary and appropriate for the profession of internal auditing. It is grounded in the fact management and stakeholders place a level of trust in the function of internal auditing.

The Institute's Code of Ethics extends beyond the definition of internal auditing to include two essential components:

- Principles that are relevant to the profession and practice of internal auditing.
- Rules of conduct that describe behavior norms expected of internal auditors. These rules are an aid to interpreting the principles into practical applications and are intended to guide the ethical conduct of internal auditors.

The term internal auditor refers to institute members, recipients of or candidates for IIA professional certifications, and those who perform internal audit services within the definition of internal auditing.

As we examine the following attributes of the internal auditors' ethics policy, let's discuss the challenges auditors face in upholding the policy. Internal auditors are expected to apply and uphold the following principles:

Integrity

> The integrity of internal auditors establishes trust and thus provides the basis for reliance on their judgment.

The Institute of Internal Auditors Code of Ethics

Integrity is a critical skill for any internal auditor. Integrity goes far beyond doing the right thing. Integrity relates to how others perceive your actions or inactions. You may have experienced a situation in which you felt you took the appropriate and necessary steps to address the issue. Yet, management may have seen the action in another light. They may have felt the issue should have been communicated differently, handled differently, or even evaluated differently. How does their view impact their opinion of your integrity?

If other individuals do not agree with your view of integrity, does this mean that you did not comply with the standards of integrity? Not necessarily; but it may mean that management perceives integrity issues based their view of how an action is managed. This is where being an internal auditor can be a difficult challenge. You must be able to justify and explain the manner in which you managed a situation and obtain management's understanding on that action. Otherwise, you may have ongoing concerns related to how management perceives your individual integrity. Notice I did not say you are required to obtain management's agreement on how you handled the issue. This is because perception is a very powerful thing, and it is often difficult to change or control a person's perception.

A simple example is where an internal auditor confides in another auditor regarding a finding on his or her project. Confiding in the other auditor is not meant to gossip or blow the issue out of proportion but rather to gain another perspective on the particular finding and its relative importance. However, there are cases where management sees this as a breach of confidence. This could ultimately have an impact on their view of your integrity. It is hard to guess when this may or may not be an issue, but auditors need to be cognizant of the sensitivity of certain audit areas and what management or other audit personnel not specifically involved in the project need to know.

Objectivity

> Internal auditors are required to exhibit the highest level of professional objectivity in gathering, evaluating, and communicating information about the activity or process being examined. Internal auditors should make a balanced assessment of all the relevant circumstances and are not unduly influenced by their own interests or by others in forming judgments.

The Institute of Internal Auditors Code of Ethics

The previous statement is the theory behind the ethics principles. It is always easier to say something than to actually execute it. Internal auditors are a part of the organization. Distinct objectivity is often a challenge. The manner in which an auditor goes about gathering, evaluating, and communicating information may depend very much on the individuals involved in the process. For instance, where auditors have close relationships with auditees, they often feel certain methods of gathering and evaluating the evidence are sufficient in meeting the objectivity principle. But, you must challenge yourself. Is it really objective? Just because a professional has been a manager in an area for many years, or because you regularly engage in social activities with the manager, does not necessarily mean you should assume every bit of information they provide you is accurate. Auditors must still ensure they exercise professional skepticism and ensure the validity of the information. Auditors must apply the principle of objectivity in a similar manner for any project they undertake. They cannot be swayed by the organizational positioning or their personal relationship with the auditee.

Confidentiality

> Internal auditors must respect the value and ownership of information they receive and not disclose information without appropriate authority unless there is a legal or professional obligation to do so.

The Institute of Internal Auditors Code of Ethics

It is important for internal auditors to understand the chain of evidence requirements and apply those procedures in all engagements. They must understand the value of information ownership, regardless of whether the information relates to customer or shareholder records or information privacy issues. These issues often arise in areas where fraud or improprieties are found. Auditors must treat all information gathered as private and confidential. Any determination as to whether information will be released to outside individuals must be discussed with appropriate legal professionals.

Competency

> Internal auditors must apply the knowledge, skills, and experience needed in the performance of internal audit services.

The Institute of Internal Auditors Code of Ethics

This is an area where many internal auditors experience difficulty. Again, words are much easier to say than to execute. Most internal auditors understand the knowledge and skills required to perform their work. However, there are many cases where auditors are placed in roles where the specific project area and its technical aspects are unfamiliar to them. In those cases, is true competency being served? Also, when auditors apply true competency and then are stringently challenged and threatened by management, it can become difficult to maintain a firm standing on issues. Auditors may often look for ways to justify management's explanation in order to avoid conflict. In some cases, where the issue is of minor concern, this tactic may be acceptable. But, auditors must ensure they are exhibiting their full competency and are capable of supporting their opinion and position in the face of management disagreement. If the issue cannot be resolved between the auditor and management, then the issue should go to the audit committee to hear both sides of the argument.

Rules of Conduct: Integrity

In relation to the rules of conduct for integrity, the *Standards* state that internal auditors shall:

- Perform their work with honesty, diligence, and responsibility
- Observe the law and make disclosures expected by the law and the profession
- Not knowingly be a party to any illegal activity, or engage in acts that are discreditable to the profession of internal auditing or to the organization
- Respect and contribute to the legitimate and ethical objectives of the organization

The Institute of Internal Auditors Code of Ethics

It is easy to tell someone they should possess integrity and outwardly exhibit integrity. But, when it comes to the corporate setting, individual limits can be challenged. For instance, the audit team may be working to perform their work honestly, diligently, and with responsibility, but when pressured by audit management to complete a project, the auditor may feel that he or she has to cut corners.

As a young auditor in a public accounting firm in the early 1980s, I recall specific budgeted hours were set aside for on-the-job training. The audit senior often made it known that he or she didn't want to use all the budgeted hours, and if the auditor wanted a good review, he or she should make sure the work was completed within budget and without using on the job training hours. The young auditor was faced with working extra overtime, researching issues, and trying to identify the proper answers on their own.

The second rule of conduct refers to "observing the law and making disclosures expected by the profession." The challenge with this rule of conduct is that auditors are not necessarily lawyers. We look to legal counsel to provide advice regarding the proper legal action. As we have said in the past, "Just because it's legal doesn't mean it's ethical!"

So auditors will most likely follow the advice of their internal legal counsel. Young auditors may not feel it is appropriate to challenge legal counsel's advice. More experienced auditors may feel conflicted because of the direction they are given by legal counsel. In this situation, the auditor has the fiduciary duty to explain his or her position to the audit committee. This is not an easy task to accept.

Rules of Conduct: Objectivity

In relation to the rules of conduct for objectivity, internal auditors shall

- Not participate in any activity or relationship that may impair or be presumed to impair their unbiased assessment. This participation includes those activities or relationships that may be in conflict with the interests of the organization.
- Not accept anything that may impair or be presumed to impair their professional judgment.
- Disclose all material facts known to them that, if not disclosed, may distort the reporting of activities under review.

The Institute of Internal Auditors Code of Ethics

The first rule of conduct speaks to "not participating in any activity or relationship that may impair or be presumed to impair unbiased assessment." The difficulty here is auditors are a part of the company. They build relationships with internal customers or process owners. Sometimes, the line between relationships and unbiased assessment can become blurry. This is when the CAE must be aware of the varying relationships in the department and do his or her best to ensure assignments are appropriately allocated.

The second rule of conduct speaks to "not accepting anything that may impair or be presumed to impair professional judgement." Many may ask, what does this mean? Does allowing a client to pay for lunch impair professional judgment? What about accepting tickets to a major baseball game within the suite of a vendor or the external auditors? Another issue may be accepting gift baskets sent during holiday time to the audit team. Each of these has varying levels of acceptance. Your organization may have rules within the code of conduct that speak to the dollar value of items that can be accepted. Unfortunately, when you start talking about sporting tickets or concert tickets to major events, people begin to question independence. There are numerous cases where the external audit team will take the finance, accounting, and internal audit staff to a major league baseball game or a national league football game. These outings often involve expensive suite tickets. Even if the games are not play-off games, it is obvious the face value of the gift is above the lower dollar level normally stated in the company's conflict of interest. How does this action appear to others within the organization? Do they perceive this to be one of the reasons the company does not regularly bid out the external audit? Could observers assume the relationships established are too close? These are things each group must understand and think about.

Rules of Conduct: Confidentiality

The rules of conduct for confidentiality of internal auditors directs auditors to

- Be prudent in the use and protection of information acquired in the course of their duties.
- Not use information for any personal gain or in any manner that would be contrary to the law or detrimental to the legitimate and ethical objectives of the organization.

The Institute of Internal Auditors Code of Ethics

When contemplating the meaning of confidentiality, consider how you obtain another person's trust or confidence. You may also view the meaning as entrusting a person with secrets or private affairs. In today's world of confidential and private information, the concept of understanding how auditors are expected to execute the rule of confidentiality is very important. It is not enough to simply speak to your auditors about confidentiality. It is important auditors understand the how, when, where, what, and who in relation to the receivers of that level of trust. If an auditor is told something in confidence, but that something indicates there is a problem somewhere in the organization, how should that auditor react? Also, consider when auditor's are placed on a specific audit, are they expected to keep the details of the audit and review fully confidential, even as they relate to other auditors in the organization? As internal auditors, we sometimes treat this rule liberally. It is important CAEs and audit managers reinforce to their staff the issues considered confidential and how to manage and handle those issues.

Rules of Conduct: Competency

The rules of conduct for competency for internal auditors state

- Internal auditors shall engage only in those services for which they have the necessary knowledge, skills, and experience.
- Internal auditors shall perform internal audit services in accordance with the *International Standards for the Professional Practice of Internal Auditing*.
- Internal auditors shall continually improve their proficiency and the effectiveness and quality of their services.

The Institute of Internal Auditors Code of Ethics

We will further dissect the meaning and implications of the Code of Ethics principles and rules of conduct for internal auditors in Chapter 2.

The rule of conduct related to competency covers two very important concepts. The first is "auditors should engage only in those services for which they have the knowledge, skills, and expertise." Think about this statement for a minute. As a professional, would you want to admit you may not have the skills or expertise to work on a project? Isn't that why we have seniors and managers to help auditors learn a process? This *Standard* most likely does not imply that everyone on the engagement has the exact technical knowledge and experience to review all issues; however, it is very important those assigned have access to someone with the proper knowledge and background to lead the efforts of the audit.

The other important concept for the competency rule of conduct is the statement auditors must abide by the *Standards*. Auditors must take a close look at what they are doing, how they are executing their roles, and whether they are fully abiding by the *Standards*. If not, this may be interpreted as an ethical concern.

The Realities of How Internal Auditors Can Work with Ethical Concepts

In the early years of the internal audit profession, it was a rare instance when internal auditors were allowed to evaluate ethical conduct issues. This responsibility was typically given to the human resource department or possibly the legal group. As corporate America has evolved, and ethical and fraudulent issues have occurred, the IIA has promulgated that internal audit take a role when ensuring the company's control environment is adequately established and managed. This requires internal auditors to have an understanding of ethics and ethical concepts.

When the SOX legislation was passed after the Enron issue, internal auditors and the profession became more involved in understanding aspects of the control environment, tone at the top, and ethics programs. In order for companies to attest to SOX, they had to examine their overall control environment and evaluate its design and effectiveness. Since internal auditors were the primary source for performing SOX compliance in the early years of the legislation, the responsibility of examining the ethical processes became an integral part of evaluating the company's control environment.

In the early years of SOX, I was a CAE with a large publicly traded organization. The company was going through many issues similar to those experienced by Enron. Due to the magnitude of many of the issues, it was important for internal audit to identify methods to fully evaluate aspects of the control environment and the ethics program. This meant we needed to employ evaluation methods that went further than the simple checklist approach established by many of the external audit firms. Our board was interested in knowing the company's culture was on the right track and that any existence of ethical issues was adequately communicated and dealt with. In addition, they wanted to ensure the company's overall compliance and ethics process was reinvigorated and well communicated. This was to assure employees management was diligently addressing issues of the past.

Typically, for or our company, issues related to the code of conduct or ethics program had been managed by the legal or human resource area. It was difficult for those groups to accept the need for internal audit to become a part of the evaluation process. However, because we had experienced several incidents that bordered on questions of ethical behavior, the audit committee supported the need for internal audit to be involved.

You might think having audit committee support would help smooth the way for internal audit to execute on various analysis processes. However, our organization had been in existence for over 45 years, and the political silos developed over that period of time made it very difficult for legal and human resources to open up their process to individuals who they considered outsiders. At one point, the chief legal officer even proclaimed he felt internal audit was hampering the ethics and control environment process rather than helping it.

In trying to understand his concerns, you have to understand the history of the company. It was difficult for his area and the human resource department to have internal auditors question some of the standard legacy processes around the ethics program that had not been changed in many years. Our organization had experienced significant flux. In 2001, the company was listed as number 33 on the Fortune 50. Revenues were over $40 billion, and stock traded at an all-time high of over $37.55 per share. By late 2002, we had divested of our merchant trading operations, and our revenues fell to $2 billion. With that change, the stock price plummeted to $4.39 per share. It would be logical to assume that due to these dramatic shifts in the organization's operations, some elements of the code of conduct and compliance program would have also changed. However, during an audit review, it was identified that many aspects had not been reviewed, or updated, in several years. To have the internal audit group question some of the processes was akin to a subtle act of pointing at the processes and questioning whether individuals had been adequately performing their responsibilities.

Although the concept of having internal audit asking ethical and tone-at-the-top questions was not popular, we were able to develop an alternative approach to evaluating the soft components of the control environment such as ethical concepts, management philosophy and operating style, and ethical actions. This process involved executing facilitated sessions with senior management using a maturity model approach to evaluate a multitude of ethical and compliance issues. This process resulted in the ability for internal audit to present the outcome and results of the evaluation as a true management product and not just internal audit's opinion. The process proved to be successful, and we continued to utilize the method to improve aspects of the ethical culture through the remainder of the company's existence.

This method helped to eliminate some of the perceived controversy and negativity around the topic. Individuals felt as though they had a say in how things were being evaluated. They also felt as though their concerns were heard, and management took appropriate actions. The process utilized was modeled after the maturity model approach and will be reviewed later in this book.

Summary

For internal auditors to be successful in evaluating ethical programs and concepts, they must think outside of the box and identify procedures relevant to their organization. This means moving away from a checklist approach or one-on-one interview processes where much of the input is left up to interpretation. In addition, when individuals are interviewed directly, or asked to complete a survey, the auditors lose several capabilities. This includes the ability to adequately ask follow-up questions that may be relevant due to other professionals input. It also includes the typical difficulties with the survey process where ratings can be interpreted in various ways.

In the end, as we have indicated the topic of ethics is not necessarily black and white. It involves a great deal of judgment and interpretation. Internal auditors should look for innovative methods to evaluate and assess their ethics program and control environment.

2

PRINCIPLES THAT IMPACT
ETHICAL BELIEFS AND
ETHICAL CULTURE

Section 1: Psychology of Ethics and Impact on Work Culture

Are you the type of individual who enjoys watching television shows such as *Criminal Minds*, *NCIS*, *CSI*, or other dramas where the characters are focused on the psychology of the criminal mind? I find it interesting to watch the analysis tactics utilized in these characterizations to determine why criminals behave in the manner they do. If you pay close attention in order to solve the crime, the characters of the show evaluate the many variables that comprise the makeup of a person's psychological mind, behavior, and thinking process.

Many years ago, there was an article in *Time* magazine that discussed how the human brain matures. The article discussed the brain functions of logic and reasoning, which reside in the brain's frontal lobe. The article mentioned the frontal lobe does not fully mature until an individual reaches the age of approximately 24. So, if you ever wondered why your teenage son or daughter may act the way he or she does, it is most likely because, to the teenagers, their actions are completely logical. When adults observe a teenager's actions, we will question: "What in the world is that child thinking?" Possibly, that question is the exact fact—the child is not thinking or processing issues in the same manner that a more mature person would. What a teenager may view as logical may not be the same as what an adult may see as logical. You can also correlate the phenomena to those individuals in their later age who fall prey to dementia or Alzheimer's disease. The brain begins to function differently, and logic and reasoning often go out the door.

Several years ago, I personally witnessed how a person's brain function and capacities can degrade due to illness. A relative was diagnosed with stage four brain cancer. This gentleman was a brilliant professional who had made a fortune in business before the age of 50. After he sold one of his businesses, he spent the next few years performing day-trading on his home computer. One evening, his wife and young girls returned home to see their husband and father having a serious and active brain seizure. This was the first noticeable sign of any potential medical issue. The ambulance was immediately called. Upon the man's arrival at the hospital, the doctors diagnosed stage four cancer residing in the frontal lobe of the brain. He was given only a few months to live. Although the family had not recognized earlier that he was exhibiting signs of an illness, looking back over the previous 12 months they began to piece together actions he had taken that were not typical of the rational and brilliant professional he was. In addition, over the remaining months, his capacity to process even the simplest thoughts became extremely impaired. It was as if he was regressing to a childhood brain function. Many things witnessed in those months were due to the psychological and medical impact of how the cancer and tumor were impacting the logic and reasoning portion of his brain. In his mind, there often was no right or wrong, good or bad. Events that occurred were individually processed, with little to no regard for anything or anyone else.

I relay this story to enforce the theory that these same correlations can be utilized when contemplating ethical views in today's world. Ethics is a moral and personal trait impacted by many factors. Organizations are composed of a diverse number of individuals who are brought together under one work setting. Those individuals will have varying opinions on how they assess issues such as:

- Distinguishing between right and wrong
- Distinguishing between virtue and vice
- Determining when their personal black or white line begins to turn gray

Each person utilizes their own individual sense of ethics based on upbringing, personal and professional experiences, beliefs, cultural experiences, and chemical brain functions as well as body chemistry. Taking all of these variables into consideration, you can begin to imagine the many types of behavior and thinking that can exist in any one particular corporate setting. These variables all complicate the ability to establish a single set of ethical guidelines that are acceptable to all individuals within the organization.

To begin to understand the elements that may be involved in how a person's ethical attitude is developed, it is important to understand basic theories embedded in the field of ethics. Organizations that understand the various theories and work to evaluate how these theories may be exhibited within their own work culture may be better able to establish policies and procedures that are acceptable at all levels of the organization.

Section 2: Theories behind Ethics and Ethical Principles

Introduction

One of my children obtained a psychology degree. I found it intriguing that this was an area of interest for him. In his latter college years, he explained that he recognized his personal logic process and how his view of even the simplest day-to-day activities was different from other individuals. One of his reasons for studying psychology was to try to determine what made his own sense of morals, ethics, and behavior so different from his own family or other peers.

As I think back about his childhood, I now recognize many signs he displayed at various points in his upbringing. Had I recognized these signs at the time, it may have helped me to recognize he had a different emotional and moral side to his personality. Some of the signs I noticed may have been from social influence while others may have related to his own personal body chemistry. When he was very young, he would experience night terrors. We had been told that a night terror is much like a nightmare, only the child appears to be fully awake. No amount of soothing or consoling can bring the child out of the terror state. Their own body or chemical brain reactions must resolve the terror. It was like micro bursts going off in the brain and the child had no control over what was occurring.

Another factor that contributed to his psychological state was related to how he transitioned through puberty. Doctors commented they regularly witnessed that young boys who entered puberty at an early age and then advanced through the stage quickly would develop a sense of logic at an earlier age than their counterparts. Those boys who entered puberty at a later age and transitioned through the stage slowly seemed to have a delayed maturity in their brain's logic and reasoning function. This explanation seemed to describe exactly what we witnessed with our middle son. Our older son had entered puberty at a very young age and advanced through the cycle quickly. During his teenage years and early 20s, he exhibited very logical and rational behavior. His organization skills were more advanced. However, my middle son entered puberty at a later age, and the stage lasted much longer than the typical teenage boy would experience. The manner in which the two boys viewed events as right or wrong was very different and seemed to have a lot to do with their mental maturity.

I relay these examples to reinforce the importance of an organizations' ability to understand the basic principles and theories behind psychology, logic, and reasoning and their link to individual ethical behavior. By understanding these principles, and how different individuals may process their individual thoughts, organizations may be better equipped to develop relevant processes and procedures that could assist in better managing their own ethical culture.

Ethical Principles and Ethical Theories

First, we will evaluate the variance between an ethical principle and an ethical theory.

An ethical theory is a tool used to come to an ethical solution for an issue. Ethical theories, along with ethical principles, form the viewpoint to guide a person's path to a decision. For an ethical theory to be useful, the theory must be directed toward a common set of goals.

Ethical principles are the common goals that each theory attempts to achieve to be successful. These goals typically utilize several terms, including:

- *Beneficence*: Guides the ethical theory that a professional should do what is good. The concept asserts individuals should attempt to generate the largest amount of good versus evil.
- *Least harm*: Comes into play and deals with the situation where there does not appear to be one choice that is more beneficial than another. In this case, the person should select the choice that will result in the least harm to the fewest people.

- *Respect for autonomy*: States that individuals should make decisions that apply most appropriately to their own lives. In other words, people have control over their own decisions.
- *Justice*: States that ethical theories should prescribe actions that are fair to every person involved. This means that ethical decisions would be consistent with ethical theory.

Philosophy 101: Introduction to Ethics

As discussed, ethical theories are based on various ethical principles. The various theories emphasize different aspects of an ethical dilemma. The expectation is that the ethical theory chosen will lead a person to the most ethically correct resolution according to the guidelines within the theory. Individuals will typically base their choice of ethical theory on their own life experiences.

Ethical Theories

Philosophers generally divide ethical theories into three groups. Each group has different underlying principles to apply when arriving at an ethical decision. To understand these theories and how they may apply to your own behavior, as well as that of your organization, you must contemplate the different types of moral or ethical judgments people are faced with. First, we will discuss the general categories of ethical theories.

As depicted in Figure 2.1, ethical theories are classified into three categories:

- Meta-ethics
- Normative ethics
- Applied ethics

As you read through the following narrative, evaluate which theory most accurately describes your individual thought processes and behaviors. Then compare that theory with the one which most accurately describes the organization you currently are associated with. You will find there are many complicating factors, depending on which ethical theory the individual or organization follows.

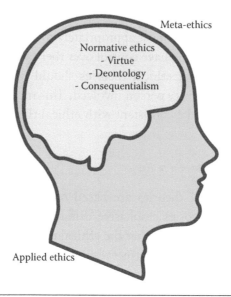

Figure 2.1   Ethical theories: three categories.

Meta-Ethics   Meta-ethics is the study of the origin or meaning of ethics. It is considered to be the area of ethics that seeks to understand the nature of ethical properties, statements, attitudes, and judgments. Meta-ethics will address questions such as:

How is moral reasoning different from other types of reasoning?
How can we tell right from wrong or good from bad?
What are the motives for acting ethically?

In essence, meta-ethics seeks to understand the nature of how we make ethical evaluations.

Meta-Ethics in Business   Consider how your organization determines what is right from wrong. What factors are utilized when making these determinations? Is it simply the opinion of one or more individuals, or is it based on some fact, rule, or law the organization is required to follow?

An example is to assume your organization is developing a code of conduct. How is it determined what directions will be given about right versus wrong within the code? The effort the organization contributes in designing a code which reflects the values the organization wishes to be known for may provide some insight into their dedication to creating a strong ethical culture. If ethical policies are developed solely by one person or a few individuals, the organization is advocating its culture to the personal ethics of the few individuals creating the code. However, if the policies are developed by a group of individuals who research various concepts, the policies may be more reflective of an organization that values the opinion of a wide range of cultures and individuals.

Normative Ethics   Normative ethics is the study of ethical action, or how people should act. Understanding this ethical theory will enable organizations to understand how individuals within their culture may exhibit ethical behavior.

Normative ethics examines standards for how individuals determine what actions are right or wrong. As an example, consider the topic of committing an act of theft. Normative ethics would be concerned with the question of whether committing theft is a proper and acceptable behavior. When applying how normative ethics may be interpreted, consider the Robin Hood character. Robin Hood and his gang of merry men acted on the principle that it was proper to "steal from the rich to give to the poor." In this example, their version of normative ethics would have supported the theory that theft is an acceptable behavior, as long as you are taking something to give to a person less fortunate.

There are typically three types of normative ethical concepts.

Normative Virtue Ethics   Virtue ethics was advocated by Aristotle. It focuses on the inherent character of an individual rather than on any specific actions. Within virtue ethics, the outcome of the action and the determination of whether it was an "ethical" action may be based on the perception of the character of the individual rather than the act committed.

If an organization follows virtue ethics, they are placing all beliefs and values in the personal character of their leaders. Consider how this theory may reflect the behavior of the German Nazis. Individuals who followed Hitler's direction believed in his inherent character and deemed his actions as virtuous or proper. Those who opposed Hitler would not classify his actions under virtue ethics.

Scenario Virtue Ethics   Using the example of a corporation, assume the organization's chief executive officer (CEO) has risen to power through the ranks of the company. The CEO is a brilliant gentleman and shows a strong level of competence in his technical field. However, he has never been known as an upstanding leader of people. The very fact that he is now in the CEO position may influence the perception of employees related to the acceptable way to act in the corporate setting. Some individuals may deem any action the CEO takes must be viewed as virtuous, simply because of his organizational standing. By recognizing this concept may exist, organizations can step away from the belief that any one individual should or could set the moral code for a company.

Reflect on the many organizational leaders who have succumbed to ethical scandals. Ken Lay, Jeffrey Skilling, Andy Fastow, Bernie Madoff, Bernie Ebbers; the list continues. At some point in the evolution of their organizations, each of these individuals was most likely viewed as virtuous in his actions by the simple aspect of his organizational standing. It wasn't until the organization recognized improprieties in operations and actions that the person's ethics were questioned. These factors outline the difficulty with an organization assuming a particular individual's opinion is ethical by virtue of his or her *perceived* character or based on his or her corporate organizational standing.

Normative Deontology Ethics   This concept argues that decisions should be made considering factors such as a person's duties as well as the rights of others. Individuals who subscribe to this concept would base the evaluation of whether an action is ethical on whether the action is indeed the responsibility of the person who performs the action.

Scenario Deontology Ethics   Consider the example of military troops. Generally, most individuals will argue the act of killing another person is not ethical. However, when it comes to military tactics, the act may be one of the responsibilities of the military troop to instill order within a region. Now, using the example of an organization, consider a group that rescues mistreated animals. The organization's purpose is to attempt to protect animals, potentially save their lives, and bring to light the improper behavior of those who mistreat the animals. Assume the organization has rescued a dozen pit bulls bred for fighting. Seven of the pit bulls have been fiercely treated and trained. The group concludes there is no possibility for rehabilitation of these dogs. To protect the rights of others, the organization chooses to put the animals down. This was not their original intention, but using both the theory of their responsible duty and protecting the needs and rights of others, the action of putting the animals down is deemed proper.

Normative Consequentialism Ethics   This concept argues the morality of an action is contingent on the action's outcome. Consequentialism is considered grounded in actual effects, and, from a theoretical viewpoint, moral action is considered to always improve life on Earth. Consequentialist theories are often attentive to the particulars of the situation. These theories allow for exceptions to the rule when warranted by the outcome. Individuals using this theory may come to different conclusions based on what they consider most valuable. Examples may include:

- Will the action lead to the greatest happiness for the greatest number of people?
- Will the action maximize good for the individual executing the action?
- Will the action result in the most loving result?
- Does the action promote or foster knowledge?
- Could the action increase economic well-being?

For consequentialism ethics, the organization may judge how ethical the issue is, based on its final outcome. Using this theory, consider the fact that Enron's actions increased corporate value and stock price until the issues were revealed. Did this make those actions ethical during the time they were not public knowledge?

Business (Virtue Ethics)   For each of the normative ethic principles discussed, a short example has been provided of how the theory may be applied in a business setting. We will now further dissect the principle and extend the thought of application to business.

Assume your organization (or senior management) subscribed to the concept of virtue ethics. Ethical decisions made by the organization are based on the organization's perception of the character of the individual involved in the incident. As an example, consider the following:

Virtue Ethics Scenario One   The organization maintains travel guidelines which outline expectations for travel reimbursement. Some of the information outlined in the policy includes:

- Personnel are expected to travel economy class.
- Travel is to be booked at least 14 days in advance.
- Hotel stays should be in compliance with corporate rate structures.

The organization's CEO is known for his extravagant business spending. He regularly books travel less than seven days in advance with no substantive explanation. He travels first class on each flight taken, and the costs are paid for by the company. In addition, he does not always abide by the corporate hotel cost guidelines. He is a member of a frequent hotel-trip club. The club is considered to include extravagant hotels. The CEO prefers to book his business travel with this hotel chain. The organization does not address any of these issues because they deem the character of the CEO to be beyond reproach, and they choose to accept his actions even though the same action is not allowed for other employees. This would be an example of where the organization has applied the concept of virtue ethics to the actions of the CEO alone.

Virtue Ethics Scenario Two   Assume one of the organization's top sales personnel was recently found to have overstated a commission sale. The individual has been with the organization for several years and is consistently a top salesman. The overstated commission is identified by the company's internal audit department. When reported to senior management, the issue is dismissed because management perceives the character of the individual as trustworthy. Rather than further evaluate the issue, they dismiss the overstatement as unintentional. There are no ramifications to the sales individual. However, during the same month, a younger, less experienced sales individual is also found to have overstated a commission sale. Although the overstatement on this sale was significantly less than the one of the top salesperson, the organization chooses to reprimand the newer salesperson. This would be an example of the organization applying the concept of virtue ethics based on their presumption of the character of the individual involved. (They applied a presumed higher value of personal integrity to the experienced salesperson than to the inexperienced salesperson.)

Business (Deontology Ethics)   A person who follows this theory will produce consistent decisions, since the decisions will be based on the individual's set duties. A deontologist adheres to their obligations and duties when analyzing an ethical dilemma. This theory assumes there is no rationale or logical basis for deciding an individual's duties. Consider the following scenarios.

Deontology Ethics Scenario One   A professional may decide it is his duty to always arrive to work early. This may appear to be a good action. However, the reason the professional chooses to arrive early is to utilize company' assets to perform personal work. In this case, the person following the deontology theory will deem the behavior is ethical if they are only considering the fact the person always arrives early to work.

Deontology Ethics Scenario Two   What if the deontologist, in his attempts to arrive at work early, puts the welfare of others at risk? Assume the deontologist left his home late and had to speed to get to work because he needed to complete some personal business using the company computer. Would this be considered in the best interest of others, or is it breaking the law? This provides a scenario of conflicting obligations and does not lead to the clear, ethically correct answer. This example demonstrates a flaw in the deontology concept.

Deontology Ethics Scenario Three   The CEO and several of his executives have chartered a plane for a business trip. The plane crashes in a desolate and wooded area. Several people are injured, some more critically than others. Utilizing the deontological theory, what should the CEO do? Is there any rational logic to guide the CEO's decision? If he chooses to stay put, the whole group may die due to lack of food and extreme temperatures. If he chooses to take those who are most capable to hike out of the wreckage, he can save a few of the executives but will have to leave others behind. Is this the correct and ethical choice?

A consideration that may be helpful in following the deontological theory is the theory contemplates all of the following concepts and considers them as ethically important:

- Individual rights
- The idea that someone deserves, or does not deserve, something
- Fairness

Using this additional information, consider the wreckage example. In this instance, the scenario to attempt to hike out of the woods with individuals who are physically capable may be ethically correct and proper because some individuals will be saved.

Next, using this additional information, consider the question of who deserves to be saved. Think about what the CEO must evaluate in this circumstance. What if one of those critically injured is his right-hand man? Certainly, this person deserves to be rescued. What would the CEO do? What is ethically correct?

Now consider the third factor of fairness. How does the CEO reconcile his decision in relationship to fairness? Will he be biased by his own personal relationships with the various individuals? Does one person deserve more consideration than another? How would a person following the deontology theory determine his or her action?

This is obviously a very difficult theory to apply and reconcile. Remember, the person applying this theory may not always apply all of the concepts listed here. This will make the application of the theory debatable.

Business Consequentialist Theories   Consequentialist theories assume ethical judgments involve issues that consider what may be intrinsically good or intrinsically bad. The concept behind consequentialism is the consideration that an action should produce the best balance of good over bad. The theory involves many questions and complications. As most realize, consequences are difficult to predict. Although actions may have good intentions and an expected high probability of good results, there is always the chance that something happens and the consequences are actually bad. In this case, you have to consider whether the action was morally right or wrong. In addition, a situation could involve a multitude of individuals as well as alternatives. How is it possible to determine which action may result in the best outcome?

A person who follows the consequentialist theory may justify many actions that would normally be considered wrong, even if it turned out that the consequences were good. Consider the following scenarios.

Consequentialist Theory Scenario One   Many people do not like visiting doctors for any reason. However, the experience of undergoing medical tests as a routine part of health screening is viewed as intrinsically good. The action is viewed as an act that may help a person avoid a future significant health issue, which would be intrinsically bad. However, the consequentialist who visits a doctor and finds out they have a serious health issue may view their action as wrong or bad. In other words, they associated the act of learning about their illness with the act of visiting the doctor. When making a decision, you must consider that visiting the doctor is a good action. It is an action that will most likely provide a good outcome, as opposed to not visiting a doctor.

When evaluating actions within the corporate atmosphere, which actions would you consider good and which actions would you consider bad? Contemplate the following examples:

Actions That Are Good

- Establishing budgets: This is intrinsically good. It provides the organization with a guideline for controlling spend.
- Internal controls: This is intrinsically good. Internal controls help to mitigate inappropriate or improper acts in the organization that may result in a bad outcome.

- Internal audits: This is intrinsically good. Internal audits help identify areas where control gaps may exist. Management can then address the control gaps in a timely fashion to prevent something bad from happening.
- External audits: From a public viewpoint, external audits are intrinsically good. They provide investors with a level of confidence in the organization's financial information.
- Board and governance oversight: Again, from a public viewpoint, the existence of a board and adequate governance oversight is intrinsically good. It provides investors and stakeholders with a level of confidence that the organization is being properly managed.

Actions That Are Bad

- Management dictatorial behavior: This is intrinsically bad. Dictatorial behavior may minimize innovation as well as open and transparent communication.
- Disrespect of other personnel: This is intrinsically bad. If an organization disrespects personnel, this will reflect poorly on the tone of the organization's culture.
- Dishonesty in the workforce: This is intrinsically bad. Dishonesty in the workforce may encourage greed, selfishness, and acts that are inappropriate and not in the best interest of the company.
- Backstabbing other employees: This is intrinsically bad. Individuals who are allowed to backstab coworkers with no repercussions will contribute to a poor culture.

These are examples of items within a corporate setting that may be intrinsically good or intrinsically bad. Keeping these things in mind, it is easier to apply the consequentialist theory. Those things considered intrinsically good would be considered ethical. Those things considered intrinsically bad would be considered unethical.

To determine the moral status of an action, the organization must evaluate the overall quality of good the action will bring to the company.

Consequentialist Theory Scenario Two   There are two other versions of consequentialism. They consider the ideas of pleasure and pain or happiness and unhappiness. This version holds that the only things intrinsically good are happiness or pleasure, and those things intrinsically bad are unhappiness and pain.

Let's examine this version within a corporate setting:

Happiness

- Employees get along, and there is a culture of empowerment: This is intrinsically good. It creates a positive work environment and individual innovation.
- Respect, integrity, and ethics are demonstrated actively throughout the organization: This is intrinsically good. An organization where individuals exhibit these qualities would be assumed to be an organization that would thrive in their operations.
- Individuals like their job and respect the company they work for: This is intrinsically good. Individuals who are happy in their job and respect the company will work hard to ensure they do an effective and efficient job.
- Individuals feel they are fairly treated by their employers: This is intrinsically good. Individuals who feel they are fairly treated will more likely be loyal to their employers.

Unhappiness

- Employees are stuck in a stale culture that is dictatorial in nature, and there is no alignment of power for decision making: This is intrinsically bad. Employees may become disgruntled in their job. This could result in a lack of effort toward effective completion of assignments.
- Actions often come with harsh repercussions, and individuals are rarely given a second chance: This is intrinsically bad. Individuals who feel they are not fairly treated or given a chance to correct mistakes may feel that the organization's standards are unfair.
- Individuals are not compensated fairly and in line with benchmark statistics: This is intrinsically bad. Individuals who feel they are not compensated fairly may become disgruntled in

their jobs and work less effectively. They may choose to leave the organization.

- There is a great deal of corporate politics played within the organization: This is considered intrinsically bad. Employees who perceive they must participate in corporate politics to be recognized or promoted, they may feel this is unfair treatment and choose to leave the organization.
- Individuals fear for their job: This is intrinsically bad. Individuals who fear for their job may not look forward to being at work and not put forth their best effort in completing responsibilities.

Pleasure

- All employees are paid and treated equitably: This is intrinsically good. If employees see the organization values their professionals and is careful to ensure individuals are fairly paid and treated equitably, they will most likely show a stronger level of loyalty.
- The organization culture is one in which employees and their careers can thrive: This is intrinsically good. Cultures that allow professionals' careers to thrive, will result in happier and more loyal employees.
- Employees enjoy their job tasks: This is intrinsically good. If employees enjoy their jobs, they will be more conscious of the quality and effort put forth in completing work. As a result, the employee will be happier.

Pain

- Employee compensation is varied based on who management deems important: This is intrinsically bad. Employees may view this as favoritism. The employee will not be happy and may feel a sense of emotional pain over the issue.
- The organization culture is toxic, and issues are not addressed in a timely manner: This is intrinsically bad. Employees cannot thrive in a toxic culture. If issues are not addressed, the organization will not be able to perform effectively. The employee may actually experience stress and pain resulting in health issues.

- Employees do not enjoy their job tasks: This would be intrinsically bad. If employees do not enjoy their job tasks they will find ways to cut corners, not show up for work, or not put forth their best effort.

In the aforementioned examples, the items listed under happiness and pleasure would be deemed ethical by the consequentialist, while the items listed under unhappiness and pain would be considered unethical.

Consequentialist Theory Scenario Three   Another version of consequentialism asserts the only thing intrinsically good is a person getting what they want and having their personal desires satisfied. On the other side, the only thing intrinsically bad is when a professional does not get what they want, and as a result their desires are not satisfied.

Some consequentialists believe pleasure and pain are very closely related to satisfaction and dissatisfaction. However, consider the following analogy, and see if you agree.

The television show *Survivor* is built on the premise of placing individuals in extreme living situations that are painful. The saving grace is the money and potential fame that will come with winning the *Survivor* title. Some people are willing to accept the pain and anguish for the pot of gold at the end of the rainbow. So, in this scenario, would a consequentialist agree the pain contestants endure is ethical, because they may win $1 million?

Consequentialist Ethical Theory Four   This form of ethical theory maintains that whether an act is right or wrong is a matter of how the consequences of the action compares with the consequences of other actions that could have occurred. The right action is the one with the best consequences or the best balance of good over bad effects. Let's examine this theory in a corporate setting.

Assume a decision has to be made regarding whether a power plant will be closed due to concern over air emissions. Management has decided it does not want to accept the risk of emissions that may result in a fine or regulatory scrutiny. Management closes the plant. Later, when performing maintenance, it is discovered that emissions controls are well established, and there was no environmental threat. In this case, the act of closing the power plant may have been the wrong decision because of the outcome. But, the question remains—how could management have known? The company was risk averse and took the risk-averse action of closing the plant. This was ultimately the proper ethical choice, regardless of the outcome identified during the maintenance procedures.

Applied Ethics   Applied ethics is the examination, from a moral standpoint, of issues that are matters of moral judgment.

Now that we have discussed and provided examples of the various forms of ethical theories, let's summarize by comparing the three types of ethical theories in a simplistic format.

- Meta-ethics: What does right or wrong mean?
    - Example: How is information within the company's code of conduct determined? Who decides right from wrong?
- Normative ethics: How should individuals act?
    - Example: Does the organization follow virtue ethics, deontology ethics, or one of the consequentialist ethical theories?
- Applied ethics: How can individuals take moral knowledge and put it into everyday practice?
    - Example: What does the company do to educate and instill ethical principles within the organization?

Everyday Moral/Ethical Judgments   As if having three ethical theories (and subtheories) to choose from isn't enough, individuals may apply moral and ethical judgments utilizing varying attributes that may include:

- Circumstance of an issue
- Individuals involved
- When an issue occurred

Consider the various types of ethical judgments individuals make on a day-to-day basis. These can run the gamut of:

- Moral judgments made about the actions of others based on a variety of parameters including individual perceptions of the person as well as the act itself.
- Moral judgments about specific incidents that occur without any consideration of the individuals involved.

- Judgments about the traits of a person's character. This may include his or her level of honesty, trustworthiness, respect, and friendship or dishonesty, unfaithfulness, rudeness, or cruelty.

In today's business world, when evaluating a moral judgment, you must consider whether the judgment is exclusive or whether the judgment is impacted based on the presumption of the personal character of an individual. Consider the following scenario:

Everyday Moral Judgments Scenario One   The CEO of a well-respected company is known as a person who exhibits a hard hand when managing employees. Even with this trait, the CEO has done a tremendous job in advancing the strategy and earnings of the company. There have been times when the CEO's actions are questionable in relation to ethical theories. Employees have noticed cases where the CEO does not follow proper protocol and policy when dealing with new customers or vendors, or the CEO is extremely brash to his subordinates. Many times his brash behavior borders on disrespect.

Given this scenario, it is obvious there are cases where individuals might judge the CEO's actions as improper or unethical. Typically, individuals judge a person who exhibits these traits based on the person's actions. In this circumstance, the employee is conflicted. He or she observes the CEO acting in a way that would be considered improper for other individuals, yet the CEO is allowed to exhibit the traits with little or no ramification. Here is where the ethical dilemma comes into play. When employees observe individuals acting in ways that do not display their personal view of right or wrong, the employee may rationalize why it is OK to act in the same manner.

Summary

By now you may be thinking, "I'm totally confused on how these theories and principles relate to evaluating corporate ethics within an organization!" Also, you may ask how auditors should employ these concepts when examining the ethical and corporate culture of their organization. From a simplistic viewpoint, it is important that management, auditors, and all employees understand there are many variations of ethical principles. Those variations can manifest themselves in the workplace based on a professional's own personal morals and attitudes. This may assist in understanding that each ethical theory has its own flaws, and there is a possibility the organization may need to use a combination of theories in its application of ethical behavior.

It would be helpful to examine various ethical incidents that have occurred in the organization and determine if you can identify what ethical theory was applied to the particular incident. Assume you identify the organization follows virtue ethics because it has handled similar situations in different ways based primarily on the perceived character of the individuals involved. If the organization formally states in its policy that "ethical issues will be evaluated equally regardless of the person involved," you have a fact to present to your governing body that indicates the organization is not following its own ethical principles.

Let's consider another example. Has the organization been known to make a decision on the status of an issue based on its outcome? In other words, is it OK to undermine other employees as long as the job is completed? This may seem to be an illogical concept. But, often organizations will take the position of no harm no foul. That may be true with regard to the outcome of the particular issue, but they must consider there may have been harm to the other employees involved. If you determine issues are being handled in this manner, management should be made aware of the potential overall consequences of maintaining this theory.

Section 3: University Organizational Theory and Behavior Curriculum

Over the years, the university educational system has placed greater focus on the topic of ethics and ethical behavior. Many universities have experienced their own "ethical" dilemmas that range from inappropriate behavior in sporting activities (recruiting, selling tickets and even events extending to sexual harassment or misconduct) to classroom issues. However, our focus in this section is to evaluate whether the current ethical courses provided to students will prepare them for the dynamic workforce they may face.

Depending on an individual's chosen field of study, his or her exposure to ethical topics may vary. Individuals who study in the health field will be exposed to ethical concepts relevant to the profession of treating and caring for patients. Individuals who study in the legal field will study ethical behavior as it relates to the execution of the type of legal work they may engage in, whether that be contracts or criminal defense. Almost all fields of study have their own version of ethics and standard guidelines by which the profession should act.

When students first enter their college years, they may enroll in a course on organizational theory and behavior. It would be interesting to review the textbook literature taught on this topic 20 years ago and compare it with what is covered in today's school setting.

I began my college years in the late 1970s and took an organizational theory course. I have to admit it didn't mean a lot to me at the time. Since I had not been exposed to the corporate organizational setting, many of the concepts were difficult to comprehend or even relate to. Ten years later, as I was working on my master's degree, I was required to take another course similar to organizational theory and behavior. It was interesting to note how conversation during the class seemed to be much more relevant to students who had been in the working world for a period. The university where I obtained my master's degree catered to the nontraditional student. Many of my classmates were individuals who had been in the workforce for some period of time and were returning to school to pursue their advanced degree. There were a few students who were entering their master's courses right after completing undergraduate work. When the topic of organizational behavior, ethics, or organizational politics came up, those students had a difficult time understanding some of the realities of the working world. Their undergraduate work had immersed them in the theory of how an organization should act. As is often the case, theory is not reality.

In reality, it is difficult to fully grasp the concept of ethics and how it may manifest itself until a professional enters the workforce. This is one reason why the previous section covered ethical theories and concepts. Often, courses focus on the methodology or textbook wording of ethical policies for a given profession. As a young student, it may be difficult to embrace and truly understand how those concepts will impact individual job performance.

With the prevalence of university courses moving to online instruction, a looming question exists as to how effective this type of instruction will be for our new professionals. Ethics and corporate culture is written about extensively by multiple professions. However, absent the ability for interactive class discussion, instructor question and answer, guest speakers, and real-life scenario role-play, the topic of ethics in our future work culture may become even more difficult to prepare for. If you question this theory, think about how your own organization currently instructs or informs employees about ethical procedures and conduct. It may be completed through online training modules which employees take during their downtime. Over the past few years, the online modules have become more effective, utilizing animation and avatars that speak directly to the employee. In addition, they have incorporated requirements for the professional to answer questions prior to proceeding through the module. However, those who have experience with online training tactics often learn certain tricks of the trade to facilitate completion of the module as quickly as possible. This does not provide for the most effective learning atmosphere.

Tricks of the Trade Scenario

Several years ago, I was a chief audit executive (CAE) at a publicly traded company. We were in an audit committee session, and our corporate compliance officer began touting how effective the company's online ethics training was. He was quoting statistics indicating that 99% of employees completed the training by the mandated deadline. In addition, the employees acknowledged their completion through an electronic sign-off at the end of the module. As I sat in the meeting, I debated how to interject a concern into the conversation.

The discussion about the code of ethics training was occurring because there was an agenda item for the audit committee to reapprove the company's code. The audit committee and corporate compliance officer knew internal audit was evaluating the current code of conduct process; however, I had not been informed the code was placed on the agenda for approval prior to our audit being completed. As the corporate compliance officer asked for the committee's approval of the code, I felt I had to speak up. I asked for the approval to be tabled until the next quarterly meeting. I mentioned that, by that time, internal audit would have the final results of the review. My request did not fare well with the compliance officer, but it gained the attention of the audit committee. They asked if there were any initial observations about the code of ethics and the training process.

One of the cardinal rules of internal audit is to be cautious of communicating findings prior to ensuring you have obtained all the relevant facts. I attempted to deflect the question by indicating we had preliminary observations but needed time to ensure our information was accurate. However, the cat was out of the bag, and the audit committee pressed for highlights of the initial observations. With caution, I explained we had reviewed the online training module process, and, indeed, 99% of employees completed the module. However, my concern was the module had been designed as a 40-minute training session. During our review, we found almost 50% of the individuals taking the module completed it in less than 20 minutes. If professionals had gone through the training that quickly, they may not have fully comprehended the various sections of the code of ethics. In addition, although they had technically signed off on the code at the end of the module, the fact that many of the employees had completed it in less than half the time expected begged the question whether the employees truly understood what they were acknowledging.

This incident occurred several years before the Committee of Sponsoring Organizations (COSO) 2013 *Integrated control framework* was released. COSO 2013 stresses the importance of an organizations' ability to effectively exhibit procedures and processes in place are well understood and communicated. Had COSO 2013 been around at the time of this incident, I may have been able to leverage it as another reason why it was important to table the approval of the code of conduct and training program.

In the end, the audit committee agreed to table approval of the code. Upon completion of the audit, the compliance department instituted additional procedures to ensure employees were diligent when completing the training. In addition, face-to-face sessions were held to reinforce the company's code of conduct. These improvements gave stronger assurance that individuals who worked at the company had an understanding of the concepts and principles behind the company's code of conduct.

Section 4: Understanding the Internal Auditors Code of Ethics and Related Principles

Introduction

Individuals who study the practice of internal auditing during their educational years will be provided with an overview of the Institute of Internal Auditors (IIA) *Code of Conduct and Ethical Standards*. This is an important document to understand, but it does not necessarily prepare the professional to evaluate ethical processes within their future organization.

Individuals who study for the Certified Internal Auditor examination will study to understand the IIA Code of Ethics. It is important for auditors to deeply examine the Code of Ethics and understand the meaning and words as well as the potential challenges that may be faced when trying to abide by the Code. To fulfill the role of internal audit as identified by the profession, you must be able to accept and understand the various elements of the Code of Ethics and come to grips with how the concepts may be manifested once you enter the workforce.

Within the following section, we will take excerpts from the IIA Code of Ethics and dissect those concepts. We will examine the reality and the challenge that internal auditors may face when attempting to follow the Code of Ethics and apply it within the workforce.

Internal Auditors Code of Ethics

The first section of the Code speaks to the purpose of why the profession has outlined the *Standards*.

The purpose of The Institute's Code of Ethics is to promote an ethical culture in the profession of internal auditing. Internal auditing is an independent, objective assurance and consulting activity designed to add value and improve an organization's operations. It helps an organization accomplish its objectives by bringing a systematic, disciplined approach to evaluate and improve the effectiveness of risk management, control, and governance processes.

IIA Code of Ethics

A Code of Ethics is necessary and appropriate for the profession of internal auditing. The Code exhibits the trust placed in the objective assurance about governance, risk management and control that internal audit provides.

Objectivity, Independence, and Assurance

As you will notice, the introduction to the Code of Ethics defines the meaning of internal audit. This is where the internal auditor's first challenge will come into play. Let's start by dissecting the first sentence of the definition of internal auditing:

> Internal auditing is an independent, objective assurance and consulting activity designed to add value and improve an organization's operations.

The Institute of Internal Auditors

Partial Definition of Internal Auditing

The challenge internal auditors have is evident when examining the words independent, objective, assurance, and consulting. Although this is how the profession defines the role of internal audit, the concept of true independence is almost impossible to execute in the corporate world. Independence means the individual is free from influence or pressure. Internal auditors are employed by the companies they work for. The companies provide benefits, a paycheck, a job, and a corporate atmosphere. Along with each of these comes a supervisor. The head of internal audit will also have a supervisor who is someone employed by the company. Inherently, this fact makes it almost impossible to be fully independent. However, the internal auditor must recognize the word used immediately after independent. That word is objective. Although it may be difficult to be truly independent from an organizational perspective, internal auditors must understand the concept of objectivity and be able to adequately execute the concept. Execution of objectivity will help balance concerns of independence. If the internal auditor can successfully execute objectivity within their work, this will significantly mitigate potential negative impacts of the inability to be organizationally independent.

Recognizing this theory, let's further explore the concept of objectivity. Objectivity is based in moral philosophy. It is generally defined as the state of being true even outside your own personal biases, interpretations, or feelings. To be objective, a person must be able to set aside their own individual personal feelings and biases about an issue. This can be a very difficult task. In addition, many professionals confuse the organizational attribute of objectivity with the concept of independence. This is a strongly debated issue for internal audit and compliance functions. Some assert to be objective in mindset, the professional must be fully independent in how they performs their assessments.

Objectivity requires the ability to utilize and exercise professional skepticism. Professional skepticism is an attitude that includes a questioning mind and a critical assessment of evidence. It is composed of three elements: personal attributes, mind-set, and actions. Each of these attributes can be very personal in nature. They often are the foundations of an individual's personality. A good example of exercising professional skepticism is to consider whether your workplace encourages individuals to openly ask questions and work to understand why things are done in a certain manner. When contemplating the ability to execute professional skepticism, consider the following scenario. The scenario may assist in understanding why the concept of professional skepticism is often easier said than performed.

Professional Skepticism Scenario   Assume you are an intern with a large public accounting firm. You are given an assignment to inventory paintings in the vault of a well-known and reputable art center in your city. Your supervisor hands you a checklist, which provides guidelines and instruction on how to execute the inventory. The instructions indicate you are to go to the vault and record the serial numbers on the back of each painting. You then go to the books and records and vouch the serial numbers to the art center's accounting books to ensure each painting is properly recorded. This may seem like a simple and straightforward task. However, for the inexperienced auditor, the act of following a checklist approach that simply instructs the person to record serial numbers is akin to limiting professional skepticism. Can you identify why this might be? Consider that the auditor will do exactly as he or she has been instructed. In so doing, the auditor may overlook glaring red flags that may point to something inappropriate with the serial numbers on the paintings. If the auditor uses individual professional skepticism and judgment, he or she may observe the serial numbers are written on tabs or stickers which can be easily removed and transferred to another painting. Or, the auditor may identify the painting is covered with a false backing that masks the true serial number. In other words, the young auditor's professional skepticism has been limited because of the direction given by the supervisor. Since professional skepticism is defined as an attitude that includes a questioning mind and a critical assessment of evidence, in our scenario the intern was not adequately exercising professional skepticism.

Now, let's take this scenario a bit further. Assume the intern speaks to another auditor who is experienced in reviews similar to the one described. The young intern begins telling the auditor about the project. Since the experienced auditor is a bit more skeptical and has actual experience performing inventories, he begins to question the intern about how he ensured the paintings were not falsified. Can you imagine how the intern's supervisor might react if the intern begins to ask probing questions that may infer the audit procedures are not sufficient to ensure fraud potential is adequately mitigated? One scenario may have the supervisor patting the intern on the back and praising him for the use of professional skepticism. Another scenario may have the supervisor becoming upset because the intern's questions have resulted in the audit team's need to perform additional tests or examinations. In either case, if you are the intern, you may be worried about how your supervisor will react if you begin to question the audit steps. The simple fact the intern may have concerns expressing his own observations is in essence, putting pressure on the ability to exercise professional skepticism.

Internal Audit Definition

The next part of the internal auditor's Code of Ethics continues with the definition of internal auditing.

> It helps an organization accomplish its objectives by bringing a systematic, disciplined approach to evaluate and improve the effectiveness of risk management, control, and governance processes.

Institute of Internal Auditors

Partial Definition of Internal Audit

Since the definition of internal auditing is embedded within the Code of Ethics, we must further examine what impact the definition will have on how internal auditors may be able to execute their fiduciary duties.

This part of the definition indicates internal auditing "helps an organization accomplish its objectives by bringing a systematic, disciplined approach." Before we go any further in evaluating the principles within the internal auditor's Code of Ethics, you must question whether your own procedures and processes are representing a systematic and disciplined approach. Many internal audit functions do not have well-defined methodologies for the execution of individual audit engagements. This can extend from financial reviews, operational reviews, compliance reviews, or even fraud evaluations. If your department does not maintain a systematic and disciplined approach to auditing, you may need to question whether the department is abiding by the profession's Code of Ethics.

The Institute's Code of Ethics includes two essential components. The first component is the principles relevant to the profession. The following excerpts from the Code of Ethics outline the principles internal auditors must abide by.

Code of Ethics: Principles

Internal auditors are expected to apply and uphold the following principles:

Integrity

> The integrity of internal auditors establishes trust and thus provides the basis for reliance on their judgment.

Institute of Internal Auditors Code of Ethics

Objectivity

Internal auditors exhibit the highest level of professional objectivity in gathering, evaluating, and communicating information about the activity or process being examined. Internal auditors make a balanced assessment of all the relevant circumstances and are not unduly influenced by their own interests or by others in forming judgments.

Institute of Internal Auditors Code of Ethics

Confidentiality

Internal auditors respect the value and ownership of information they receive and do not disclose information without appropriate authority, unless there is a legal or professional obligation to do so.

Institute of Internal Auditors Code of Ethics

Competency

Internal auditors apply the knowledge, skills, and experience needed in the performance of internal audit services.

Institute of Internal Auditors Code of Ethics

Each of these principles is critical to maintain ethical standards. However, simply listing the principles and including them within a charter or policy does not ensure the principles are executable within the organization. Consider the following scenario.

Integrity Scenario   Contemplate the meaning of integrity. It is often referred to as doing the right thing when no one is looking. Are you certain the auditors within your organization will perform and act appropriately when they are not being evaluated or supervised?

A CAE relayed a story regarding an incident that occurred with staff members. Several of the staff were sent to a conference by the CAE. Company policy dictated that when several staff members dined out together, the most senior individual at the table would pay for the meals and submit the expenditure for reimbursement. The purpose was to ensure the proper level of supervisory approval. In this instance, the CAE sent a senior manager and four staff individuals to a conference. The senior manager should have been paying for the meals when the group dined out together. When the group returned from the trip and the CAE began to approve expense reports, he noticed the senior manager was not reporting meals on his travel and entertainment expenses. The CAE began to wonder why and went to the senior manager to inquire what had occurred. After a series of questions and exchange of information, the CAE identified the senior manager had requested one of his direct reports to charge the meals on his company credit card. The senior manager knew that by having his direct report handle the charges he would then receive the report for final approval. This would keep the CAE from seeing the total amount of the bill or what was purchased. When the CAE discovered the issue, he further evaluated the expenses and found the group had dined at expensive establishments and had consumed a good deal of liquor (which was not in line with company policy). The CAE confronted the senior manager with the incident. The senior manager acknowledged he had asked his staff person to charge the meals but indicated the reason was he forgot to bring his credit card to the dinners. However, when speaking with other staff members, they indicated the senior manager did, in fact, have his credit card. The senior manager told the other staff members that having one of them use their travel expense card would be the easiest way to facilitate the charges without having to ask the CAE for approval of the lavish dinner expenses.

Think about this scenario for a bit. Was the senior manager acting with integrity in this situation? When the CAE discovered the full story, he had a long talk with the senior manager. The manager had been a long time employee of the company and was typically a very trustworthy and hard-working individual. However, this incident resulted in a significant distrust by the CAE of many of the actions of the senior manager. Even though, in the grand scheme of expenditures, the amounts were not significant, the long-term impact of this event caused the CAE to question many aspects about the integrity of the senior manager. If the senior manager could not display the proper integrity within his own group, how could the CAE trust he would act in the proper manner in situations that may involve process owners? One other question in this scenario is of concern. Each of the staff auditors knew and understood the company policy for payment of group meals. However, they went along with the senior manager's suggestion to bypass the payment going to the CAE for approval. Should one of these staff members have questioned the issue or informed the CAE? You be the judge in this situation.

Objectivity Scenario   We've previously defined objectivity as "the state of being true even outside of personal biases, interpretations, or feelings." We have discussed the dilemma faced when combining the words independent and objectivity. But, let's consider the act of being able to act in a truly objective manner.

Assume you are performing an audit on safety procedures at your company. The city where your organization's headquarters is located passed a conceal-and-carry law for guns. In the past, your organization prohibited firearms on company premises. However, they now must abide by the city law for conceal and carry. The organization alters their internal policies to indicate that conceal and carry is permissible, but those who do so must take extra precautionary actions to ensure the safety of employees and customers. From your own personal perspective, you have a strong opposition to the conceal-and-carry law and agree with the company's original internal policy. You feel the conceal-and-carry law could result in danger and harm to innocent individuals.

To adequately perform the review or engagement, you must be able to put your own personal biases aside. Your organization has included within their policies that conceal and carry is not forbidden. During the audit, you find numerous individuals who frequently interface with customers are carrying firearms under the conceal-and-carry law. You inquire of the precautionary procedures utilized by the individuals but your own personal bias prevents you from objectively analyzing the situation to evaluate whether there is any potential threat. You must be completely objective in this circumstance. Unless you can factually show the conceal-and-carry process could pose an imminent threat to employees or customers, your desire to report the issue as an unacceptable or high risk would demonstrate an inability to use objectivity. (Remember, the city has passed a conceal-and-carry law, and the organization has shown their support of the law through acknowledgment within their own policies.) You have allowed your own personal biases to impact your judgment.

This is obviously an extreme and personal issue. But often, when objectivity comes into play, our own personal biases and beliefs impair the ability to fully exercise the trait. We may decide our opinion is the correct one because of our own experiences and beliefs. When this happens, a person tends to block out the information provided by others. The person may see things as black and white and have a hard time objectively evaluating a situation.

A separate example may relate to the judicial process. Consider those individuals who act as judges in a court of law. They are required to put their own individual thoughts and prejudices aside and evaluate the facts of the case in an objective and unbiased manner regardless of personal beliefs on the issue.

If you, or anyone within your department, has difficulty with examining issues outside personal biases, the concept of objectivity will be very difficult to execute. In this instance, you are not abiding by the Code of Ethics.

Confidentiality Scenario   This portion of the Code of Ethics indicates that

> Internal auditors respect the value and ownership of information they receive and do not disclose information without appropriate authority unless there is a legal or professional obligation to do so.

The Institute of Internal Auditors Code of Ethics

Again, this is an excellent theory or concept, but the dynamics of the workplace can often overshadow the best intentions of workers.

An internal auditor relayed a story regarding confidentiality of information. In this instance, the auditor was on a team evaluating executive expenditures. The team had identified issues that appeared to be egregious actions, if not fraudulent, and purposefully deceptive toward the organization. The challenge was the auditors on the assignment were fairly inexperienced. Instead of speaking with their direct supervisor in a confidential manner about the observations, they chose to brainstorm thoughts and ideas with other staff members. This resulted in some individuals inadvertently mentioning to others outside the department about the discrepancies in executive expenditure habits. Of course, the word spread quickly, and before the young audit team knew it, their observations were informally communicated throughout the company. As you can imagine, this caused quite a stir with executive management as well as the audit committee.

There may have been a couple of errors within this process. First, the young audit team should have taken their observations directly to their reporting supervisor rather than discussing them during a brainstorming session with other auditors. Second, even though it would have been better not to discuss the issue with other members of the audit department who were not involved with the audit, those individuals were still under a fiduciary obligation to not communicate the issues outside the department.

In this instance, the young auditors fell prey to a situation many auditors experience. Auditors often consult with departmental coworkers to obtain new ideas and brainstorm risks. However, when it comes to discussing specific findings, especially if they are sensitive in nature, the internal auditor must be cognizant of the sensitivity of the issue and the relative requirements to maintain confidential information.

Competency Scenario   The competency scenario can become a bit difficult. According to the Code of Ethics:

> Internal auditors apply the knowledge, skills, and experience needed in the performance of internal audit services.

The Institute of Internal Auditors Code of Ethics

Even though the definition of internal auditing may sound like an internal auditor can provide any service management may request, it is important to keep in mind the relative competency required to complete specific audit requests. Use the example of the need to evaluate the adequacy of a new information technology system. If the audit department does not maintain staff with the expertise to understand and examine typical information technology threats, this factor must be acknowledged, and the proper resources must be obtained to efficiently execute the project. As an internal audit group, you may have individuals who obtained their degree in the information technology sciences. However, that does not necessarily qualify the person to be the lead auditor on a new systems implementation. This is a similar thought to considering an auditor who has passed the certified fraud examiners accreditation. This certification displays the auditor has learned the basic techniques and methodologies to apply when evaluating potential fraudulent situations. However, if the person does not have experience with an investigation or is new to an organization and does not fully understand the various processes involved, he or she may not be the correct person to assign to a fraud investigation. In other words, the individual may not have the true competency to execute the project.

The internal audit department must critically evaluate the skill level and experience of their personnel and ensure they have the knowledge, skills, and expertise needed to perform the assigned work.

Section 5: Understanding the Internal Auditors Code of Ethics and Rules of Conduct

The second part of the Code of Ethics is Rules of Conduct that describe behavior norms expected of internal auditors. These rules are an aid to interpreting the principles into practical applications and are intended to guide the ethical conduct of internal auditors.

The Integrity Rules of Conduct indicate internal auditors shall:

- Perform their work with honesty, diligence, and responsibility.
- Observe the law and make disclosures expected by the law and the profession.
- Not knowingly be a party to any illegal activity, or engage in acts that are discreditable to the profession of internal auditing or to the organization.
- Respect and contribute to the legitimate and ethical objectives of the organization.

The Institute of Internal Auditors Code of Ethics

The Objectivity Rules of Conduct indicate internal auditors shall:

- Not participate in any activity or relationship that may impair or be presumed to impair their unbiased assessment. This participation includes those activities or relationships that may be in conflict with the interests of the organization.

- Not accept anything that may impair or be presumed to impair their professional judgment.
- Disclose all material facts known to them that, if not disclosed, may distort the reporting of activities under review.

The Institute of Internal Auditors Code of Ethics

The Confidentiality Rules of Conduct indicate internal auditors shall:

- Be prudent in their use and protection of information acquired in the course of their duties.
- Not use information for any personal gain or in any manner that would be contrary to the law or detrimental to the legitimate and ethical objectives of the organization.

The Institute of Internal Auditors Code of Ethics

The Competency Rules of Conduct indicate internal auditors shall:

- Engage only in those services for which they have the necessary knowledge, skills, and experience.
- Perform internal audit services in accordance with the *International Standards for the Professional Practice of Internal Auditing* (Standards).
- Continually improve their proficiency and the effectiveness and quality of their services.

The Institute of Internal Auditors Code of Ethics

Many of the concepts discussed within the scenarios presented for the Code of Ethics principles are evidenced in the information outlined within the Rules of Conduct. Let's take a few minutes to examine those rules a bit further and discuss where challenges may occur.

Rules of Conduct: Integrity

Our scenario for integrity principles provided insight into the concept of integrity as displayed within the workforce. The Rules of Conduct specify internal audit will perform their work with honesty, diligence, and responsibility. This statement also addresses the manner in which internal auditors should act when performing their day-to-day responsibilities or executing projects. Yet, many internal auditors understand the reality when attempting to abide by rule. Auditors face challenges when management wants the hurry-up-and-finish approach. This may create difficulties in utilizing appropriate diligence in performing work. Also, the rule of performing work with responsibility can be challenged when auditors request information management cannot readily provide, or feel the request is not warranted. The internal auditor is attempting to be responsible and ensure documentation is obtained to ensure the auditor arrives at the proper conclusion. But, when barriers are placed in the path, it may be difficult to find an alternative route to executing responsibility.

The second rule listed for integrity speaks to observing the law and making disclosures as expected by the law and the profession. You would think there would be little room for waiver in relationship to this rule. However, remember that internal auditors are not necessarily lawyers who have been trained in all legal aspects of the multitude of issues they may encounter. Also, remember "just because it's legal, doesn't mean it is ethical." Auditors may face challenges when issues are identified because management may defer to legal counsel to determine the ultimate severity or impact of the issues. They may even be informed by legal counsel that the issue is one the legal department will handle, and the auditor does not need to take further action. If, as an internal auditor, you come upon an issue where you question the legality of the circumstances, ask yourself what you would do. Of course, the first step would be to consult with the organization's legal counsel. Now assume the legal team has taken ownership of the issue, and you have been informed that further evaluation or communication by the audit team is not necessary. What would you do? The Rules of Conduct say you should observe the law and make the proper disclosures expected by the law and by the profession (internal audit profession). You have informed by legal counsel and senior management of the issue and have been told it is time for internal audit to step away. This is one of those challenges where, until you actually experience the issue, it is difficult to know what steps you might actually take. In essence, you have fulfilled your fiduciary duty by disclosing the issue to management and the legal counsel. However, how do you know when you must take further action and inform the audit committee or relevant governance body?

Integrity Scenario   A CAE relayed an incident in which the audit team had identified a violation by the company of an aspect of the Foreign Corrupt Practices Act. The information gathered clearly supported the findings. The CAE took the issue to the chief legal officer (CLO). The CLO informed the CAE that the legal group would handle the issue moving forward. The CLO hired outside counsel experienced in aspects of the Foreign Corrupt Practices Act to evaluate the auditor's findings. Outside counsel informed the CLO the findings were accurate and the company may face liability, but there were some legal loopholes that could minimize the issue. The CLO told the CAE he was not to inform the audit committee until outside counsel had reviewed all the facts of the case. When outside counsel made mention of the potential legal loopholes, the CLO engaged counsel to begin building a rebuttal case. Over the next 14 months, the CAE periodically revisited the issue with the CLO. He expressed his concern that the issue was still outstanding and indicated he had a fiduciary duty to inform the audit committee. The CLO, who was a higher-ranking executive, informed the CAE he had fulfilled his fiduciary duty by telling the CLO, and he had no further communication obligations. He also informed the CAE he was not authorized to inform the audit committee until the outside legal firm had prepared their defense.

What would you do? Put yourself in the place of the CAE. In some respects, the CAE did indeed follow the guidelines outlined in the Rules of Conduct. He informed internal legal counsel of the issue. In other respects, the CAE knew the outside firm had validated the issue was a true threat, and yet no communication had been provided to the audit committee. This is a difficult circumstance for the CAE. To abide by the Code of Ethics, it would seem appropriate the CAE must ensure the audit committee is informed of the issue. However, the CLO has executed his authority and intimidation over the CAE to attemp to keep him from informing the audit committee of the issue prior to a loophole defense being developed. How would you handle the situation?

Rules of Conduct Illegal Actions

The Rule of Conduct related to not knowingly being a party to any illegal activities is one that would be expected by any organization or internal audit function. However, the second part of the Rule of Conduct, which states "not engage in acts that are discreditable to the profession of internal auditing or to the organization," can be left open to various forms of interpretation.

All companies have varying views on the purpose and authority of the internal audit function. Regardless of whether the company is privately held, publicly traded, not-for-profit, or even a sole proprietorship, there may be polarizing views on acts that would be considered discreditable to the profession of internal auditing. For instance, in our example where the CLO has directed the CAE not to discuss the issue with the audit committee, could this be considered discreditable to the profession?

Rules of Conduct Legitimate and Ethical Objectives

The last Rule of Conduct under integrity states, "respect and contribute to the legitimate and ethical objectives of the organization." Through training hundreds of auditors, I have often heard comments and concerns expressed by auditors regarding whether certain objectives of the organization are truly legitimate or ethical objectives. Yet, the auditors stay in their positions without raising the issue with management. This can occur due to a fear of confrontation on an issue, an assumption that the objectives and strategy of the organization are not considered part of the scope of internal audit, or simply a fear of retribution. However, to abide by the Rules of Conduct, if an internal auditor has an observation of this type, he or she must find a way to bring it to the attention of the proper governing body.

Rules of Conduct: Objectivity

In our discussion of the principles of objectivity, we discussed the challenges faced due to personal biases and pressures. Within the Rules of Conduct, further clarification is made regarding participation in activities or relationships that may impair or "be presumed to impair" an unbiased assessment.

Objectivity Scenario   A CAE relayed an issue that deals with this specific Rule of Conduct. He assigned a new audit to one of his senior staff. Approximately halfway into the audit, the CAE discovered the senior staff member was a distant relative of a manager of the department being audited. When the CAE approached his senior staff about the issue, the staff member acknowledged the manager was a distant relative, but she indicated they rarely had interactions. The staff member did not mention she maintained a close family relationship with the parents of the manager. The senior staff felt she could still be objective and review the audit area without bias. A separate staff member informed the CAE of the close relationship of the senior staff member with the parents of the manager. The CAE informed the senior staff that regardless of how she felt about evaluating the issue, the existence of a conflict of interest may be perceived. In this case, the CAE removed the senior auditor from the review and reassigned the review to another staff member. This action raised questions with the department being audited. The senior auditor and the department manager both filed complaints against the CAE with the human resource department contending improper utilization of personal information. They felt their personal privacy was being invaded, and the personal relationship should have no impact on the audit.

In this instance, the human resources group did not have an understanding of the Code of Ethics for internal audit. Although the CAE outlined the Code to the human resource director, the company did not recognize the *Standards* as policies required to be followed. They sided with the senior auditor and the department manager. The CAE was reprimanded for an invasion of privacy. What would you have done in this circumstance? The CAE followed the Code of Ethics and Rules of Conduct, yet the issue came back as a reprimand. The CAE indicated he even discussed the issue with his direct reporting line in the company. However, he was told since the company didn't regard the *Standards* as requirements their auditors must abide with, the issue was deemed a human resource issue.

Accepting Gifts

The Rule of Conduct stating the internal auditor "will not accept anything that may impair or be presumed to impair their professional judgment" is another concept that can be broadly interpreted. Most individuals would agree acceptance of a complimentary lunch or other small token is not something that would impair a person's ability to exercise their professional judgment. But how and when is the line drawn?

Accepting Gifts Scenario   I reside in Kansas City, home of the Kansas City Royals. In 2014, the Royals faced the San Francisco Giants in the World Series, and in 2015 they faced the New York Mets in the World Series. Ticket prices to the series came at an extreme premium, and access to suites during the World Series was equivalent to a small fortune. Yet, there were several circumstances in which internal auditors (as well as external auditors), in addition to company management, accepted complimentary tickets to the series from vendors and consultants. Of course, this was a tremendous benefit, but you have to question whether this constitutes a potential conflict. Would management or the auditors be more or less willing to contest an issue because they had been provided with this gift as a "thank you" or gesture of trust? There are probably many instances in which this issue had absolutely no impact on any type of impairment of judgment. But there is always the perception of what expectation accompanied the gift. Auditors must be cognizant of these issues. They may seem minor on the surface but ask yourself, is the gesture or gift offered to other personnel who do not have a relationship with the vendor or consultant? If not, possibly the offer is an attempt to sway a future favor. Even if it is not an attempt to sway a future favor, how would the acceptance of the gift be viewed by others within the organization who regularly abide by the company's gift acceptance policy?

The final rule related to objectivity under the Rules of Conduct addresses the need to "disclose all material facts known to the auditor that, if not disclosed, may distort the reporting of activities under review." This rule comes with ensuring you have validated the material facts are indeed facts, and not presumptions. Auditors can sometimes feel they have adequately evaluated an issue and examined all relevant facts. However, the auditor is not as well versed in the area as the process owners. It is always possible facts gathered do not fully represent the issue. If an identified issue appears to be one whose outcome could result in a distortion of the activities under review, the auditor must ensure the facts and circumstances are fully vetted.

Rules of Conduct: Confidentiality   The scenario discussed under the principles for confidentiality covered the concept of the use and protection of information acquired in the course of performing auditors' responsibilities. Specifically, we discussed the communication of issues. However, the rule also relates to the adequate protection of work papers and work product, especially during sensitive reviews. Many audit groups have shared hard drives for their archived work papers. These shared drives are typically accessible to everyone within the department. The internal audit group must be cognizant of who has access to specific work papers and work products and be assured that when individuals enter or leave the group, the relevant work documents remain accessible only to those who need to have the information.

The second rule of conduct related to confidentiality indicates the internal auditor will "not use information for any personal gain or in any manner that would be contrary to the law or detrimental to the legitimate and ethical objectives of the organization." In today's world of sophisticated information technology, it is important internal audit groups maintain proper security over work products. Auditors rotate in and out of departments, and the Rule of Conduct should apply regardless of when and how access to the information is obtained.

Rules of Conduct: Competency   The scenario provided under the principle aspect for competency provided some validation and support behind the Rule of Conduct that internal auditors should engage only in those services for which they have the necessary knowledge, skills, and experience. Often, audit departments and CAEs are eager to please management and to exhibit their value to the organization. Periodically, they may stretch the limits when it comes to accepting certain assignments or engagements. It is incumbent on management of the internal audit department to ensure they can effectively execute assigned work with relevant competency.

The second Rule of Conduct under competency speaks to performing internal audit services in accordance with the *Standards*. This may be one of the most challenging areas for auditors when attempting to fully abide by the Code of Ethics. As we have stated, often management is not aware of the *Standards*. This makes it difficult for auditors to fully abide by those *Standards*. In other cases, management may feel the *Standards* are simply guidelines, and do not apply to their organization. This puts the auditor in an even more difficult position. CAEs and audit management must ensure management and the audit committee understand the *Standards* as well as the requirements of the Code of Ethics. Absent adequate understanding, it may be difficult to abide by this Rule of Conduct.

The last Rule of Conduct under competency is the statement that internal audit should "continually improve their proficiency and the effectiveness and quality of their services." Auditors must remember there are numerous ways to continually improve their proficiency. Those methods extend far beyond attending formalized training or conferences. Think back to when you were in grade school. How did you improve your proficiency in math or writing? In some cases it was through your studies, but much of the improvement came through continual practice. This relationship can extend to your working years. The more you practice or are involved with your profession, the more proficient you will become. As a result, audit departments must strive to implement strong standards for supervision, mentoring, work paper review, on-the-job training, and regular group interaction and meetings to share learning. Remember, proficiency does not solely equate to having a certification. Proficiency comes with practice and execution.

Section 6: Corporate Ethics in the Future— Could There Be an App for That?

Introduction

A couple of years ago, the American Institute of Certified Public Accountants magazine published an article which indicated that certain organizations were working toward creating a computer application which could help guide professionals in their ethical decision making. What an intriguing thought! However, as with our definition of the various ethical theories and individual traits and morals, it is hard to conceptualize an effective application could be created that would provide employees with the proper ethical answer to a dilemma for every situation they may encounter. But, "never say never." Many people thought it was impossible to walk on the moon. Think how long ago that occurred. As technology becomes more sophisticated, there may be the possibility of some application where employees can enter parameters, and the application will provide a guideline by which to make an ethical decision. In thinking through the possibilities, I began to imagine what an ethics application may look like. Just for fun, let's brainstorm what an application of this kind may incorporate. Consider these thoughts, and then also consider what other concepts could be added.

Steps for Application

Step one: Enter your profession (e.g., doctor, lawyer, certified public accountant)

Step two: Does your profession have an ethics policy? (Yes or No)

Step three: Categorize the type of company you work for (e.g., public/private/government)

Step four: Categorize the company's geographical reach (e.g., local/national/international)

Step five: Categorize workforce generational and gender composition (e.g., male/female; millennial, baby boomer, Generation X)

Step six: Categorize the makeup of the workforce's religious faith

Step seven: Categorize industry appetite (Are they tolerable to ethical issues?)

These may be a few of the initial questions an application may need to establish parameters around an ethical situation. There may be others, but let's assume we've covered the most significant ones at this time. What would the next step be? The organization would have to establish parameters that classify their opinion of how severe an incident might be. Consider Exhibit 2.1 as a potential example of a company's tolerance guidelines around ethics.

You may examine this exhibit and have your own personal opinions as to whether this could actually work. Assume for a minute that it does. Possibly, an employee comes across an ethical issue, so he or she uses the application and inputs the basic parameters outlined in steps one through seven. Next, the employee would need a method to categorize and classify the type of incident (as indicated in row one on Exhibit 2.1). There may be another input which allows the employee to add information the application can consider when arriving at an estimate of the severity of the issue. Assume this all occurs, and the application does its thing and comes back and tells the employee

Bad	Really bad	Horrible
Lying to other employees	Lying to your boss	Lying for your boss, to senior management, or the board
Taking small dollar items	Taking large dollar items	Blatant misuse of corporate assets
Skipping process steps to complete a task	Utilizing organizational authority for your own benefit	Mental or physical harassment to get what you want
Disrespecting other personnel	Upward disrespect	Taking advantage of vendor relationships
Accepting small dollar gifts	Not disclosing a potential conflict of interest	Accepting large dollar gifts or using position to advance your own needs
Taking advantage of paid time off	Misreporting time	Blatantly and regularly falsifying time
Concealing records	Destroying records	Falsifying records
Petty fraud	Large dollar fraud	Collusion and major fraud

Exhibit 2.1   Tolerance guidelines for ethics.

the incident witnessed falls into the "horrible" category. Now what? The organization would need to have a protocol in place to escalate each type of issue based on severity.

This may all sound impossible or difficult because of the many parameters involved in ethical decision making. But, tougher problems have been solved, and it is amazing what information technology can do these days. So, don't dismiss the idea too quickly. Just as we now witness the many tasks our smartphones and iPads can accomplish the day may come where the ethics application is a reality.

Section 7: Global, Diverse, and Expanding Workforce

Introduction

As the corporate climate continues to evolve and become more global, we will experience a greater combination of professionals interacting who maintain various beliefs, morals, and ethical boundaries. The advancement of technology and the method in which companies manage their workforce can itself be an ethical question. Consider the following true scenario.

Diverse Workforce Scenario One   Company ABC decided to begin a virtual work environment. The original expectation was the arrangement would enhance worker satisfaction, decrease overhead costs, and increase productivity. This assumption considered the fact that professionals would not spend a great deal of time commuting to and from work. However, after approximately 2 years, the company found they were experiencing a vast array of new challenges.

First, they found productivity had not gone up; it had actually gone down. Professionals who worked in the virtual environment became protective of their personal time and were not flexible in requirements for scheduling meetings with other professionals. In addition, it was difficult for supervisors to judge whether a professional's lack of productivity was due to the inability to focus on work while away from the office or whether it was a technical issue where the employee needed more handheld guidance to complete a task. The organization found itself asking supervisors to make determinations as to which employees would be allowed to work virtually. This created an atmosphere of perceived arbitrary decision making. Employees accused supervisors of being unfair or unethical because they allowed certain professionals to work virtually, while other professionals could not. There was a trend where some supervisors observed professionals with young children would experience a lower rate of productivity when working from home. The organization concluded that professionals with children could not effectively work from home, because their focus would be on their children and not on work. Rather than working with the employees to ensure there were effective day-care alternatives, the supervisors mandated specific standards based on arbitrary observations. Was this ethical?

Another trend to emerge was the employer found although professionals were saving time by not having to endure a long commute to the office, they were utilizing the expected commute time as part of their allocated workday. In other words, if it normally took the employee 45 minutes to commute to the office one way, the employee was equating that to a 90-minute daily commute. Rather than logging an 8-hour day, some employees would count the commute time and only put in a 6.5-hour day. You may ask yourself whether the professionals who were doing this were acting ethically. That is what the employer considered. What wasn't considered was that often, those individuals who made this assumption actually were the more productive workers, who turned their work in on time and with fewer errors. However, for other employees who knew this was occurring, the issue became an ethical question. Less productive workers felt it didn't matter if a person was able to do 8 hours of work in 6.5 hours. They felt if they had to work 8 hours, everyone should have to work 8 hours. Anything else was tantamount to favoritism or unethical treatment of varying employees. Whether this issue is or isn't considered an ethical dilemma is debatable. The argument is, many employees perceived the inconsistent treatment as unethical. What should the organization do?

By considering these examples, you can begin to imagine the wide range of issues that will begin to be raised as the workforce continues to diversify in age, gender, religion, and culture. As we discussed in Chapter 1, morality is a very personal trait. All of the varying factors that comprise an organization's work culture will impact the manner in which individuals consider the topic of ethics. Corporations will need to identify methods to effectively address these variances and merge them into a code of ethics or code of conduct that employees can understand and feel they can abide with. Organizations that blindly dictate a code of ethics without considering the diversity of their workforce may find they experience increased ethical dilemmas.

Actions for the Diverse Workforce Scenario One   Recognizing the many factors cited may impact how an organization's professionals perceive the ethical culture of the company, organizations must begin to gain a complete understanding of various facets of their workforce composition. By studying and gathering this information, organizations can utilize various techniques to assist individuals in understanding the reason and purpose behind the organization's adoption of a particular stance on an issue. Let's examine this theory with a scenario.

Diverse Workforce Scenario Two   Company ABC has experienced rapid growth in the past five years. They have gone from a small regional manufacturing company with approximately 20 locations throughout the United States to a large international company with approximately 60 locations that span the United States and four European countries.

During this period, to keep up with their rapid growth, they have outsourced some facets of their back-office operations to other companies based in various countries and locations.

Since the company's product is manufactured primarily in the United States, they have found it is cost-effective to locate their manufacturing facilities close to U.S. borders and utilize immigrant labor. Individuals employed within the manufacturing facilities are typical blue-collar workers with little to no education. In addition, the typical workers in the manufacturing facilities are young men between the ages of 20 and 35 who have young families. The workers possess minimal knowledge about information technology processes but understand building products and the company's manufacturing business.

The headquarters of the organization is located in a large city on the East Coast of the United States. Most employees who work at the corporate offices are typical white-collar workers. They have obtained college educations and live a fairly affluent life. The majority are individuals between the ages of 35 and 50. Approximately 65% of the headquarters employees are men who were educated at East Coast colleges. To attract younger employees to the headquarters business, the company has established a management trainee program. They recruit individuals directly out of college but focus on males rather than females because of their belief that building products is a male profession.

Based on the information provided, what aspects may be important for the company to understand when communicating and teaching their code of conduct?

Actions for the Diverse Workforce Scenario Two   Consider the following factors as they relate to the manufacturing facilities:

- Large population of immigrant workers
- Age demographics of workers
- Small population of women workers
- Language barriers
- Family obligations
- Cultural variances

With these things in mind, there are several concepts that will be important to ensure the company has integrated into its ethics program.

- Since the majority of workers are immigrants, it would be important to ensure the code of conduct has been appropriately translated into the language of the workers.
- The fact many of the workers do not have a strong educational background means the company will need to be cognizant of having formal training and communication sessions on various aspects of the code of conduct to ensure workers understand concepts outlined in the policies. If the company were simply to ask the workers to sign the code, a gap may exist in their understanding of what is required due to language or educational barriers.
- The company will need to be cognizant that the lower population of women workers could create varying dynamics at the facility. Consideration will need to be given to the needs of women workers versus their male counterparts.
- It may be important for the organization to insert experienced supervisors in each facility who can oversee work and actions, properly exhibit work expectations, and train on the company's code of conduct.
- It was stated that the majority of the working population were in their early careers. The organization could establish a mentoring program to ensure workers have the opportunity to learn about company expectations firsthand and on the job.
- The company may also need to find methods to ensure employees understand aspects of the U.S. fair trade laws and Foreign Corrupt Practices Act. Since many of the workers are immigrants, they may be accustomed to work practices in their home countries that are not necessarily acceptable in the United States.

Aspects of understanding and training on the code of conduct may be very different within the corporate headquarters. Consider the following factors related to headquarters.

- The predominance of an older-generation male executive workforce as compared with the composition of workers in the manufacturing facilities
- Highly educated individuals with a strong concentration of workers who have attended prominent East Coast universities
- The establishment of a new management trainee program that will attract the younger millennial worker
- The composition of women in the workforce and their relative positioning in the company

Knowing these factors, there are several efforts the organization can take. Since the majority of the workforce are educated professionals, they should be able to comprehend the written code of conduct, and the aspect of training may be effectively executed through various online methods as well as periodic management forums. In addition, we cannot overlook the age variance of the individuals in the corporate headquarters versus those at the manufacturing facilities. The company will need to consider how best the workforce will comprehend and understand the training. The older generation may be more receptive to face-to-face training, while the younger generation may be comfortable with online methods.

The addition of the management trainee program will bring an influx of new millennials into the workforce at the headquarters. The organization should ensure they have an adequate understanding of the manner in which millennials learn most effectively and their expectations for work environments. This is not to say the company should adjust their code of ethics to meet millennial expectations; however, if there are aspects within the code that could be troublesome or questionable to millennial workers, the organization must be prepared to explain their rationale for those items.

Although the facts of the scenario stated the majority of the workforce is male, there are female workers mixed throughout the organization at varying stages of their careers. The organization should evaluate how this mix of women in the workforce may be perceived and treated within the organization. For instance, if women are relegated to lower-level positions and there are no women in upper management, the organization may experience ethical concerns related to diversity issues. This may be an issue the organization will need to address. They should ensure they have a proper management training program in place that provides equality to all professionals who exhibit relevant skills to move into management.

Management should take into account the age variance of the workforce within the headquarters. Millennials often have very different expectations with regard to work practices than older-generation workers. They may have different philosophies regarding a virtual work environment, standard work hours, travel expectations, or even time-off expectations. The organization should ensure all professionals are treated fairly and equitably related to these issues. In addition, often technology comes as second nature to the millennial workforce. Their ability to quickly adapt to technology changes could be perceived as a threat to the older worker, who is challenged to simply remember his or her password. This could create an atmosphere where the older executive male or female workforce resists new technology suggestions and changes. This diversity in opinion can quickly result in organizational tension and resulting ethical issues. The organization must ensure adequate processes are in place to fully vet needs for technology changes. Changes deemed necessary will require effective training for all levels of the organization.

Summary

Ethical culture changes are not as easy as simply writing a code of conduct or ethics policy. A CAE of a very large multinational company relayed her company was in the process of translating their code of conduct into various languages. She was very proud of this action. Indeed, it was a strong enhancement, but the fact the organization was only then taking the action of ensuring their international workers had a document in their native language was a bit troublesome. The company had been in existence for well over 20 years, and international workers had been a strong part of the workforce for more than 10 years. This example points to the fact management must be conscious of the makeup of their workforce and make timely changes to their code of ethics. They also must recognize a multidimensional workforce will have a vast array of beliefs and morals. This does not mean the organization must bend its rules to meet those cultures. But, it is important to be cognizant of what facets exist so the organization can take appropriate training and communication steps to ensure professionals understand why the organization has included certain items within their code of ethics.

Section 8: Internal Auditors Working with Diverse Cultures and Beliefs

Introduction

When an internal audit is involved in evaluating the company's code of conduct, their first actions may be to research best practice or leading code of conduct statements and compare those statements with company policies. If you consider the issues discussed on corporate ethics in the future, this action may not be the best first step. Just as the organization must have an understanding of the composition of its workforce, internal auditors evaluating the effectiveness of the code of conduct must work to understand how the organization translates the varying beliefs of its workforce into expectations as listed in the code of conduct.

A simple example is the issue related to the acceptance of gifts from vendors. In the United States, many codes of conduct have thresholds for this activity. However, in certain countries, the activity is considered a way of doing business. How will the organization ensure its international employees understand the company's position on the acceptance of gifts? If employees do not understand the concept behind the requirement, they may revert to their own cultural beliefs. Another example may relate to how women are treated in the workforce and efforts made to appropriately segregate specific facilities such as bathrooms or locker rooms. In the United States, most companies place value in maintaining appropriately segregated and private facilities. In other countries, this may not be the norm, and management in those countries may have a hard time reconciling why they should spend extra budget dollars to provide for these facilities. For international workers to understand and buy into the organizations stated code, they must have a good understanding of the purpose and reason behind the policy statement.

Another example auditors may want to consider is the utilization of the words honesty, respect, and communication and how they may be exhibited in the workforce. Many companies have inserted the words into their codes of conduct and mission statements because they are expected items in today's business world. However, auditors must be cognizant of how those attributes are actually displayed within the work environment. If respect is listed as an important attribute of the company's code of conduct, the organization should maintain a policy of respect that extends both up and down the ladder or organizational ranks.

Respect Scenario   A CAE relayed a story about his concern over the display of respect within his company culture. The organization regularly touted its focus on maintaining a respectful working environment. However, the CAE would often observe acts of disrespect by management individuals towards lower-level employees. This disrespect extended from individual instances to meetings. It would often manifest itself in ways that appeared to be calculated methods to undermine an employee's ideas or actions. In one event, the CAE experienced the issue personally. His group had been working on several audit reports. The CAE's reporting line in the organization was through the chief financial officer (CFO). Because some of the reports dealt with areas under the responsibility of the CFO, their continued to be significant pushback by the CFO on the release of the written reports. The CFO required the audit team to validate and revalidate findings, rewrite the reports, and then revisit with management. The CAE was finally able to obtain approval to release the reports to the audit committee and the process owners approximately two weeks before the scheduled quarterly meeting. He had reached out to the external auditors and reviewed the issues, obtained agreement on the issues from process area management, and reached out to the audit committee to try to explain the difficulties encountered in releasing the reports. However, he did not have success in getting the audit committee to return his e-mails or phone calls. The CAE was aware the CFO had a preconference meeting with the audit committee chair and asked to be involved. He was told his involvement was not required and the CFO would explain the reason why the reports had been delayed. At the actual audit committee meeting, it was evident management had utilized their influence with the audit committee to convince the members that issues stated in the reports were blown out of proportion. In this case, the CAE faced significant questioning during the actual audit committee meeting, where approximately 20 members of management and the board present. The meeting became accusatory and disrespectful toward the CAE. The CAE pointed out he had obtained all the necessary approvals of the identified issues and had made several attempts to speak to the committee members, but his efforts were to no avail. It was clear the audit committee was accepting the opinion of management, and they had little to no interest in the opinion of the CAE. The CAE left the meeting with a significant feeing of disrespect. In the succeeding days, although the CAE attempted to speak further to the CFO and audit committee chair about what had occurred, they had no interest in revisiting the issue. The CAE left the company within a short time. He felt his previous observations of the concern over corporate respect had been validated by his own experience.

The scenario points to the need for auditors to look further than the written word outlined in the code of ethics. Some specific suggestions include:

- Can the code be effectively implemented based on the workforce cultural diversity?
- If elements such as honesty and respect are listed, are there identifiable issues that display how this requirement is regularly exhibited throughout the organization, regardless of a professional's organizational standing?
- Are requirements related to behavior, or possibly acceptance of gifts, consistent for all individuals within the organization? There should be no exceptions.
- Do employees and management actually display the activity listed in the code, or is it simply a document for compliance purposes?
- Is training and acknowledgment of the understanding of the code required by all employees? (Methods may be different, but all employees and management should fall under the same requirement.)
- When violations are identified, are they handled consistently and completely, or does it depend on the individual involved?
- Is the code readily available to employees for review?

- Do strategic vendors, customers, or consultants of the company obtain information related to the company's policies on code of conduct?
- Does the board or governing body take an interest in how violations of the policy are remediated?
- Do employees know how to report issues regarding violations of the code of conduct?
- What types of issues have been reported in the past, and how have they been resolved?
- Do management and the board take a strategic interest in maintaining an open and ethical culture? If so, how is that displayed?
- Do employees feel they cannot express their opinions and observations openly? If not, why?
- When issues are reported to the audit committee, do they appropriately question details around the issue? Are issues dismissed because senior management tells the audit committee they are of no significance?

There could be additional questions you may ask within your own operating environment. Those cited here are a few to assist brainstorming processes that may help the auditor effectively evaluate the company's code of ethics.

Summary

The evaluation of organizational culture and the code of ethics is not an easy task. Auditors must use their personal professional skepticism while evaluating various aspects of the cultural environment. Just because a code of conduct exists is not proof of a strong ethical environment.

3

ESTABLISHING AN ETHICAL CULTURE AND THE CONNECTION TO COSO 2013

Section 1: Committee of Sponsoring Organizations (COSO) 2013
Control Environment Principles and Corporate Ethical Culture

Introduction

In 1992, the Committee of Sponsoring Organizations (COSO) released its *Initial Internal Control—Integrated Framework*. COSO is a joint initiative of five private-sector organizations:

- American Accounting Association (AAA)
- American Institute of Certified Public Accountants (AICPA)
- Financial Executives International (FEI)
- Association of Accountants and Financial Professionals in Business (IMA)
- Institute of Internal Auditors (IIA)

COSO provides thought leadership through the development of frameworks and guidance on enterprise risk management, internal control, and fraud deterrence. COSO was formed in 1985 to sponsor the National Commission on Fraudulent Financial Reporting (Treadway Commission). The Treadway Commission recommended organizations sponsoring the Commission work together to develop integrated guidance on internal control.

Post the passing of Sarbanes–Oxley in 2002, companies struggled to determine what procedures should be in place to meet the Act's compliance requirements. The COSO 1992 framework was recommended as the framework organizations should look to when developing their methodologies. The trouble was, many companies and personnel were not intimately familiar with COSO 1992. Sure, the framework had been in existence for over 10 years, but it was never as a requirement mandated by the Securities and Exchange Commission (SEC) to adopt the framework. When SOX was passed, many accounting, finance and internal audit professionals didn't fully comprehend the requirements of COSO. Organizations began working to dissect and understand COSO while also attempting to understand the requirements of SOX. Simply learning the terminology included in the framework became a significant task. Organizations had to determine how to employ the COSO concepts within their organization. When the 1992 framework was released, it had always been intended to be an internal control methodology organizations would use throughout all areas of operations, compliance, and financial reporting. Companies considered if they were required to adopt an approved internal control framework, whether this action needed to be applied throughout the whole company, or if it just be applied to financial reporting? Most companies chose the financial reporting route.

In 2002, the organization I was employed with was a $3 billion company with international operations. Our audit team gathered in a conference room with our external auditors to evaluate the COSO 1992 cube and decide how to develop our compliance. One of the senior managers from the public accounting firm stood up and circled the top of the cube titled "financial reporting" and then drew an arrow down to the five COSO attributes: control environment, risk assessment, control activities, information and communication, and monitoring. He declared, "This is where to focus!"

This meeting was held in the early stages after the passing of the legislation and prior to the establishment of the Public Companies Accounting and Oversight Board (PCAOB). The compliance date was December 2014. The public accounting firms, as well as every company expected to comply, were understandably concerned about the compliance requirements. No one wanted to be the next Enron or Arthur Andersen. There were news reports that Senator Paul Sarbanes and Congressman Michael Oxley indicated, the *COSO 1992 Integrated Control Framework* had been in existence for over 10 years. As such, initial expectations were it would take companies only a few hundred hours to comply with the legislation. The assumption was organizations were already using the COSO framework. The problem with that thought was the framework had never been mandated by the SEC. Companies allowed it to sit it on the shelf without paying much attention to the detailed components outlined in the framework.

During my organization's planning meeting to prepare for SOX, compliance we determined the need was to focus on the components of control over financial reporting. Even though the SOX legislation included 11 separate sections including specific references to fraud, audit firms and companies felt the requirements were primarily linked to internal control over financial reporting. As an audit and accounting group, our company, like many others, applied the key control concepts to internal control over financial reporting.

Although there was discussion about review of the control environment and entity level controls, organizations did not seem to place as great of a focus in those areas. Looking back, some may question why the focus of work became so transaction oriented. After all, the Enron downfall did not occur because someone forgot to document accounts payable from start to end. It occurred because of inappropriate actions on the part of senior management. These actions expanded into the operations of the organization. However, most companies were using the COSO components and only evaluating compliance for the financial reporting level. Even the attribute of control environment was typically evaluated in the form of management's financial reporting philosophy, entity level controls, tone at the top, and the establishment of sound financial procedures. But realistically, when fraud occurs, it often manifests itself in the operations of the organization. By neglecting to apply the COSO attributes through to the operations, there was a risk organizations would miss key identifiers of unethical behavior and fraudulent actions. But, in those days, companies were grasping for guidance on how deep to apply compliance procedures within the organization. When the external auditors seemed satisfied to apply procedures at the financial reporting level and scope out the operations, companies were relieved because it reduced the level of work required for compliance.

The Updated COSO Framework

In May 2013, more than 20 years after the release of the original framework, COSO released an update to the *Internal Control—Integrated*

Framework. The update was deemed necessary due to the many changes in the business environment, including:

- Globalization of markets and operations
- Greater complexities of business
- Demands and complexities in laws, rules, regulations, and standards
- Expectations by stakeholders and shareholders for competencies, accountabilities, and governance oversight
- Evolving technologies
- Expectations for preventing and detecting fraud

The COSO 2013 framework was expanded to include 17 principles and 77 points of focus. These elements were added to assist organizations when evaluating their internal control structure.

COSO 2013 identified a specific fraud principle that resides under the risk assessment attribute. The principle states the organization considers the risk for fraud in assessing risk to the achievement of objectives. This principle specifically directs organizations must take actions toward active evaluation of fraud risks. Fraud and ethics can be closely correlated so it is important auditors and organizations fully understand and embrace the concept of fraud evaluations. The principles that underlie the control environment attribute can also be related to processes that involve establishing an ethical culture. The five principles supporting the control environment indicate the organization must:

- Demonstrate commitment to integrity and ethical values
- Ensure the board exercises oversight responsibility
- Establish structures, reporting lines, authorities, and responsibilities
- Demonstrate commitment to a competent workforce
- Hold individuals accountable for internal control responsibilities

For internal auditors to effectively evaluate a company's ethics program, they must fully comprehend and employ procedures to demonstrate the control environment principles as well as principle eight related to fraud are in place and consistently executed. COSO emphasized the need for organizations to ensure policies and procedures were more than paper documents. There must be evidence to demonstrate how the organization is effectively executing the procedures.

In the early years of SOX, many companies would positively attest to their control environment by pointing to the existence of ethical policies, conflict of interest statements, or a whistleblower hotline. COSO 2013 reinforced the concept that policies can be easily written and adopted in form, but it is also important to ensure they are fully executed and abided by.

Let's examine each of the five control environment principles and consider how each may impact an organization's ethical environment. We will then identify methods to determine if procedures are in place to ensure the principles are adequately executed.

Section 2: COSO Principles One and Two—Demonstrates Commitment to Integrity and Ethical Values and Ensures the Board Exercises Oversight Authority

Introduction

The board of directors' primary responsibility is to provide proper governance and oversight for the organization. This requirement can be vast and extend to many organizational processes and strategies. The role of the board of directors comes with many duties. These duties include maintaining an ethical environment while displaying integrity and respect. The board's responsibilities regarding ethics can include:

- Approving the code of conduct and conflict of interest process
- Oversight of the company's whistleblower hotline
- Oversight of the internal and external auditors
- Executing proper governance over the actions of the organization

Responsibilities do not end with these few bullet points. The board must ensure the code of conduct and any ethical programs are executable for the organization, and are embraced and regularly practiced. Recognizing board members are not necessarily on company premises eight hours a day, it is still critical they take a strong interest to ensure ethical concepts are established and effectively and consistently executed. Board members should not be satisfied with the role of simply signing off on the code of ethics. They must understand each element within the code and ensure it meets the goals and expectations of the organization and its stakeholders. They must also understand how each element of the code is put into practice by the organization.

In addition, the audit committee of the board must exercise authority over the internal audit function and maintain a close relationship to facilitate open and transparent communication. This is a concept that is viewed in various manners by organizations. Organizations may include charter statements such as "the internal audit department reports to the audit committee," but often these charter statements are not fully embraced and practiced within the organization. For the audit committee to provide proper oversight of internal audit, they must establish a strong relationship with the chief audit executive (CAE) and have a strong understanding of how the internal audit plan is established and executed. They should also work with internal audit to establish the proper risk thresholds for reporting issues identified during an internal audit. These are just a few of the links between the first two COSO principles and ethical behavior.

Acknowledging board procedures are more formalized and focused since the years prior to SOX, there remain an abundance of situations where internal auditors find themselves in positions where the actual execution of board oversight for internal audit is insufficient. If auditors observe the board's relationship with management has become one that hampers the board's ability to be truly objective, auditors have a fiduciary duty to discuss the issue with management and the board. However, when board members cross the line from being independent, objective and utilizing professional skepticism to taking information provided by the leadership team as gospel, they are not fulfilling their fiduciary duty. If board relationships become so close to management that their ability to ask probing questions and exercise professional skepticism is impaired, it is time the organization take a second look at the composition of the board.

Consider the following situations that auditors may face. As we cover the various scenarios, ask yourself if these situations occurred at your company, would you be able to affirmatively attest to COSO principles one and two?

Scenario One: Board Composition

The board of directors is composed of 12 external directors. All directors have been on the board for a minimum of 15 years. Several of the members are close friends of the chief executive officer (CEO) and regularly engage in social outings and trips with his family. During board meetings, the directors rarely question management strategies. They listen to information provided by internal audit; however, they defer to management for determination of any need for issue remediation. Considering the facts provided, if you were the CAE, would you have concern as to whether the directors are acting fully independently?

Scenario Two: Internal Audit Oversight

Leading practice and the *IIA Standards* indicate the internal audit department charter and audit committee charter should state the audit committee's responsibility for oversight of internal audit. At ACME Inc., both the audit committee and management have directed that any meetings between the CAE and the audit committee, outside of quarterly private sessions, must include the CEO or chief financial officer (CFO). The CAE is not allowed to reach out independently to the audit committee. If he does, the audit committee does not return the call. In this situation, would you say the audit committee is exhibiting proper oversight over internal audit? Are the decrees of management and the audit committee within the realms of transparent and ethical behavior? If you were part of this internal audit group or the CAE for this company, do you believe you could positively attest to COSO principles one and two?

Scenario Three: Audit Committee Communication

A new member of the board has been elected for ABC Inc. He is assigned to be a member of the audit committee. Management has developed a one day orientation for the new board member. The orientation includes presentations by the CFO, CEO, chief legal officer, chief administrative officer, and chief operating officer. The CAE has requested time on the agenda to present information about the internal audit process. Management has declined the request. They have indicated since the CAE administratively reports to the CFO, information the audit committee may require about internal audit will be communicated by the CFO. If you were the CAE in this instance, what would you do? Do you believe this is acting with integrity and respect in relationship to the CAE position in the organization? Considering the audit committee has oversight responsibility of internal audit, would the denial of allowing the CAE to be part of the orientation be any reflection on ethical behavior and conduct for the organization? Could you attest to COSO principles one and two in this circumstance?

Scenario Four: CAE Selection

Your company has experienced significant turnover in the internal audit department over the past several years. The company has struggled to find the proper fit for the CAE position as well as recruit internal audit staff. They have recently lost their fifth CAE in a period of seven years.

The company has begun a search for a new CAE. The audit committee chairman agrees it is important to be part of the selection process. However, he has agreed he will only interview the final CAE candidate presented by management. Several candidates interview for the position and, after an eight-month search and exhaustive interview process, a candidate is selected by management to interview with the audit committee chairman. The individual is an external candidate whose background is from a different industry but who has performed the role of CAE for other organizations.

During the interview, the audit committee chairman expresses his belief in the internal audit process and the need to establish a close relationship with the CAE. He expresses his wish that the company establish a true risk-based process for internal auditing. He also indicates he will be available to the new CAE at any time to speak about issues or concerns.

The candidate accepts the job, and upon his arrival at the company he begins working to establish a risk-based audit process. During his first week of employment, he meets with the CEO and several presidents of various business units as well as the CFO, to whom he will administratively report. During these meetings, he is informed of several points. Each of these statements raises a level of concern with the new CAE related to his authorities within the company. He is told a few of the following facts.

- The organization is slow to change.
- The budget of the internal audit department is managed by the CFO, and the CAE has no authority or input regarding decisions relating to the budget.
- Hiring of internal audit staff is managed through human resources and the CFO.
- The CAE is not allowed to issue audit reports without the approval of the CFO.
- The CAE is not allowed to make any changes to the audit plan without the explicit approval of the CFO.

The new CAE is also told that, although the audit committee indicated they were looking for an open relationship with internal audit, management expects communications should only occur if approved by them.

If you were the CAE, what would you do? Do you think management was completely open and honest and displayed integrity during the interview process? What about the information you discovered in your first week? Would you call and speak to the audit committee, regardless of management's request? Also—to make this situation a bit tougher, assume you have been out of work for about a year and you have some financial issues. You really need to keep your job! What would you do?

Scenario Analysis

In contemplating these scenarios, you may initially feel issues such as these don't really happen. Each scenario is true and was relayed by a CAE. Ultimately, each felt they would have difficulty attesting to COSO principles one and two. In addition, each CAE had strong feelings about how management had been able to control the audit committee and whether there was any true independence or objectivity on the part of internal audit or the audit committee. In some instances, the CAE questioned the ethical manner in which various communications and issues were handled.

Each CAE took different actions to attempt to resolve the issues in line with the *Standards* and with the intent of COSO. In the case of the board member composition, the CAE spoke to the audit committee in private session and explained the inherent difficulties of executing independence when individuals were long-standing board members. The CAE also inquired about how the process for elect-ing board members or selecting potential candidates was executed. He was informed by the audit committee and by management that the issue was not part of his responsibility. The CAE stayed with the company but changed positions within a few months.

In the scenario of internal audit oversight, the CAE attempted to provide the audit committee and management with information regarding the *Standards* and the responsibility of the audit committee as it pertained to oversight of internal audit. The CAE was informed by both management and the audit committee that, since the *Standards* were merely guidelines, the company did not feel obligated to comply. The audit committee supported management's directive for communications between the CAE and the audit committee to be filtered through the CFO. In this situation, the CAE remained in the position for almost 18 months and attempted to make periodic strides toward improving communication with the audit committee. However, due to the deeply established culture and processes of the organization, his attempts were viewed negatively and did not result in any improvement in overall relationships. In this case, the CAE chose to move to a different position within the company.

In the scenario of training and communication for the new board member, although the CAE had been informed he would not be given time within the orientation session, he individually reached out to the new board member. The CAE offered to spend time with the new board member, at his convenience, to review internal audit processes and procedures. In this instance, although management was not thrilled with the situation, the new audit committee member viewed the initiative of the CAE as a positive move. This action served to assist in building a stronger communication process with the entire audit committee. However, the action also created internal political difficulties with the organization's management. They viewed the CAE's action as stepping over the line of responsibility. Although the new audit committee member formally relayed his appreciation of the CAE's initiative, the audit committee chairman supported management's opinion that the CAE should not have reached out without the proper approvals. These conflicts resulted in a period of politically sensitive relationships.

In the scenario of the CAE selection process, the CAE was very conflicted on what action to take. He had relocated his family to a new city. His on-site interviews seemed to go very well, and information relayed by management during interviews was in line with how the *Standards* suggest an internal audit function should be run. After the CAE's first week on the job, he was unsure what steps to take. In this instance, he chose to pick his battles and tackle one issue at a time. However, after 12 months it was evident that much of the information he had been told in interviews was more fiction than fact. Eventually, the CAE left the company because he felt there was a lack of trust, integrity, and ethics on the part of management as well as the organization as a whole.

Section 3: COSO Principle Three—The Organization Establishes Structures, Reporting Lines, Authorities, and Responsibilities

Introduction

The manner in which an organization is structured can run the gamut from complex to simple. When an organization is initially established, management works to most effectively align the structure with the needs of the organization, while keeping overhead costs in mind. As the organization expands, it is easy for this intention to take a back seat. Positions may be added because of a specific request or a perceived need by a department leader. In another scenario, when organizations merge, the structure and reporting lines can become a difficult aspect of the merger and due diligence. Management is required to evaluate the needs of the combined companies and determine what structure will best meet those needs. Often each organization may work to keep their employees.

The key to attesting to COSO principle four while ensuring proper ethical practices is to periodically revisit organization structures and reporting lines to ensure they meet corporate objectives and expectations. If an organization has experienced exponential growth, the structure and reporting lines should be revisited to ensure they align with the goals of the company. If the organization has experienced downsizing, the concept of reevaluating structure and reporting lines may be even more important to ensure approvals, authorities, and decisions are within the realms of the organization's tolerance levels.

Downsizing Scenario

A CAE relayed an instance in which his organization was going through a difficult financial time. The company determined it was necessary to reduce the workforce. The total reductions equated to 45% of personnel. As the downsizing for this organization rolled out, it was imperative for management personnel to reevaluate reporting lines and authorities to ensure organizational processes would be effectively managed and professionals were aware of their individual job requirements. A downsizing as significant as a 45% reduction in workforce will undoubtedly have an impact on individuals who remain with the company. Some may begin to question their longer-term viability and rationalize why it is OK to cut corners on job responsibilities. Personnel may feel they have been personally impacted by the mistakes of the company, and this could lead to questionable (unethical) actions or decisions.

Section 4: COSO Principle Four—Commitment to Competence

Introduction

When you think of the term *commitment to competence*, how would you relate it to the ethical principles we discussed in Chapter 1? Competency implies not only intelligence but also having the appropriate knowledge, qualifications, and experience to accomplish assigned tasks. The connection to an ethical culture is that organizations work to ensure individuals who are hired and placed in roles have the relevant skill sets and capabilities to execute the work within the parameters of the organization's expectations. In today's competitive workforce, it is not unusual for individuals to embellish information on their résumés. This is a strong concern when the job being filled requires specialized skills. To exercise adequate commitment to competence, the organization must have processes in place to attract, develop, and retain individuals who have competent skills to perform the objectives of the role assigned. They must also have procedures in place to ensure that résumé credentials are valid.

In 2015, CareerBuilder conducted a survey of more than 2,500 hiring managers. The survey results were quite interesting. The results point to concerns about the ethical morals of prospective employees. Following are a few of the observations from the survey.

- Fifty-six percent of hiring managers completing the survey caught job candidates lying on their résumés. The most common lie was embellishment of skills or capabilities.
- Fifty-four percent of respondents indicated they caught applicants taking liberties when describing the scope of their responsibilities.
- Twenty-five percent of people claimed to be employed by companies they never worked for.

Executing Commitment to Competence

Organizations typically have defined hiring policies which include validation of a prospective employee's education and previous work experience. But when it comes to exhibiting commitment to competence, we must consider whether the process of education or work experience validation is sufficient. To fully exhibit the organization's dedication to commitment to competence, the auditor should consider the following procedures and processes and how well they are established and engrained in the workplace.

- Has the organization fully defined the skill sets required to perform the respective roles of personnel they are hiring?
- Are there well-defined policies and processes in place to ensure employees placed in positions have been adequately informed of the position requirements and expectations?
- Do employees understand the variance between their listed job tasks and the expectations surrounding the internal control aspects of their duties?
- Do employees have the requisite education or experience to perform the responsibilities of the position?
- Have facts stated on the new employee's résumé been vetted and validated?
- Is there a sufficient on-boarding process for the employee that includes ongoing mentoring and on-the-job training?
- Are employees given regular and constructive feedback regarding their job performance?
- Has the organization identified relevant ongoing continuing education requirements for professionals?

- Does the organization provide all employees with some level of ongoing job education?
- Do supervisors adequately monitor employees' work and provide relevant and timely feedback regarding the accuracy and completeness of the work?
- If the organization has a management trainee program or provides reimbursement for advanced management education, is there a fair and equitable process established to ensure that employees receive fair and relevant consideration for this benefit?
- Are employees trained on procedures required to monitor the external (legal, political, etc.) and internal environments to ensure required changes are identified and brought to management's attention in a timely manner?

Commitment to competence extends far beyond procedures used to evaluate the initial qualifications of a prospective employee. An organization which does not regularly provide employees with opportunities to enhance competency level may face a work environment that is unstable and full of controversy. These attributes will inevitably lead to an environment where employees rationalize why certain questionable or, possibly, unethical acts are not a concern.

Section 5: COSO Principle Five—Individuals Are Held Accountable for Their Internal Control Responsibilities

Introduction

Some professionals would contend the very foundation of ethics lies in how individuals execute their specific duties. COSO principle five sets the theme for that theory. The requirement for individuals to be held accountable for their responsibilities can be viewed as an ethical outcome.

In life, we are ultimately responsible for our own actions. There are always ancillary circumstances that may impact the outcome of those actions. Outcomes may not always be what we expect or anticipate. When this occurs, individuals can fall into the it's-not-my-fault syndrome. In some respects, that might be true. In other respects, you as an individual have the final say and control over your life. If something doesn't go as intended, you still have choices to ensure your own personal life maintains a sense of control.

In the corporate world, many professionals focus on the tasks assigned or the job description outlined in their human resource file. Today's business requires individuals to understand not only the individual tasks but also why those tasks must be performed in a certain way and how they contribute to the overall internal control of the company. Professionals must take responsibility for their influence over internal control. Let's consider a real-life scenario.

Scenario One: Internal Control   Company JK is a small facility that generates power for a military base. The facility is sparsely staffed. There are three employees of the facility. They include a maintenance engineer, a CFO, and a mechanical engineer. In the past, the facility has not been part of a publicly traded company, so there have been no requirements for SOX compliance. However, the parent company has undergone an external audit every year for financing purposes. Traditionally, because the facility has been a small portion of the parent company's overall portfolio, the external auditors have not examined the procedures at the facility at an in-depth level. The auditors are aware of the staffing limitations and the processes executed at the facility but it has not been an area of focus because of the deemed immateriality.

The parent company has chosen to spin off certain assets. The facility becomes part of the portfolio of a separate company which is publicly traded and must abide by SOX rules. As the accounting staff of the new company begin work on documenting processes for the facility, they discover the following with regard to how the CFO position has been managed at the plant:

- The CFO works out of his home office, where all the records for the facility are stored in metal, unlocked file cabinets.
- The CFO manages all aspects of accounting, which includes billing, payables, payroll, receivables, treasury, banking, and financial statement reporting.
- The books and records are managed using QuickBooks. There are no procedures in place to regularly back up or secure the electronic information.

- The CFO receives all payments in the mail, opens the mail, records checks for payments on customer accounts, organizes the deposit, takes deposits to the bank, and reconciles the bank statement at end of the month.
- The CFO negotiates all contracts with vendors.
- The CFO handles processing and payment of all invoices.

These are a few of the responsibilities the CFO has managed over the past four years. As the accountants begin to realize the scope of the CFO's role, they begin to ask questions surrounding adequate segregation of duty. The CFO laughs and jokingly remarks, "I could take out $40,000 from the bank and be in Aruba before anyone noticed!"

The accountants begin to ask the CFO if he has any concerns over the lack of segregation of duties. He defends his role by indicating the facility has been part of an organization that has undergone an external audit every year since its existence. The external audit has been conducted by a Big Four accounting firm that never raised questions or concerns regarding the CFO's role or responsibilities. The accountants continue to inquire about which responsibilities the CFO feels would be most important to segregate. His response is, "There is no possible way to segregate responsibilities. We only have three employees. I was hired to manage the accounting process, and that is what I am doing."

What is your analysis of this situation? The CFO is a younger individual but has a finance degree and is a sharp professional. Should he have been concerned over the lack of segregation of duties when he was placed in the role? Should the external auditors have previously made mention of the control issues that may be at the greatest risk related to the lack of segregation of duties? Should management of the parent company previously have raised a concern about the operations of the facility?

This is a classic example of a person performing assigned tasks without having a strong understanding of the impact of internal controls and the need for relevant checks and balances as well as segregation of duties. In this scenario, the CFO was extremely offended by the insinuation that he may not be properly performing his job or that there could be any ethical concerns in the way he executed his responsibilities. He felt since the auditors had never mentioned concerns in the past, and since management allowed him the authority to execute his job in the manner described, he was now being unduly criticized. The accountants explained to the CFO the intention of segregation of duties is to protect the company and protect the employee. If something questionable were to occur, the CFO would not have much recourse to support the fact of adequate internal controls.

The CFO was performing his job based on the identified job tasks listed in his position description. He did not understand, or take time to evaluate, how some of those tasks could create a poor internal control environment. This example supports COSO principle five, which states the organization must hold individuals accountable for their internal control responsibilities. For this to be effective, individuals must have an understanding of the variance of tasks versus controls. If you observed this situation occurring in your company, could you positively attest to COSO principle five?

Scenario Two: The New CFO and CAE   Assume approximately six months ago, you joined a growing software company as the CAE. Recently, the CFO of the company announced he would be leaving due to health reasons. He had been with the company more than 15 years. The company executes an exhaustive search for a new CFO. They identify a gentleman who has over 20 years in public accounting and is experienced in the software industry. Each candidate is asked to interview with the audit committee, CEO, COO, and several other executives. They are not allowed to speak to the CFO who is leaving the company due to his health situation. As the CAE, you are not included in the interview process, even though you will be a direct report to the new CFO. The gentleman from the public accounting firm is offered the position and accepts.

His start date is a couple of weeks after the end of the company's fiscal year. During the first week of his employment, you and the new CFO attend a meeting held by the CEO. He announces the company had an excellent fourth quarter, and due to several large contracts being finalized in the final month of the quarter, the company will meet their projected earnings target, which also results in strong bonus payouts.

When you leave the meeting, you speak privately to the CFO and express your surprise at the news of the finalized large contracts. Your group completed a review of revenue recognition and contracting during the third quarter of the year. Although you did not find validated evidence of manipulation of revenue recognition principles, the audit group found concerning circumstantial evidence regarding how the various business units were applying revenue recognition standards. More importantly, you did not find any evidence of potentially large contracts being negotiated that would close prior to the end of the year.

You tell the new CFO that you reported your concerns to the past CFO. When this communication occurred, you were informed that since there was no physical or validated evidence of any issues, there should not be any mention of potential control gaps within your audit report. Because you were fairly new to the company and not as familiar with processes as the CFO, you agreed to his request. However, you informally spoke to the external auditors and suggested that it may be beneficial to provide some revenue recognition training to the area controllers. The external auditors agreed. They had also found evidence in the past of some aggressive revenue recognition procedures.

After listening to the CAE's story, the CFO returns to his office. He decides it would be prudent to speak to each of the area controllers and understand more about the large contracts finalized in the last month of the fiscal year. His conversations with the various controllers surface significant concerns as to whether the recording of these contracts was proper. One area controller informed the new CFO that her area had two large contracts, which were in the process of negotiation and scheduled to close within three days after the fiscal year-end. She was instructed by the old CFO to record the revenue on those contracts in the current fiscal year. They have now identified that both contracts were not finalized prior to year-end. This results in a major increase in the pricing of the contract and has further delayed the finalization of the agreements. When the CFO questions the controller about revenue recognition processes, she informs him the request was not out of the ordinary. Most quarters the CFO and CEO would direct the controller to recognize revenue on contracts that appeared would be finalized, even if it wasn't certain. In addition, if the contract was recorded in the period and not finalized until later, no adjustments were made.

As the CFO, you now have a problem. You request support documentation, and from what you can identify, the contracts should not have been recorded at the end of the year. Since the CAE was the person who first brought the issue to the CFO's attention, the CFO confides in the CAE.

To make matters worse, one of the area controllers informs the new CFO about the true reason the old CFO resigned. He was concerned that the external auditors were getting close to discovering his scam. The former CFO has now left the country.

So, the ethical question relating to responsibility for internal controls is "What should the CFO and CAE do now?" Here are some options.

- Speak directly to the CEO, even though he may be complicit in the matter.
- Contact the former CFO and attempt to speak with him further.
- Go to the audit committee and explain your findings.
- Go to the external auditors and explain your findings.
- Contact internal legal counsel and obtain their support in resolving the issue.

There are many red flags in this situation. The answer as to what should be done is not an easy one. From an ethical viewpoint, the new CFO and the CAE should ensure the audit committee is aware of the issues and the external auditors are appropriately informed. The proper protocol for communication of these issues may depend on the culture and hierarchy of the company. It does not appear beneficial to attempt to reach out to the ex-CFO. The new CFO may want to first inform the CEO and then involve internal legal counsel and inform the audit committee. In any event, the CFO has a fiduciary duty to disclose what he has found.

As for the CAE, what is your opinion regarding his apparent lack of knowledge of the situation? Remember, the CAE has only been in his position for six months, so it is possible that nothing came to his attention that would raise his suspicion. However, the scenario stated several comments made during the internal audit review of contracts. The statements regarded the manner in which revenue recognition was completed. Should the CAE have expanded his scope on the audit?

Scenario Three: ABC Consulting Company ABC consulting firm has contracted a professional to perform the role of interim leader for one of its business segments. The contractor's initial responsibilities are to perform an analysis and evaluation regarding the expertise of the group. He is to evaluate the current product offerings of the group, determine if the proper skill sets are available to execute work being offered, and manage and mentor employees. The new leader begins his assignment with these requirements in mind.

He begins by evaluating staffing, examining past work products, evaluating the expertise of the individuals currently employed, and asking for past working papers and current planning documents for the work being conducted. Staff members are confused, because they have not been officially informed the interim leader has been assigned to be their supervisor. However, the contractor is not aware of the confusion because the firm's management has continued to indicate he is to work as the supervisor of the group. The staff continue to side step the contractor's efforts. After a short period, the contractor learns the reason for the staff's reaction. Although management has told the contractor to act as supervisor, they have directed another internal manager to also act as the supervisor of the staff. This is not how the contractor's role was outlined or how the contractual description was written. The situation has created conflicts and some ethical dilemmas. The difficulty in this situation is the person who brought in the contractor did not clearly communicate the agreed to role with the staff. After a short period, the interim leader realizes things are not working as described in the contract. He outlines the issues and presents them to the person who brought him on. No response is received. In the end, the interim leader steps back from the contract, because the work has not proved to be effective.

After the contractor has stepped away from the arrangement, he hears from an individual within the firm. The person informs the contractor that he was brought in on contract to determine if he could attract new business for the consulting company. This responsibility was never discussed and was not included in the scope of work for the contractor. The person from the firm relays that although this responsibility was not in the written scope of the contract, the firm was most likely attempting to determine if the contractor would be able to attract new business. The contractor expresses concern since he had no authority to sell services for the firm.

Think about this scenario—do you believe this was an honest and forthright way of managing this contract? Was it transparently handled by the consulting company? If, indeed, the consulting firm was trying to determine if the person could attract new clients, would it have not been better to be forthright with the expectations of the position? How would you view this situation if you were the contractor?

Summary

Internal auditors can obtain significant insight by using the COSO control environment principles when evaluating ethical culture. They must be able to extend these principles past the normal check-the-box processes and look deep within the organization to evaluate how the principles are applied and how they can impact the ethical environment. In addition, they must be prepared to utilize their professional skepticism and questioning mind to examine the current environment and transparently and fully evaluate its effectiveness.

Later in this book, we will discuss utilizing specific ethical evaluations within each audit; it is important to keep in mind the COSO principles when utilizing the process.

Section 6: Organizational Requirements to Align with the New COSO Framework and Ethical Principles

Introduction

When COSO 2013 was released in May of 2013, the initial expectation was that companies would transition their internal control framework for SOX purposes by December 14, 2014. According to reports released by the SEC, a strong majority of organizations adopted the revised framework in line with the stated time requirements. For almost 1900 annual reports with fiscal year-ends after December 14, 2014 (the date COSO ceased support of the original 1992 framework) filed through March 4, 2015, 80% had transitioned to COSO 2013. Statistics from December 31, 2015 filers indicated that 99.5% had transitioned to the COSO framework.

Principle Mapping Process

Upon initial release of the framework, the COSO Foundation provided guidance regarding how principles should be mapped to COSO attributes and how current controls should be evaluated. The original expectation was for organizations to begin with the 17 principles, evaluate what it would take for the company to meet the principle, and then determine if the proper policies, procedures, and processes existed within the organization.

Companies took varying approaches to the mapping process. In some cases, organizations began with their current set of key controls and tagged them to specific principles. There are many different debates on whether this type of mapping approach fully meets the original intent of COSO. In theory, since the five attributes of COSO did not change, companies could expect they would have policies or procedures in place to meet the various principles. However, some would contend by performing cross-mapping in this manner, organizations may miss obvious gaps which existed because they are only considering what is currently in place. Mapping current key controls to the principles would not ensure organizations took a fresh look at procedures as COSO suggested. In addition, it would not ensure that because a policy exists, it is enforced and fully enacted in the company.

In other circumstances, organizations took the suggested approach and began with evaluating the principle, determining what the organization needed to have in place to meet the principle, and then examined their current processes to determine if any new key controls should be added.

Regardless of the approach taken, many companies will continue to refine their mapping and COSO 2013 compliance processes. As this occurs, companies should continue to place focus on the aspects that contribute to an ethical culture and ethical control environment.

Consider the five attributes defined by COSO:

- Control environment
- Risk assessment
- Control activities
- Information and communication
- Monitoring

As mentioned, the control environment is the very foundation for an organization. This is where the company establishes policies, procedures, methodologies, management structure, tone, human resource processes, and overall ethical culture. It is critical for organizations to seriously consider procedures and processes that support all COSO principles to attest to internal controls. As it relates to ethics, organizations should take a transparent view of current processes, perceived processes, and how each are actually executed. They should then determine if the execution supports the relevant control environment principles and, ultimately, an ethical atmosphere.

As companies continue their evolution to COSO 2013, they will undoubtedly begin to refine their key controls and processes to more closely align with the 17 principles. Organizations should challenge themselves to look beyond the obvious, especially when it comes to soft controls like tone at the top and ethical conduct.

Procedures to manage ethical conduct will continue to evolve. This is one of the reasons we have discussed the psychology behind ethics in early chapters. Organizations must be aware of workforce dynamics. They must understand how employees may view ethical concepts and how this view may be impacted by workforce dynamics. Internal auditors must also understand ethical concepts and ensure that they appropriately consider outside factors when evaluating ethical issues.

Considerations When Examining COSO Alignment

Considerations that auditors may take to ensure the organization fully aligns with COSO 2013 include:

- Support strong education on COSO 2013, its intent, and the reason behind the 17 principles and 77 points of focus.
- Allow internal auditors to evaluate ethics and control environment within audit projects.
- Include the 17 principles within individual audits to effectively evaluate ethical concepts at the process level.
- Ensure management and the board agree to the role of the internal audit in ethical evaluations.
- Ensure internal auditor knows the proper reporting protocol when ethical issues are identified.

Continually re-evaluate the effectiveness of key controls for meeting ethical principles. Ensure the organization understands as processes mature, controls and concepts may change. In addition, as the workforce evolves, additional efforts may be needed to ensure ethical conduct concepts are understood.

Section 7: Nontransition to COSO 2013 and Implications to the Ethical Culture

Introduction

What are the implications for a company's ethical environment if an organization does not effectively transition to COSO 2013? What could occur if companies and employees do not understand the related principles and points of focus? These questions may be difficult to evaluate, and the outcome may depend on the organization and the professionals within the organization. What we do know is that COSO 2013 provides additional guidance and examples organizations can use to ensure they have an effective control environment and their ethical programs are strong and contribute to the overall goals and objectives of the organization. For those organizations who have transitioned to COSO 2013, they must continually reevaluate their processes to ensure they are meeting the intent of the 17 principles.

If you are an experienced professional who has worked in various organizations, you may have witnessed all organizations have their individual culture and idiosyncrasies. What may be considered proper or ethically correct in one organization may be very different from the expectations in another organization. The variances may occur due to the type of organization, the size, the geographical territory the organization personalities involved, the industry of the organization, or the manner in which the company has evolved over time. The COSO framework was established to be relevant to all types of organizations, regardless of their industry category, size, or complexity. This should allow any organization to evaluate the concepts and apply them to their own ethical environment.

Over a career of 30-plus years, I have been employed with six separate companies and performed consulting work for dozens of others. In addition, I have trained internal auditors from thousands of organizations that stretch across international boundaries and many industries. One of the common themes I hear from auditors is the difficulty they experience in attempting to evaluate ethical culture. In some instances, the auditors cannot identify effective methods to make an assessment; in other instances, the organization does not accept the need for internal audit to assess ethical culture.

Challenges in Evaluating Ethical Culture

Companies have made significant strides over the past decade related to ethical concepts. Granted, many of these strides were the result of governmental legislation placed on organizations due to corporate scandals. In any event, organizations have placed a greater focus on ethical elements such as the code of conduct, conflict of interest, tone at the top, whistleblower hotline, and human resource processes as well as other procedures that may contribute to an ethical culture. Even with this focus, internal and external auditors continue to express concern that although the theories are written into policies, the actual execution of these policies is not always successful and, many times, questionable. When internal auditors face challenges in evaluating ethical culture, part of the challenge may relate to management's view of whether this is an area internal auditors should even be examining. Ethics and control environment are considered soft controls. It is difficult to find tangible evidence that some aspect is actually being effectively executed. From a management viewpoint, they may believe internal auditors should only be validating controls with tangible evidence that can be examined. When you consider an ethics policy, auditors can validate a person has acknowledged receipt of the policy by obtaining a copy of his or her signature on the document. However, this type of validation does not ensure the person completely and adequately understands the policy and expectations. In addition, there are always the political implications of evaluating ethical culture. The topic itself is one management would prefer internal auditors not to become involved with. In their view, internal auditors aren't psychologists or lawyers, and they aren't specifically trained on all aspects of ethics. Evaluating ethics is often a judgment, and management may not agree with the internal auditor's judgment on a particular issue. Any observations identified by the internal auditors can be perceived by management as an accusation. This creates further difficulty when internal audit attempts to be involved in ethical processes.

Earlier chapters described a process utilized by an internal audit department during the early years of SOX to more effectively evaluate the control environment and aspects of an ethical culture. This method is often referred to as the maturity model approach. In Chapter 4, we will further outline this concept and provide ideas and thoughts for executing this approach within your company.

Section 8: Internal Audit's Role in the Evolution of Ethics in the Corporate Culture

Introduction

Earlier, we presented a scenario where a CAE was informed by the CEO that she was expected to be the moral compass of the organization. The statement of being the moral compass took the CAE by surprise. Although the CAE appreciated the confidence placed in her, the actual moral compass and ethical direction of the company was one that must be set by senior management and the board. In her situation, she was not a direct report to the CEO and did not have the authority to act as an ethics officer or a moral compass for the entire company.

Internal Audit's Role in Ethics

Internal auditors can still take a value-added role in facilitating the evolution of ethics within their organizations. Internal auditors have vast knowledge of various areas of the company and often see how individuals and departments act and interact on a day-to-day basis. They can utilize this information to develop improvement recommendations when completing reviews or working on SOX processes. However, to be able to impact ethical culture, the internal auditors must be perceived as having the relevant knowledge and appropriate authority to evaluate issues and incidents and to raise the issues, when observed, to the attention of management and the board.

Some internal audit groups consider the evaluation of the control environment or ethical culture as a once-a-year task. It may be a process executed when performing work to comply with SOX, or it may be related to work performed for external audit. However, internal auditors should consider how to be proactive in their observations and evaluations of ethical behavior and procedures. With the evolving business world, the diversity of individuals within the workforce, and the changes occurring in our communication methods (e.g., e-mail, Twitter, LinkedIn, instant messaging), auditors should always maintain an awareness of the ethical culture of the organization and how it is manifested in everyday actions. Internal auditors often mention they regularly hear concerns or comments about their organizations ethical atmosphere via watercooler talk. In essence, they are referring to hearing and observing behavior and discussion when they are not officially conducting an audit. Internal auditors must use care when assuming the watercooler talk is a true reflection of the company's control environment or ethical culture. Personnel often like to vet frustrations about an issue in an informal manner. Things overheard can be taken out of context. However, there is still something to be said for maintaining a continued awareness of the culture, tone, and ethical conduct of individuals within the company. This can be accomplished through everyday actions and interactions as well as during officially scheduled audits. Consider the following scenarios regarding the role of internal audit in establishing an ethical culture.

Scenario One: Internal Audit and Evolution of Ethics   You are a member of the internal audit group for a medium-sized financial organization. The audits performed by your department are primarily compliance related and support banking regulations. The department is considered understaffed for the company's size. Audits do not include a formal evaluation of the control environment for the audit area. This is because management does not believe an evaluation of this type is relevant to compliance auditing. However, your CAE has instructed the audit team to stay aware and informally record observations of how the control environment operates in the area they are reviewing.

At the end of the year, the CAE gathers the audit team together to discuss the completion of the annual audit plan. The audits executed throughout the year have identified issues, but none considered significant in nature. However, during the discussion, each auditor brings up concerns that areas reviewed seemed to have questionable practices that may lead to an unethical environment. The practices extended from the manner in which work was performed to the philosophy and management style of the area being audited. As each auditor provides input, the team and the CAE become concerned that although their audit procedures did not identify any significant compliance issues, there may be an issue with the control environment and ethical culture of each process area that could impact the organization. In addition, the auditors indicate the areas they reviewed continually have a significant amount of personnel turnover. When the auditors inquired regarding the turnover, they were told it was because of the competitive workforce, and personnel were always looking for the next best job. However, when speaking with employees and observing the management of the department, the auditors observed the work environment is very tense and stringently controlled. Employees are generally dissatisfied with their jobs.

If you were the CAE, what would you do in this circumstance? Remember, you have already issued audit reports for the year, which have not revealed any issues which may relate to a concern regarding the control environment or ethical conduct. Would you go directly to the audit committee to express your concern? Would you speak to your direct supervisor the CFO? Would you ask to speak to the CEO about your concerns?

This is a good example for considering how internal audit can contribute to the ethical culture of the organization. In this scenario, circumstances inhibited internal audit from providing relevant and timely input about the control environment. These included:

- Understaffing of internal audit
- Limitations on audit scope
- Management's perception of internal audit's role in compliance auditing and evaluation of ethical culture
- Strict compliance focus for audits

However, it is interesting the CAE instructed his auditors to pay attention and observe the control environment and ethical processes within each audit area. Possibly, the CAE had questions regarding the overall ethical culture, or possibly he is simply attempting to expand the knowledge base of his auditors.

The difficulty in this scenario is there were obvious issues auditors noticed during their reviews. Those issues were not communicated to management. As such, waiting until year-end to hold a discussion on the issues observed puts internal audit at a disadvantage.

If the internal audit group were following the *Standards*, any observations identified related to the control environment should have been communicated during the course of the audit or in the formal audit report. Of course, this would have required management to understand internal audit's fiduciary duty to evaluate the control environment and their acceptance of listening to the identified issues.

COSO 2013 can provide a supporting position for auditors who wish to incorporate an evaluation of the control environment into their audits. To be able to effectively execute a compliance audit, the auditor would need to ensure policies and procedures of the audit areas are up to date and relevant. It would also require the auditor to ensure staffing of the audit area was sufficient to execute the compliance procedures. In addition, it would be important to ensure there were proper procedures in place to ensure segregation of duties and ethical management philosophy toward the compliance issues. These are all elements of a company's control environment. However, many auditors view compliance audits as a check-the-box review. They rely on predetermined procedures validated at the back end. In this instance, the CAE has to determine how he will communicate the various observations to the relevant management. This will be difficult, since management does not see the evaluation of ethics or the control environment as being within the purview of internal audit. Also, the CAE has informally asked his auditors to document observations of the control environment. The CAE will need to be able to adequately explain to management why this was done, and why the items observed were not communicated earlier.

A more transparent approach for the compliance audits would be for the audit team to take a step back and first evaluate the foundation and structure of the control environment within each audit area. This approach requires management to understand the work will include elements that may examine procedures used by management when directing their compliance personnel in their daily tasks. A strong and ethical control environment will be the basis for ensuring a strong compliance program.

Section 9: Dissecting Ethics

Introduction

Inability of an organization to adjust to the requirements for a complete and open ethical culture can have many ramifications. Shareholders, stakeholders, and regulatory agencies have set the bar high when it comes to the ethical actions of organizations. The difficulties of the past continue to plague the economic markets and erode investor confidence. Investors must have faith in organizations they have interest or invest in. Employees must feel their organizations are ethical and they treat people fairly to maintain a proper work environment. From a perspective of how ethics impacts an organization—take the word "ethics" and assign a phrase to each letter of the word. This may assist in understanding why organizations must adjust to maintaining and improving their ethical environment.

> E—Everyone is responsible.
> T—Tone at the top is essential.
> H—Honesty is the best policy.
> I—Integrity is a measure of ethics.
> C—Corporate social responsibility is expected.
> S—Silence is not acceptable (or silence is acceptance).

Take these concepts and translate them to how your organization manages its ethical culture. In reality, everyone in the organization is responsible for an ethical culture. Of course, tone is set from the top, but each individual must display the proper attributes of respect, integrity, and honesty for an ethical culture to be effective.

Everyone Is Responsible   All too often, when the word ethics is brought into a conversation, individuals tend to promulgate its primary responsibility lies with the leaders of the organization. Although it is true ethical behavior must be demonstrated at the top, it is imperative for everyone in the organization to display ethical behavior. Just as we learned in kindergarten to be personally responsible, each employee must be committed to ethical behavior for a company to be successfully moral. Think about your first real ethical dilemma. It probably occurred long before you entered the business world. It may have happened when you were faced with some decision as a child, or later in your teenage years. Often, those experiences and how they evolved impact our overall sense of ethical responsibility. For some, ethics is an unquestionable choice, while others may find that certain elements can be rationalized. Standardizing every employee's understanding is a difficult task. However, the existence of a written, well-communicated and well-taught code of ethics that is made an integral part of the organization can go a long way for ensuring an organizations ethical culture. As we have learned from past examples, the code must be more than a written document; it must be practiced and evident in the behavior of the organization.

Tone at the Top   Tone at the top is a phrase management likes to tout. Many will assert the attribute is present in their organization, even without the claim being proven. However, if management does not act in an ethical and forthright manner, it may be difficult for employees to model the proper behavior.

Many writers claim ethical behavior and conduct must start with tone at the top. I agree this is a critical attribute, but we must accept that not all individuals will have the same morality and opinion as ours. Simply addressing tone will not ensure the organization acts appropriately when faced with an ethical dilemma. If there is a question as to which path is the most appropriate to take, individuals can find it easy to rationalize alternatives that may not be in line with the company's overall code. This is exactly why organizations must not only rely on what they deem as tone at the top but also ensure tone is actually exemplified in day-to-day practices. Tone at the top must be communicated frequently, openly, and honestly and put into practice by every individual within the organization. Individuals will follow their leaders and learn from their actions. These actions should show an undeniable compliance with ethical values.

Honesty   All too often, ethics and corporate responsibility don't necessarily equate to honesty in the workplace. As Agent Jethro Gibbs states on the popular *NCIS* television show, "Never say you are sorry. It is a sign of weakness." Unfortunately, this is a sentiment that sometimes spills over into the business world. Honesty may mean admission of either wrongdoing, poor judgment, or even an honest mistake. But that admission isn't to say the wrongdoing was unethical. When employees are conditioned to act with caution when discussing issues in public, they may feel they must hide the truth from management because of potentially negative implications.

No one wants to be responsible for having to point out areas where work is not being done as effectively as possible. This can become quite a dilemma when your job involves internal audit, process improvement, or quality assurance. The professional is put in the position of calling out gaps which may have existed for a period of time. Organizations must ensure all professionals feel that when a potential issue is identified, they can openly discuss the situation with the appropriate management. This does not mean everyone's word or opinion is taken at face value, but when employees feel they cannot freely express thoughts and ideas, the culture may be sending the wrong message. In addition, remember the phrase "Just because it's legal, doesn't mean it's ethical." Ethics deals with morality issues, and most people's level of morality will reach different tolerances. So, when you are personally faced with an ethical dilemma, ask yourself whether you are looking at the situation as honestly and transparently as you can. If questions still arise, it is your obligation to raise those questions with individuals in positions of responsibility. The legality of the issue may not be the right answer when looking at the morale side of the issue. This is when you must enlist the assistance of others to help ensure the organization's needs are being appropriately met.

Integrity   Integrity is a virtue essential to proper ethical concepts. Integrity represents doing the right thing when no one is watching. If management cannot trust employees will act in accordance with their outlined responsibilities, irrespective of how closely the employees are managed or monitored, integrity will come into question.

If someone asked you to name the top three people in history who you felt displayed unquestionable integrity, would those same individuals measure high on the ethics scale? Integrity is adherence to a moral code, reflected in honesty and harmony in how a person thinks and acts. Individuals regarded as having high integrity normally possess a strong set of moral ethics. From a corporate viewpoint, ask yourself if the members of your leadership team are individuals whom the employee population will view as having strong integrity and moral ethics. These are the individuals who employees will look to emulate. This is the mirror into your future organization.

Revisiting the earlier scenario, when the CAE was informed by the CFO that she was to serve as the moral compass of the organization, may give some insight into how management perceives internal audit's role. In this instance, the CEO may have been trying to relay he felt the CAE should be the moral compass as it relates to the trait of integrity. Management understands internal audit is supposed to exercise objectivity, and along with that comes the attribute of executing their role with full integrity and ethics.

Internal audit certainly has a role in assisting in the establishment of a proper ethical culture. But, it is not their role alone. The true moral compass of an organization is the responsibility of management and the board. Internal audit should execute their responsibilities with proper ethical actions and integrity, but the tone of the organization its culture and ethics will be established from top-level management in the organization.

Internal audit departments who find themselves in a position of being informed they are the moral compass of the organization should have a discussion with management on the perception of the role. In addition, internal audit should review the *Standards* with management and ensure they understand the internal auditor's role versus management responsibilities.

Corporate Social Responsibility   Since the early 1960s, when business ethics came into vogue, the topics of corporate responsibility, ethical behavior, and compliance have been on the radar for the SEC and other federal and state regulatory agencies. Yet, corporate social responsibility goes far beyond environmental initiatives, community support, and being a good neighbor. Corporate social responsibility is owned by each and every employee. Whether it is a dedication to recycling efforts, contributing to community causes, or providing appropriate feedback to supervisors on how to make the business better, this is the true intent of corporate social responsibility. Organizations must learn to embrace the concept that individuals who work in the organization have day-to-day observations which can improve operations and business processes. The inability to encourage this feedback from employees and provide an outlet to use creative ideas is a failure of corporate social responsibility.

Silence Is Not Acceptable Silence can occur due to the fear of retribution. The only way to advance the elimination of business scandals which have pervaded our everyday life is to erase the notion that silence is golden. Many employees see things in their daily job which they may question, yet they turn a blind eye due to fear of retribution. Ensure your employees know the appropriate outlet for surfacing concerns or questions. Organizations must instill the concept that silence is not acceptable. Another way to view the issue is that "silence is a form of acceptance." If individuals chose to stay silent when they witness or experience unethical behavior, they may be, in essence, perpetuating the issue.

Summary

Ethics and corporate responsibility will continue to be hot topics in corporate America for years to come. As the economy continues to struggle, or to rebound, the ethical behavior of those within business will dramatically impact the success of that recovery. Technological advances will also impact the manner in which ethical principles are executed. It is no longer acceptable to be the Enrons of the world, where a best practice code of conduct sits on a shelf but is not embraced or actually displayed in practice. Organizations must focus on all aspects of their ethics program. You must look further than the policy itself. Understand how the policy is practiced, enforced, and updated and how compliance is measured and reported. This is the true sign of a policy in action.

4

METHODS FOR IDENTIFYING AND MEASURING ETHICAL BEHAVIOR

Introduction

This chapter will provide ideas for internal auditors to utilize when attempting to evaluate their company's ethical culture. As a profession, internal audit must begin to move past the typical questionnaire process or survey procedures. In addition, inquiry alone should not be considered sufficient to assess ethical culture. When inquiring of other professionals about their opinion of the organization's ethical culture, professionals may inherently feel an obligation to relay only positive comments or observations. This is why auditors must identify unique and innovative methods for their evaluations. Consider the following questions.

- Can internal audit effectively evaluate an organization's ethical climate and culture?
- Is evaluation of ethics only relevant at the top of the organization, or should it be extended throughout the operations?
- Should we assume that if an organization has policies on ethics, then employees will know and understand what actions are proper and which actions are not?

Answers to these initial questions may vary. According to the *IIA Standards*, internal auditors should be involved in evaluating ethical culture. The trick is, will management accept the evaluation. In addition, ethics should be evaluated at further than just the top level of the organization. As we have indicated in previous chapters, ethics is everyone's responsibility. Finally, auditors should not assume organization policies will adequately inform professionals of their ethical responsibilities. Internal auditors must ensure policies are effectuated in the daily working environment. Organizations should ensure there is an ethical culture and climate that extends throughout all facets of the company's operations. Recalling the corporate incidents since the Sarbanes–Oxley legislation was passed in 2002, do you feel your organization's work to evaluate ethical culture is sufficient and effective? Most companies would not want to admit they performed anything less than a serious evaluation of ethical culture. If this was true, would all of the scandals and ethical incidents outlined on the time line in Chapter 1 still have occurred? Maybe so, and possibly the reason is because individuals have different levels of morals and values. That was the purpose of our discussion on the psychology of ethics in Chapter 2. However, we now have an updated version of the COSO framework which provides additional guidance toward evaluating an organization's control environment and attributes that link to ethical conduct. Internal auditors should begin their evaluation by closely examining each of the principles under the five attributes of the control environment and ask, "How could unethical behavior happen if this principle is not met?"

To understand and embrace the COSO 17 principles and 77 points of focus, auditors must be able to relate each principle to the individual organization's processes and activities. By performing this exercise, internal auditors can obtain strong insights into methods to establish, maintain, and monitor an ethical culture.

Although auditors can use COSO 2013 as a tool for obtaining a deeper understanding of ethical culture, remember the COSO Foundation stresses it is the responsibility of management to properly instill the principles within the organization. The internal auditor is responsible for only evaluating whether the principles actually exist and are being appropriately executed.

The task of evaluating a company's control environment and ethical culture is difficult because of the soft attributes which require judgment and professional skepticism to evaluate. It can be a very politically charged task. Management may be sensitive when told that attitudes, tone, philosophy, or organization procedures may not be effective to develop and sustain an ethical culture. As we have discussed in previous chapters, many companies do not feel internal auditors are capable or qualified to evaluate these attributes. It is often seen as the legal department's role, or one senior management handles.

The *Standards* outline requirements for internal auditors to evaluate aspects of the company's ethical culture and control environment. As evidenced by examining corporate scandals of the past, these evaluations must go further than examining the presence of a code of conduct. Enron had what many considered a best practice code of conduct, yet it was not effectively accepted and utilized throughout the company. Auditors must utilize other techniques and methods to examine the true identity of an organization's control environment and ethical culture. In this chapter, we will:

- Review the process of utilizing surveys and questionnaires when evaluating ethical culture
- Identify components that comprise an ethical culture
- Examine how perception of ethical culture can become reality
- Provide examples of the utilization of the maturity model approach to facilitate an evaluation of ethical culture and the control environment

Section 1: Moving Past Surveys, Questionnaires, and Interviews

Introduction

Surveys and questionnaires are utilized by many different professions for different purposes. Everyone has their individual opinion on the value of questionnaires or surveys. Regardless of your personal preference or opinion, consider for a moment the challenges presented. The following narrative is from a blog written after witnessing an unfortunate survey experience by a colleague during the 2014 General Audit Management conference. The impetus of the blog was from observations related to how the survey process was conducted and how feedback was provided to the speakers.

Critique with Etiquette

At some point in every professional's career, the opportunity to critique some element of work will be presented. It may be the performance evaluation of a subordinate; providing 360-degree feedback for a superior; evaluating some project, process, or presentation; or even providing feedback to a seminar presenter. As with any new experience, there is a learning curve for effectively delivering critique or feedback or providing an opinion on a process or topic. The manner in which the critique is phrased, worded, or delivered may dramatically impact how it is received and whether the intended recipient will accept the feedback as a learning opportunity.

In today's world of social media and the Internet, it is surprising how harsh individuals can be, even with the simple task of responding to a blog or LinkedIn remark. When Facebook first became popular, it was often used it as a vetting tool to let the world know how a person felt about something. If you are a parent, you may have used the cautionary phrase to your children, "What hits the Internet, stays on the Internet!" The interpretation is, what you put in writing in a public domain can reflect on your overall personal character.

Returning to the theme of critiquing with etiquette, let's examine a few scenarios and their pressure points. As a supervisor tasked with providing personnel evaluations to employees, you learn the manner in which improvement opportunities are relayed can impact the outcome of the message. Assuming you are focused on assisting the professional with improving their skills, the message may be more successful when delivered in a constructive, coaching atmosphere rather than one that is reprimanding or confrontational. Similarly, if you've had the opportunity to provide 360-degree feedback to a superior, you learn the art of relaying concerns in the most positive and politically correct manner possible. Even if the feedback is given through an anonymous sealed survey, you can be assured superiors will try to evaluate where specific comments came from based on the wording, phrasing, and writing style. Both of these scenarios are incidents where individual evaluators learn to be cautious with their words and delivery.

In the case of utilizing surveys to gather information about a process or procedure, especially something as sensitive as ethical culture, individuals have varying opinions on how effective surveys are in measuring the control environment. Asking an employee to complete an ethics survey or control environment survey can surface many questions including:

- How do I know the survey is anonymous?
- What if I write something negative—will it come back to haunt me?

- Why should I write my true opinion down? This is just one of those processes where nothing ever changes.

In the case of surveys handed out following a conference or at a speaker's event, professional organizations want to ensure programs made available to their constituency are providing the level of information expected. Typically, a survey or feedback form is distributed, allowing participants to rate the speaker on several characteristics in addition to providing comments. In theory, this is good practice. In reality, it can present several difficulties. In our desire to allow for open feedback, we provide for the confidentiality of the person completing the survey. This authority absent accountability can create an atmosphere where feedback may not always be constructive and can actually border on offensive.

An example involves a well-versed colleague who was making a formal convention presentation on a topic of which he had expert knowledge. The speaker was a volunteer presenter who paid his own travel to the conference event. The day of the presentation he was not feeling well, but confident he could effectively deliver the presentation (which he did). Several hours later, he was in the emergency room experiencing a heart attack. After surgery and hospital time, he recovered. But, a few weeks later, he received the participant reviews via e-mail. Overall, the reviews and ratings were satisfactory, with a couple of exceptions. One person's feedback appeared more as an offensive rant about the gentleman's presentation style and appearance. There were no comments about what the participant found inappropriate, but rather the narrative was filled with degrading comments about the presenter's physical appearance and a listing of the individual reviewer's personal credentials. The point is, the feedback was not constructive but truly offensive, to the extent the speaker decided he would no longer agree to speaking invitations. Unfortunately, this is a true loss to the profession.

When there is a large audience, you can assume there will be individuals in the room who have a different perception of the presentation. Experienced presenters learn to take the comments in stride and adjust as appropriate for future presentations. It is certainly everyone's right to have their own observations on the topic.

When utilizing surveys for evaluating processes or procedures, the auditor must keep these same concepts in mind. For those surveys returned with only a score circled, the auditor should question the usefulness of the response. If the respondent did not take time to provide comments to support the ranking, what is a simple score relaying about the evaluation? In addition, if there are a large number of survey respondents, scores can tend to cancel each other out. One respondent's high score will cancel out another respondent's low score. This information must be considered when determining the usefulness of the survey process. When considering the process of providing specific comments on surveys, there are a few recommendations participants should consider before recording their written observations.

Use Your Words   New parents may instruct children to "use your words" to discourage the child from communicating by simply using hand gestures. As professionals, we may want to consider this advice with a small twist. "Use your words constructively and with proper etiquette." In cases where the respondent is being asked to review a process, consider supporting ratings with relevant observations and comments. The critique will be better accepted if the recipient of the survey does not feel they are being unduly singled out or attacked. Ask yourself, am I willing to relay the same information to the individual or the process area personally? If not, why? Also, if not, should you write your comments and remain anonymous?

Be Specific   If you have concerns about the presentation or the process being evaluated, point out the exact area of your concern. Broad statements like "The presenter made things up or stated facts improperly" or "The ethics of XYZ area is questionable" do not provide enough feedback to help correct an issue if, indeed, there is one. Keep in mind the purpose of your critique is to provide feedback to improve the process. Ratings absent constructive suggestions do not provide the necessary information to allow organizations to ensure they improve their programs.

Avoid Personal References   Here is where accountability comes in. Prior to submitting a completed survey, consider whether you are willing to put your name and contact information on the form. If not, why? If there were strong enough concerns to express them in a critical manner wouldn't you want to have the opportunity to better outline your concerns to someone who may be able to adjust the process and make a difference? Also, consider if you were required to provide the feedback face to face, would you use the same words?

Consider What Information Is Important to Improve the Process   Whether comments are positive or negative, consider how the feedback will impact the end result of the survey process. If the feedback is unclear, those gathering the information may put it aside without realizing there is an important issue to address. Take the case of a control environment survey where a question requests the respondent to rank tone at the top on a scale of one through five. What does a three ranking mean anyway? Many individuals have high expectations when it comes to moral values. Someone may view a three ranking as poor. Another person may view the same ranking as adequate. Providing comments which explain your rating will make the survey process more valuable.

Whether you agree or disagree with some of these points, take a few minutes to pause the next time you complete a survey. Consider the following questions:

- What is the expectation of the survey?
- Has guidance been given with regard to the ratings and how they are defined?
- Will it be helpful to elaborate on ratings with specific examples or comments?
- Can you "use your words" constructively and with dignity?

There are also various elements that organizations may want to consider that may improve the overall survey process. These considerations may assist to ensure participants are providing the needed information to improve the process.

Provide Respondents with Instructions   Provide respondents with brief instructions on the purpose of the survey, what it will be used for, how it is to be completed, and how to submit the survey. Remind respondents that information is intended to assist in improving future processes. Ensure they understand the importance of providing constructive feedback relevant to the topic area being addressed. The survey should not be used as a vetting tool.

Consider Gathering Demographic Information   Any professional who has presented to a large audience may periodically see comments on the opposite spectrum of the majority of the comments. If you are executing a survey throughout your company, this can make it very difficult to pinpoint what elements of the survey topic are not meeting respondent's expectations. It can be helpful for the person executing the survey to understand basic demographics of the audience such as job level, experience level, industry, and, geographical location. This information can be easily collected through the review process and may help presenters place the comments into a frame of reference. By understanding certain demographics of the survey responses, surveyor's may be able to put certain outlying comments into the proper frame of reference.

Carefully Consider Questions for the Survey   Organizations will often mimic survey forms found on leading practice websites. In these instances, ensure questions are relevant to information being assessed. Don't assume you can ask a generic question such as "Is segregation of duties adequate?" The respondent may wonder if you are asking the question related to a particular process area or in relation to the company as a whole. You must tailor the survey to your organization's processes.

Another consideration is the rating scale. A scale of one to five may seem reasonable; however, if you intend to use the average scores of all surveys collected and present it as representative of the overall opinion of the respondents, it is difficult to determine the true effectiveness of the process being evaluated. For example, if a respondent rates a process at a one while another respondent rates the process at a five, this will result in an average rating of a three. In essence, if the internal auditors are not evaluating the break-out of the individual scores and their disparity, simply averaging the scores may not be a good indicator of why a process is handled in a certain manner.

Provide Guidance for Comments   Organizations executing any survey should consider providing soft reminders to participants of the proper or acceptable tone of comments. Request details behind opinions to enable evaluators to place the comments into the proper perspective. A topic such as ethics or control environment can be one in which some individuals will take the opportunity to vent about every little

thing they believe is wrong in the organization. The survey evaluators must to be able to appropriately measure those comments against
other responses to identify if the issue is isolated or widespread.

Overall, organizations and participants can assist in the improvement process for effective critiques. We are all trying to reach the
same result—a positive and learning experience for professionals.

Section 2: Assessing Effectiveness of a Survey or Interview

Take the survey

Introduction

Consider how often you are asked to complete a survey. Typically, the
survey will consist of a number of questions and provide a rating scale
for assessment. As alluded to earlier in this chapter under the Critique
with Etiquette section, the difficulty with this process is the concept
of aggregation and averaging of scores. Does an average provide the
evaluator with the relevant information to understand the results of
the question? Wouldn't it be helpful to know what part of the service
was or was not unacceptable? The variances may be impacted by the
time of year, day, or even month in which the service was provided.
Or it may have something to do with the individuals providing the
services. Simply having a rating that is averaged does not provide
enough information to fully evaluate the effectiveness of any process.
As many accountants will say, "We can make the numbers look the
way we want!"

Many individuals who complete surveys do not take the time to
provide comments. Either they don't care about the topic, don't want
to officially go on the record as having said something, or simply don't

have time to write a comment. This dynamic makes it even harder to evaluate the reasons behind the ratings.

Another difficulty with a survey is the manner in which a person may interpret the question. Take an example of having internal audit distribute a survey to evaluate the ethical culture of the organization. The survey includes a question such as "I believe management is ethical." The person taking the survey is asked to rank the statement one through five, with five being strongly agree. Each individual reading the survey may interpret the question in a different way. One may feel the question is asking about the perception of senior management, while another individual may believe the question relates to direct management or, possibly, a business unit head. This interpretation could result in various ratings. Without the ability to clarify the question, individuals may assign ratings that do not provide input the surveyors are intending. It is difficult to word a question in a manner everyone will interpret consistently. If this occurs, the manner in which the participants assign ratings may not provide the surveyor with the best insight into the issue being evaluated.

Utilizing Questionnaires to Evaluate Ethical Culture

In the early years of SOX, the external audit firms developed standard questionnaires, which many internal audit groups used to assess the control environment and ethical values. If your company utilized these questionnaires, try to remember some of the questions listed. Did a rating provide a transparent evaluation of the company's ethical culture? Consider the following statements that may have been included on a questionnaire.

- The company has a code of conduct.
- The company's code of conduct is effective.

Considering these two statements, would the answers truly provide the organization with a good insight into the ethical culture? Now, let's take this thought process one step further. Consider the following additional factors for each of the inquiries listed.

The Company Has a Code of Conduct   The results of the survey have shown respondents rated this question a five. Good for you! But remember what was mentioned earlier in the chapter. Enron also had a code of conduct. The simple existence of a code does not equate to an effective ethical culture. The auditor should be assessing how well the code is trained, understood, and followed throughout the organization. They must evaluate the actual execution of the code and how it impacts the organization's activities. If you had a question such as this on your original surveys to measure ethical conduct, how effective do you believe the rating process was?

The Company's Code of Conduct is Effective   This inquiry is asking the person to make an assessment. But how do you know what specific factors a survey participant is considering when making the assessment? The person will most likely be assessing the question based on their own personal moral code. This may be appropriate, but absent further understanding of why the respondent believes the code is or isn't effective, the question may not provide the answers needed to adequately assess the ethical culture of the entire organization.

As you can see, when utilizing surveys, it is important to ensure questions are carefully crafted.

Interviewing

When utilizing interviews as a method of gathering information about the organization's ethical culture, internal auditors must keep in mind the dynamics presented when interviews are executed. Assume the internal audit department developed a series of open-ended questions to be used for interviewing a select population about the ethical culture of the organization. Open-ended questions would be used in an interview process to allow the respondent to provide information they deem most relevant. The interview process could be impacted by any or all of the following:

- The person conducting the interview, their relative experience level, and with whom they are speaking.
- The manner or tone in which the original question or any follow-up questions are asked.
- Whether individuals conducting the interviews are instructed to stay strictly to the questions on the list, or whether those questions are merely guidelines.

- The location of the interview. There are some psychological theories around how and where interviews are conducted and how that impacts the manner in which interviewees may respond. For instance, if the interview is conducted in a neutral location where individuals do not feel intimidated or threatened, they may be open with their responses. If an interview is conducted in the auditor's office, the respondent may be guarded with responses. If the interview is conducted in the respondents' work area, their ability to answer openly may depend on whether they are located in an open office or closed office, or who else within the area is aware of the interview.

The lesson is that even when using a survey template as a guide in conducting interviews, the auditor must be prepared to adequately execute the process and effectively assess information obtained.

Section 3: Effective Survey Techniques

Introduction

Surveys can be a good tool to obtain information from a wide audience. However, it is critical that the survey be developed appropriately and clearly. There may be several steps to consider:

Developing Surveys

Step One: Developing Surveys Clarify the Objectives of the Survey

Ensure several questions are addressed:

- Exactly what is the survey attempting to determine?
- What actions may result from the survey process?
- Who is the target audience?
- How will the survey questions be prioritized? This can impact how individuals may answer certain questions.
- Is a rating scale appropriate, and if so, how will the scale be defined? In other words, if you use a one through five scale, many people assume a score of three is adequate. In your mind, is it adequate? Should you provide the respondents with some simple guidelines such as the following?

- One: The process is informal, and personnel must execute it utilizing their own personal expertise.
- Two: The process has some standards and guidelines, but departments have significant variability in how they apply the guidelines.
- Three: The process has documented procedures, but the procedures are not considered policies and may not be consistently followed.
- Four: The process has documented policies, which are consistently followed. The organization may not update the process in a timely fashion.
- Five: The process is executed, managed and updated optimally.

These are only examples and are geared toward evaluation of a process rather than a speaker or presenter. The point is, just like asking someone to assign a high/moderate/low assessment, you must provide the respondent with some general guidelines regarding the meaning of the scale. In addition to guidelines for the rating scale, the surveyor should carefully consider other factors when developing survey questions. The following are a few examples.

- Should the survey use open-ended questions or a yes/no response? How might this impact the results?
- Can questions be stated in a manner that will be consistently interpreted by the respondents?
- What is the best method to elicit comments from the individuals being surveyed?
- Will the survey be anonymous, or are individuals required to record their name or other logistical information?
  - If the survey is fully anonymous, it may be difficult to interpret the results.
- How many completed surveys are required to assume the results obtained are an accurate reflection of the population?

These are a few considerations when creating the survey. Also, remember surveys should be concise and short. If the individual completing the survey is required to fill out pages of questions, they may lose attention quickly. Understand objectives for the survey and ensure questions meet those objectives.

Step Two: Communicate Survey Purpose

Consider including a narrative at the beginning of the survey which clarifies the intent of the questionnaire. Keep the narrative short to ensure participants read the information. Call attention to this section with highlighting, bold type, or a different font. Make sure it is clear what the survey will be used for, why respondents are being asked to participate, and "what's in it for them." Individuals will be more receptive to completing a survey if they believe it will result in some action or change. If you allow for anonymity of the survey, ensure you explain how the process will be managed. In contrast, confidentiality is not necessarily equivalent to anonymity. Confidentiality would infer the respondents answer will not be individually relayed to another person. However, it does not mean the auditors will not ask the respondent for additional information or confirmation on some fact within the response.

Step Three: Gather Logistical Information

Determine the need to gather geographical or logistical information from the survey process. Some helpful information might include:

- Job level of the respondent
- Department or division the respondent works for
- Respondents tenure with the company
- Specific geographical location where the respondents works

This information may assist in the overall analysis of survey results.

Step Four: Determine Requirement for Anonymity

Anonymity is often the cornerstone for obtaining reliable and truthful information. As previously discussed when contrasting the term anonymity to confidentiality, the concept of anonymity has its own inferences. People who feel their responses may be used against them will be guarded when completing a survey. A friend once inquired about a survey she received through her company's internal audit process. The survey asked about the company ethics process and corporate culture. She was concerned about completing the survey because of the requirement to indicate name, employee ID, supervisor, and department.

When conducting a survey of this type, individuals must feel they have appropriate anonymity regarding specific responses or questions. Of course, comments and input will need to be provided to management, but do not disclose the individuals who made the specific comments. If individuals feel this may occur, they will not be transparent in completing the information.

Step Five: Survey Distribution

There are many methods used to conduct surveys. They include automated online, e-mail, manual, face to face, or even other forms of web-based or virtual processes. Each method has its advantages and disadvantages.

Online Surveys   Distributing a survey through e-mail or another electronic process may seem to be easier on everyone involved. However, it can also result in answers that are not in line with the intent of the survey. When completing a survey online, the survey taker does not have a sense of accountability for the ratings they assign or even comments they may provide. A respondent may not care about what is being asked, so they take the middle-of-the-road approach. Or, there may be a disgruntled employee who rates everything at the lowest extreme level and leaves harsh comments, because they know the survey is anonymous. Then, you must consider effectiveness of the overall survey responses. On the opposite end of the spectrum, some believe that anonymous surveys completed online contribute to what researchers may refer to as the honesty factor. Some believe respondents may answer a computer more honestly than if being asked to respond to a surveyor face to face. If that was true, we would have to ask ourselves why the legal system conducts the legal process in an open atmosphere in front of a jury of peers. In addition, most individuals who are familiar with information technology processes understand there are many ways to trace Internet protocol (IP) addresses to computers where the survey was taken. So in essence, is there really anonymity or confidentiality?

One-on-One Surveys There is one method of performing surveys that entails more time but can provide effective insight. This method involves conducting the survey in a one-on-one setting. The surveyor is able to clarify questions the respondent may have. The surveyor can also elicit comments and include them on the survey. In addition, if the respondent is rating a question very differently from what the surveyor has experienced with other respondents, open-ended questions can be used to clarify the respondent's view. Of course, on the downside, the respondent may feel their individual survey results may not be kept confidential. This may result in inaccurate answers. However, the surveyor may be able to identify how comfortable the respondent is with the process by observing body language and listening to voice inflection as well as gauging the interest of the respondent in completing the survey. If using a one-on-one approach, the surveyor should maintain control of the actual survey form and record the information and scoring. The surveyor should verify the responses with the participant before ending the process. By utilizing this approach, the surveyor is assured of being able to read and interpret the results.

Step Six: Test the Survey

This step can be often overlooked. Regardless of the method used to distribute the survey, it is advisable to conduct a dry run of the survey with an individual not involved in developing the questions. This will assist in ensuring the questions are worded in a manner to meet the objectives of the survey. A test run of the survey could involve utilizing a focus group to evaluate the survey questions and provide feedback regarding their interpretation of the questions. It may also provide insight into whether the scale has been adequately developed or whether individuals may feel comfortable providing comments on the surveys.

Step Seven: Analyze Results

Ultimately, the final analysis is what the auditor is working toward. The auditor is seeking the most transparent analysis that will provide information reflecting a realistic view of the issue being evaluated. Whichever method is used for executing the survey, the internal auditor must consider the advantages and disadvantages of each when analyzing the results. In addition, ensure skilled auditors with the proper expertise are available to evaluate the results. Individuals with varying experience may interpret results in various manners. It may be important to have a cross-functional analysis team to ensure results are appropriately evaluated.

In this section, we have analyzed the pros and cons of utilizing questionnaires or surveys for evaluating ethical culture. Whichever method the internal auditor chooses, be aware of the limitations of the process and ensure the results interpreted are representative of individual respondents. In the end, the auditor is working to obtain information that is a true reflection of the organization's ethical culture.

Section 4: Effective Interview Techniques

Introduction

As previously discussed, a challenge for internal audit when attempting to evaluate ethical culture is that management may not believe the responsibility is within the purview of internal audit. This is something that must be clearly addressed before internal audit attempts to execute any evaluations, surveys, or interviews regarding ethical programs. Recently, an individual inquired whether internal audit should perform a review of the company's ethics program. My response was "it depends." First, ask how your organization views internal audit's role in ethics. If the organization does not feel internal auditors have the skill or experience to truly evaluate or provide an opinion on ethical culture and concepts, observations may not be seriously considered. In essence, prior to initiating evaluations on ethical programs, ensure the appropriate backing of management and the audit committee.

Interview Techniques

There are several techniques for interviewing which may improve the outcome of information obtained. If utilizing interview techniques for your evaluation of ethical culture, consider some of the following steps.

Step One: Effectively Plan the Interview   One of the biggest mistakes any interviewer can make is to enter a session without being fully prepared. Preparation involves knowing the objective and expectations of the interview process and understanding the dynamics involved with the interviewee. When considering the needs for planning an interview, the auditor must have a good understanding of the questions to be asked. Write down initial questions, and make sure to allow for the ability to add or adjust questions based on responses. Keep the conversation on track and to the point, and avoid turning the interview into a vetting session. This could ultimately impact the effectiveness of the interview. Also, don't underestimate the importance of the physical logistics of where and how the interview will take place. Make sure to conduct the interview in a nonthreatening area and in a mutually agreed-on location. This will put the interviewee at ease.

Step Two: Building Rapport   Allow the interviewee time to adjust to the setting for the interview. Individuals may understand they will be discussing ethical viewpoints and this may result in a feeling of uneasiness or apprehension. Take time to answer questions and concerns, and provide information about how the survey results will be communicated and utilized. To the extent possible, keep individual responses anonymous, unless the respondent has given permission to utilize their name. Reassure the respondent information will be used as part of a larger body of information to evaluate results. If you have questions, consult with legal counsel.

Step Three: Control the Interview   Often, interviewers do not adequately manage the process of controlling the interview. They begin a meeting with an objective and goal in mind and allow the meeting to get off track either with small talk or by allowing the respondent to continue discussion long after relevant information has been obtained. The interviewer should begin the interview with an established agenda and time frame. Communicate to the interviewee the objectives of the interview and what the expected outcome will be. If the interview begins to move off track, pull the conversation back to the objectives of the session. Often, interviewees may feel they need to elaborate on explanations. This elaboration may result in the conversation taking a different turn and not providing the value expected. The interviewer should listen and be aware of these instances and do what is required to get the interview back on the proper track. If necessary, plan for time to follow-up on input.

Step Four: Don't Overanalyze When conducting interviews, it is easy to overanalyze information. As discussed, everyone has their own morals and values. Individuals communicate in different manners. If at all possible, it can be valuable to have two auditors attend the interview to ensure information being relayed is heard and interpreted consistently. If this is not an alternative, ensure the interviewee reviews their formal responses and affirms the responses have been properly recorded.

In addition, refrain from jumping to conclusions when performing individual interviews. Until information is obtained from the full population, you may inadvertently make inaccurate assumptions. Allow the person time to think about questions and provide examples.

Step Five: Listen The art of listening can be an overlooked skill. For auditors, it is an essential element of being able to adequately evaluate issues. Be cautious of preconceived expectations for answers. Allow the individual to provide their response. Listen carefully and without bias. Don't attempt to judge a person's tone of voice, facial expressions, or reactions. Unless you have training in the art of interview profiling, your presumptions could be wrong. Jot down notes about the conversation, and ensure you are recording the intent of the conversation being relayed.

These are just a few suggestions for performing interviews. You may have developed your own best practices which work well in your organization. Not everyone will follow these exact steps. Evaluate what works for your organization and how the organization will interpret the results. Take time to determine the most effective method for conducting interviews in your cultural environment.

Section 5: The Impact of Perception on Ethical Culture

Introduction

Perception can manifest itself as reality. If employees perceive management acting in a particular way, they will rationalize why these actions are relevant to the manner in which they conduct business. Consider the official definition of perception:

> Perception: A way of regarding, understanding, or interpreting something

Perception is one of the reasons it is critical companies develop and properly train and execute on a sound code of conduct. In the absence of sound direction, when individuals question the proper moral path, they will follow their own moral instincts. Or they may decide to treat an incident in a manner they have observed other employees or management treating the incident. Individual instincts may not be reflective of the company's ethical expectations. Let's evaluate this concept with a scenario.

Ethical Scenario One Perception   The chief executive officer of Acme Inc. frequently travels on company business. The organization has a policy for first-class air travel. First class reservations are approved only if the trip is more than eight hours of consecutive flying time. It is well known the CEO travels exclusively first class. There is potential he is using his own frequent-flyer miles to upgrade to first class. This fact is not evident within the organization. Employees perceive the CEO as taking advantage of the travel policy. As such, they may find a way to rationalize why it is OK for them to fly first class.

Ethical Scenario Two Perception   Internal audit has completed a survey process evaluating the company's control environment and ethical culture. They have segregated surveys between individuals below the director level from surveys completed by the executive team. When analyzing the results, it is evident the lower-level employees have a harsher and more critical view of the ethical environment than executive management. The lower-level employees cite issues they perceive as questionable and potentially unethical.

When the internal auditors review the issues with the senior leadership team many of the leaders are surprised and initially assume the employees are exaggerating the issue. However, the CEO indicates that even though the leadership team may believe the company has a strong ethical culture, if the employee population has a different opinion there must be a disconnect in some area of the process. Because perception can often be reality, the CEO believes they should take action on some of the employee observations.

As you can see, management must understand and recognize that perception can impact the actual culture of the organization and its ethical environment.

Ethics Examination and Obtaining Management and Board Acceptance

As visited within other chapters, the Institute of Internal Auditors Code of Ethics indicates:

> The Code of Ethics of the Institute of Internal Auditors (IIA) are Principles relevant to the profession and practice of internal auditing, and Rules of Conduct that describe behavior expected of internal auditors. The Code of Ethics applies to both parties and entities that provide internal audit services. The purpose of the Code of Ethics is to promote an ethical culture in the global profession of internal auditing.

The Institute of Internal Auditors
Code of Ethics

Internal auditors wonder what action can be taken when management does not recognize their responsibility to the IIA Code of Ethics. This can be a very troubling situation. It can be difficult to convince management that a separate code of ethics, not supported by any legislative guidance or license requirement, deserves their attention. The proper action for auditors to take may depend on how the organization views and utilizes the internal audit function.

If a company is not required to have an internal audit function (such as a not-for-profit, or nonpublicly traded company), the company may not place value in the *Standards* or the Code of Ethics. This will put the internal audit team in a difficult position. Many auditors have faced this situation. During my years in internal audit, there were several occasions when my status as a staff auditor or even audit manager did not afford me the ability to clarify the concept with management. However, once I assumed the role of chief audit executive, I utilized the opportunity to visit with the senior leadership team as well as the audit committee and review the *Standards* and Code of Ethics. I was able to convey the importance of the these guidelines and explain the differences between the company's code and the IIA professional Code. I was surprised the CEO and audit committee were not aware of the *Standards* or Code. Once I provided the rationale behind the IIA guidelines, I was able to obtain agreement for the department to have a quality assurance review. This review helped to provide further assurance to the audit committee and management that internal audit was providing overall value to the organization.

In those cases where management believes they have control over the behavior and actions of the auditors, life can become even more difficult. I have also been in positions where I was asked to affirm issues identified by internal audit would not manifest in a significant financial reporting issue. Since internal auditors are not fortune tellers, and control gaps were observed, this request was tantamount to affirming no one in the organization would take advantage of the control gap and perpetrate an issue. Management did not understand my opposition to this request. I explained the Code of Ethics for auditors. I also explained the variance between an identified control gap and a true control failure. However, management still felt they had control over the work of the internal auditors, and they wanted affirmation the issues identified could not result in a financial reporting impact. In the past, issues the group had identified as significant control gaps were explained away by management. In these cases the auditors could not provide management with a quantification of the exact dollar amount of risk the control gap presented. Management would speak to the audit committee without the knowledge of internal audit, to convince them issues were being blown out of proportion. This is a very difficult dilemma for internal audit. In this case, your personal integrity and skills are being questioned. You must be able to stand up for what you believe is correct and explain the issue in a rational manner to management.

Section 6: Utilizing a Maturity Model Approach

Introduction

Assessing the effectiveness of a company's ethics program is not a walk in the park. Just because elements exist to outline the organization's expectations for an ethical culture (e.g., code of conduct, conflict of interest, whistleblower hotline) does not mean each of these elements are effectively executed. Realistically, in today's business world, we cannot assume because a policy exists, our programs are effective. As businesses evolve, as controls evolve, so do cultures. As cultures evolve, so do people. As people evolve, ethical concepts and behavior change. As a result, procedures and processes to enable a true ethical culture must also evolve.

Utilization of a process maturity model approach can be an effective way to gain a transparent look into the true nature of a company's ethical programs. In theory, a maturity model approach incorporates a five-level process maturity continuum. The lowest stage is considered the initial or ad hoc stage. This is where processes are not formalized, and controls are often up to the heroics of individuals. The stages progress similar to steps on a ladder. The uppermost (fifth) level is considered the ideal or optimal stage. This stage represents one where processes are systematically managed by a combination of process optimization and continuous process improvement. The maturity model approach involves gaining agreement and consensus from a group of stakeholders on the maturity of the process being measured within the organization.

I have had the opportunity to utilize the maturity model approach several times throughout my career. It was successfully utilized numerous times when attempting to evaluate the overall ethical environment and culture. Using this process for evaluating ethical concepts can be an illuminating experience. When the model is adequately defined and developed, evaluators will often be very open to providing timely and relevant feedback on procedures that might otherwise be considered difficult to obtain input for. However, the maturity model itself must be carefully developed, and the execution of the assessment utilizing the model must be completed in an open and transparent manner. This means internal audit must work closely with management and other personnel to ensure the maturity model is properly represented and the definitions, expectations, and outputs are well understood by the individuals who will be participating in the assessment.

Building the Approach

When working with a maturity model approach, generally there are five levels defined along the continuum of the model.

1. Initial (chaotic, ad hoc, individual heroics): This is the starting point for the use of a new or undocumented process.
2. Repeatable: The process is documented sufficiently such that repeating the same steps is possible.
3. Defined: The process is defined and confirmed as a standard business process.
4. Managed: The process is quantitatively managed in accordance with agreed-on metrics.
5. Optimized: The process is fully defined and includes procedures to allow continual review and maximization of optimization efforts.

As mentioned, I have utilized this approach to assess the company's overall ethical culture and how well elements such as ethical policies were actually embedded and working within the organization. The most difficult aspect of this process was the creation of the maturity model and the inclusion of the relevant attributes.

Model creation takes time, consideration, and understanding of company processes while being able to outline the stage definitions in a consistent manner. It is also critical the development of the matrix appropriately identify the attributes most important to the organization. These would be the attributes important to obtain a measurement in order to evaluate the effectiveness of ethical culture. There is no standard checklist of attributes however, there are various generic attributes organizations can utilize and tailor when creating the matrix. If you believe your organization should evaluate specific elements within your code of ethics or conflict of interest policy, or even specific ways in which your whistleblower hotline operates, these are attributes which can be incorporated within the maturity model.

Maturity Model Development

Typically, the maturity model approach is used to evaluate "soft" attributes (those that cannot be easily tested). The maturity model can help the organization gain an understanding of the sufficiency and adequacy of policies and procedures as well as how well those policies or procedures are executed.

Step 1: Identifying Attributes   Step one involves identifying attributes of an ethics program the organization wishes to assess. Identify attributes that relate to the specific organization's ethical culture and those which should be measured to adequately assess the effectiveness of the culture in its entirety. Exhibit 4.1 provides general attributes to consider. Ensure when defining attributes, you include separate assessments on how the attributes are documented or developed as well as how they are executed. Often, there may be attributes unique to your specific culture. For instance, if your organization is a global company, you may have separate measurements for how well the code of ethics is understood and practiced within the various countries. The list provided in Exhibit 4.1 is a generic list of attributes to consider when developing a maturity model approach to measure ethics programs. This list should be used as a brainstorming list. It is not meant to be all-inclusive.

Ethical values–policies	Ethical values–employees execution	Ethical values–management execution
Ethical values–reporting	Ethical values–discipline	Commitment to competence personnel
Management structure and operating style	Management internal control philosophy and actions	Management incentives
Management financial goals	Organization structure and size	Ownership and accountability
Policy establishment	Approvals	Segregation of duties
HR policies and procedures	Code of conduct policy	Code of conduct executions
Ethical tolerance	Whistleblower hotline policy	Whistleblower hotline execution

Exhibit 4.1   Example Maturity Model Ethics Attributes.

Step 2: Subject Matter Experts   A valuable tactic to utilize when developing the maturity model is to enlist the assistance of subject matter experts throughout the organization. The subject matter experts will provide important insight into many cultural and ethical aspects of the organization. Utilizing their input will ensure you have adequately identified the attributes to be measured. Just as internal auditors are not subject matter experts for each process area, they are not considered the keepers of the holy grail when it comes to identifying ethical attributes that should be measured. Auditors may not know and understand various attributes that may relate to the organization's ethical culture. However, gaining input from subject matter experts who understand how the process works and is perceived is important to the effective development of the model. This may mean gaining input from individuals on the legal team, compliance team, or other areas of the organization. Properly outlining the attributes within the model and developing the proper definitions are critical components to the success of this process.

Subject matter experts can be a critical link to providing input for the definitions of each attribute within the model. For the approach to be effective, assessment personnel must understand and agree with the individual attributes as well as their individual stage definitions. It can become challenging if an attribute is defined in a manner that does not match your organization's culture.

Step 3: Defining Stages   Guidelines for the stage definitions within the maturity model can be found through various sources. For ease, Exhibit 4.2 outlines a generic approach to defining the stages for each attribute. Review this generic model and ensure definitions utilized for your chosen attributes are consistent across the various stages. This will ensure assessors are able to understand and consistently assess the attributes. For example, if the initial stage is considered one that is ad hoc and requires the individual efforts of personnel, that same type of definition should be utilized for each attribute.

Step 4: Customizing the Matrix   The manner in which the definitions are outlined in Exhibit 4.2 is generalized. Refer to Exhibit 4.3 for an example of how specific attributes may be defined within a model utilized for ethics and control environment evaluations. Keep in mind,

Initial	Repeatable	Defined	Managed	Optimal
Processes are ad hoc and potentially chaotic.	Processes are in place for highest at risk areas. Processes can be repeated with fairly consistent results.	Processes are formal, defined, documented.	Processes are very formal, well defined and fully documented.	Processes are considered optimally defined and documented for the current business.
Procedures are considered reactive.	Procedures mostly reactive; some are proactive.	Procedures are executed real time.	Procedures are a combination of real time and some proactive.	Procedures are considered pro-active.
Processes are not formal and normally undocumented.	Discipline of process may not be rigorous or consistent.	Processes are considered adequate for current business.	Processes are consistently applied with strong results.	Processes are consistently applied for all levels throughout the organization.
Procedures may be in a process of ongoing change or are considered unstable.	No formal metrics or measurements in place.	Some metrics may exist but may not be consistently applied or monitored.	Metrics are in place, regularly monitored and measured with appropriate actions taken.	Metrics are optimal, always monitored and acted upon and routinely updated.
Processes are considered ad hoc and often driven at the heroics of individuals.	Process is rarely monitored or evaluated.	Process is periodically monitored and evaluated for required change.	Process is regularly monitored and adjusted for needed changes.	Changes required are considered completed real-time.
Identified issues are addressed in an ad hoc manner and not reported consistently.	Identified issues may be "prioritized" based on management preference and expectations and not always reported.	Issues may be identified but not necessarily timely addressed and reporting procedures are not always consistent.	Identified issues are timely addressed, and reporting is fairly consistent.	Identified issues are rigorously evaluated, investigated, and reported.

Exhibit 4.2   Maturity Model Generalized Stages.

individuals utilizing such an approach should ensure they tailor the model to their organization's culture and expectations. The examples are to provide guidance to brainstorm the attributes within a maturity model approach.

As stated earlier, utilize the approach to evaluate both the execution of ethical issues (such as the true ethical actions of management) as well as the effectiveness and understanding of ethical policies and programs.

Step 5: Determine the Naming Convention for Stages   A traditional maturity model has predefined category names for the various stages. These predefined categories are typically *initial, repeatable, defined, managed,* and *optimized.* Some individuals may have a preconception of a stage definition when these generic category names are used. When personnel hear the word *optimized*, they may assume the organization expects all attributes to be at this stage because it is leading or best practice. Assessors must understand the optimized stage is not one all attributes must be at to support an ethical culture. All organizations are at different levels of maturity in their processes as well as within their ethical culture. The assessment of current stage must be made understanding how the company currently operates given its maturity, capabilities, resources, and organizational objectives. In other words, an organization may measure a specific attribute at an initial or repeatable stage. This does not necessarily reflect a bad assessment. It simply reflects how the process is currently being managed. What can be more important is the assessment of desired stage. Use the following scenario as an example:

Scenario One: Maturity Model Ethics Policy   Assessors are asked to measure the current and desired stage of the company's ethics policy. An example definition of each stage for the ethics policy attribute is shown in Exhibit 4.3.

Current stage: The stage in which the process or policy currently operates or exists within the organization, considering allocated resources.

Desired stage: The stage at which participants feel the organization should operate, considering current organizational goals and objectives.

Assume there are 50 participants assessing the ethics attribute. The participants come from cross-functional areas of the organization. Overall, the consensus current stage vote is at the initial stage. This rating was assigned because the organization does not have a formal ethics policy or any formal process for managing ethics complaints. The process has been managed ad hoc in the past. The participants indicate they feel the organization has good intentions and they believe when issues arise, they are addressed at some level. However, since there is no formal process or policy, it is difficult for the employees to know what is right or wrong or whether issues are handled consistently. The organization has not had the resources to address the issue.

When assessing the desired stage, participants indicate they believe the organization should be at a defined level, given current objectives, resources, and goals. The organization has been in a growth mode. Given the number of new personnel being added and the diversity in

Attributes	Initial	Repeatable	Defined	Mature	Optimized
Ethical values (policies)	A formal code of ethics policy does not exist.	Informal ethics policy exists, but communication of policies is weak and inconsistent. Policies do not adequately cover dealings both internally and with external parties.	A formal ethics policy exists and is considered to adequately cover most aspects of ethical behavior involving internal employees and with external parties. Communication is adequate; however, not all aspects of the policy are well understood throughout the organization. The policy is only periodically updated.	A formal ethics policy exists, covers the majority of aspects related to ethical behavior involving internal employees and external parties. Policy communication is good and the majority of policy aspects are understood throughout the organization. The policy is regularly updated.	A formal ethics policy exists, is considered best practice, and continuously updated. Policy communication is excellent and fully understood throughout the organization. Policy is considered to cover all aspects of behavior internally as well as with external parties.
Ethical values (management)	Management does not display a commitment to ethical values.	Management does not consistently display commitment to ethical values when conducting company activities with internal and/or external parties. The "tone at the top" is questionable.	Management generally displays ethical behavior in most aspects of day-to day activities. "Tone at the top" is considered adequate.	Management regularly displays ethical behavior in the majority of its day-to-day activities. "Tone at the top" is considered effective.	Management's display of ethical behavior is optimal in day-to-day activities. "Tone at the top" is irreproachable.
Ethics policy	No formal policy exists, and there is no documentation of ethical priorities. Procedures related to ethical issues are considered reactive. Procedures are developed as ethical issues arise.	Informal policy exists but is not documented or monitored. Procedures related to ethical issues are typically directed to the human resource group. There is no consistency of how ethical issues are managed.	A formal ethics policy exists and is documented. The policy is considered adequate for the current business. The policy may not be consistently applied in the organization. Some metrics exist to monitor issues, but measurement is not consistently handled.	A formal ethics policy exists, is documented, and frequently updated. The policy is consistently applied throughout the organization. Metrics for the policy are in place and monitored at an organizational level. Required changes to the policy are made timely.	A formal ethics policy exists and is considered optimal for the organization. Ethical policies are pro-actively identified and updated. Policies are consistently applied throughout all levels of the organization and regularly monitored at the business unit level. The organization pro-actively monitors the ethical culture and makes timely changes to the policy.

Exhibit 4.3   Example Attributes - Ethics Maturity Model.

the workforce, a formal ethics policy is something the organization should have in place.

The assessment between current stage and desired stage represents the assessors' opinion the organization's ethics policy has a full two-stage gap between current operation and how they desire it should operate. The assessors are not claiming the rating of the current stage is because the attribute is poorly handled. They are simply indicating the assessed stage of "initial" represents how the process has been managed in the past. Also, they have not gone to the extreme and indicated the attribute should be at the optimal stage. The assessors recognize the organization should formalize their policies due to the continued growth of the business. However, they do not feel the organization needs to be at the optimal stage to be effective. The facilitator of the assessment would work to identify actions that, if put in place, would assist the organization in moving the ethics policy attribute closer to the mature stage.

Varying Naming Conventions   The facilitator may wish to assign different names to the stages so assessors do not place perceived labels on each stage. Individuals inherently think of the initial stage as bad and an optimal stage as good. This is not the purpose of the maturity model approach. In some cases, an organization may be in an initial stage due to its maturity or limited resources. This is not meant to be a poor reflection on how the attribute is managed. Some groups choose to categorize the stages as A, B, C, D, E or 1, 2, 3, 4, 5. Assessors should not focus on the perception of placing an attribute in a certain stage based on the category name. Assessors should make their determinations based on where they believe the attribute operates, given current organizational strategies and expectations. It may be perfectly acceptable for an organization that is in growth mode to be in an "initial" stage of an attribute.

Another consideration is to identify a method to allow assessors to assign an in-between stage to an attribute. The team should anticipate this possibility and have a predefined method of how to define the in-between stage. This can be easily accomplished using assignments such as *initial plus* or *A plus*. This would mean the assessor feels the attribute is above the initial stage but not quite at the repeatable stage.

Step 6: Establish the Assessment Process   Execution of the maturity model approach is best accomplished through a facilitated session. This approach is when assessors are gathered and a facilitator maintains control over the timing and discussion of the session. A facilitated session provides many advantages.

- Assessors are performing the evaluation at the same time.
- Each participant hears consistent explanations or thoughts of other assessors.

- Assessors can anonymously make their assessment utilizing voting equipment.
- If voting is disparate, the facilitator can stop and ask questions to ensure the participants fully understand the attribute being assessed.
- By discussing the voting trend, the facilitator allows participants to express their thoughts on why they voted the attribute at a specific level. This information can be helpful to other participants and provide additional insight that had not been considered. The facilitator can then ask for a revote.

The intention is to come to a "consensus" vote, which is much more valuable than an overall "average" vote. A consensus vote represents a general agreement of the assessors. The facilitator is hoping the discussion after voting of the attribute will provide additional insight to individuals. When a revote is cast, the disparity will be less significant, and assessors can agree the new average is representative of their overall opinion.

A facilitated voting session is best accomplished utilization of voting software. This software is readily available through various forums. The software provides the ability for confidential individual voting while allowing participants to see real-time voting results.

Assume there are 30 participants in the session, and the scale for voting is 1 to 10. Participants can visually see how many individuals voted at each level (although they do not know who specifically cast a certain vote). When the voting is diverse, the facilitator can stop and inquire why some individuals feel the attribute is at one level of the continuum while others believe it is at a different level of the continuum. This does not require participants to indicate their exact vote; they may simply mention they voted at the higher end or at the lower end. In other cases, a participant may explain exactly how they voted and why. This discussion helps other participants understand the rationale behind the individual's thought processes. They may not have taken certain elements into consideration, and the additional information may form a basis for which they may decide to alter their vote.

Facilitation itself is an art and should be taken seriously. The facilitator cannot influence the participants and should not be a person who may be deemed to infer perceptions based on comments or voting. The facilitator should be an impartial representative who acts as the gatekeeper or discussion leader who will keep the conversation flowing. The facilitator must use cues and clues to initiate discussion. At the beginning of sessions, it is not unusual for individuals to shy away from speaking up. As the session evolves, it may be difficult to get some participants to limit their comments. This is where the facilitator must step in and manage the process appropriately.

Step 7: Execute the Assessment Process At the beginning of the facilitation, review the "rules for the day." Everyone must understand information discussed in the session is to be kept confidential, and no individual comments should be relayed outside the session. They must also agree to provide honest and direct feedback while avoiding negative challenge or arguments with other participants. This may require the organizers to carefully consider the composition of assessors for each session. It may be necessary to conduct several sessions to ensure supervisors and employees are not part of the same facilitation. If this were to occur, the session may result in individuals feeling that they cannot openly speak their mind.

For the facilitated session to be successful, the audit team must have efficiently completed preparation and prework. This includes:

- Complete development of the maturity model and buy-in of the definitions from the core team.
- Completion of presessions with assessors to discuss the process, how the agenda for the session will run, and also cover the explanation of how the maturity stages are represented.
- Discussion of what consideration will be given for voting in-between stages.
- Answer any questions that assessors may have about the process or voting selections.
- Discussion of whether the session will encompass voting the current stage along with the desired stage.
- Explanation of how output from the session will be used.

When voting the desired stage of each attribute, the team must recognize this is an optional element of the process. Voting desired stage may assist the evaluation team when prioritizing and measuring attributes for specific focus. When voting the desired stage, assessors must understand that "desired" does not equate to the highest stage. Desired should be voted as the stage that the company feels would adequately meet their goals and objectives.

Step 8: Utilizing the Output   Prior to closing out the voting, it is helpful to show assessors the summarized final voting of the attributes. This allows the participants to calibrate their evaluations. In some cases, they may have voted an attribute at a lower stage of maturity than another attribute. When they see the voting in sequence, it may cause them to consider a change in the prioritization of the issue.

If you have voted desired stages, assessors should pay attention to the gap between current and desired stage for each attribute. Often, those attributes with larger gaps may be those management chooses to address with immediate actions.

Summary

This chapter has reviewed methods for identifying and measuring ethical behavior. We have reviewed the concept of using surveys and the maturity model continuum. Ultimately, every organization will have its desired process. However, encourage management to try new methods to ensure you are properly identifying and measuring all elements as effectively as possible. As COSO 2013 suggests, think outside the box in your assessment methods. This will provide for the most effective overall process.

5

ETHICAL SCENARIOS AND POSSIBLE ALTERNATIVE SOLUTIONS FOR THE INTERNAL AUDITOR

Introduction

In this chapter, we will review some ethical scenarios and alternative actions the auditor may consider. The examples will also evaluate potential implications of actions.

What makes individuals do the things they do? Why do certain people see things in one light or in one view, while others see the very same issue from another perspective? Part of the answer may be found in our discussion of the psychological mind. Other answers may deal with external stressors placed on individuals within circumstances that may be outside the person's control. Whatever the reason, it is likely actions and ethics will continue to be an area of challenge for multiple professions. But, by identifying, discussing, analyzing, and examining issues, organizations can identify ways to improve their overall ethical culture.

Section 1: Sports and Ethics

Introduction

Ethics is a topic that touches so many facets of our world. Even our beloved professional sport teams are not immune to the concept of ethics. Whether it is professional or college sports, football, baseball, hockey, soccer, volleyball, weight lifting, or any other combination of sporting disciplines, the concept has become a part of universal culture. Individuals cling to the television and news outlets with interest whenever controversial issues arise that involve sports figures. Sports can have a very emotional attachment for those who follow their

Foul ball!!!!

favorite team or alma mater. Individuals fiercely defend hometown heroes or favorite players when allegations of misdoings first arise. Why does this occur? Potentially, because, in the realm of the sports world, these athletes represent the chief executive officers of their respective activities. They are viewed as individuals who set the tone for how others will or can behave. Children are especially vulnerable to this concept. A recent article contended that a city's professional sports teams actually can play a significant role in shaping the values and character of the city's culture. This is an interesting concept to reflect on. Depending on where you live, consider your hometown professional sports teams. Does the behavior of the team, the way the players present themselves in public, and the demeanor of the coaches impact your city and the culture where you live?

In 2015, my hometown Kansas City Royals broke their 30-year World Series slump and won the crown. The city was exhilarated by the success of the team. There was a great deal written all over the country about the comradery of the players, their individual morals and behavior, and how they displayed their enthusiasm as well as frustration. For the most part, the city was proud of each player and how he presented himself. If a player got out of line, the other players took it upon themselves to bring that player back into the fold.

Early in the season, the Royals were coming off their success of the 2014 baseball season. Other teams were said to be gunning for the Royals. They wanted to prove that the 2014 Royals' unexpected trip to the series was a fluke. However, the 2014 and 2015 Royals team and coaches truly believed in their abilities. They knew the 2014 season was not a fluke. Early in spring training, the team set out to prove that very fact to the baseball world.

For the young Kansas City pitching staff, the fact that other teams were gunning for the Royals became extremely frustrating. The emotion of these players came through in some of the early games. But, the coaching staff as well as the other players made sure the players represented in these scuffles knew their behavior was not how the team wished to be represented. Within a few weeks, the situation was remedied, and the more experienced players would quickly rush to calm down the young frustrated players or help remove them from the contentious situation. The Royals became known for their aggressive base running, exceptional field plays, team atmosphere, love of the game, and love and respect for each other. The culture within the locker room was said to be similar to one experienced in a home atmosphere.

The team won the World Series crown in game five of the series, amid some miraculous plays and a 12-inning game. On a beautiful November 1, 60-degree day in Kansas City, the first World Series parade and celebration in 30 years was held. Pictures captured that day show over 800,000 fans all wearing royal blue crowded into the area around the Kansas City Union Station. Fans came from far and wide to show their pride in the team. Articles were later written that Kansas City had one of the largest turnouts for any recent sporting celebration. What was more amazing was the fact there was not one arrest or injury during the whole day. The city emulated the respected behavior of the team.

Sporting Scandals

But, what happens when our sports idols of today don't act appropriately, and the issue becomes newsworthy? There are many examples of inappropriate behavior. Those examples include steroid use, child and spousal abuse, cheating in sports, inappropriate hits on the football field—the list continues. When these issues become newsworthy, they impact not only the city where the athlete resides but every single individual or child who sees and hears of the incident.

When the issue rises to the attention of the sports commissioner, the news media will debate the ethical sides of the issue. Let's reflect on recent sporting ethical issues and how they were managed.

The New Orleans Saints "Bounty"   The bounty incident involved members of the New Orleans Saints football franchise who were accused of paying out bonuses, or "bounties", for injuring opposing team players. The hits in question were never penalized or deemed illegal by game officials. The pool was alleged to have been in operation from 2009 (the year in which the Saints won Super Bowl XLIV) to 2011. The National Football League (NFL) chose to make a statement by suspending the New Orleans head coach for the full season. This penalty along with other sanctions was considered the most severe ever issued in the 92 year history of the NFL. Since that time, the NFL has strengthened protocols around concussions and the penalties assessed when a tackle or hit appears egregious in nature. Even with this known, there are many players who will continually argue to return to the field when they have experienced one of these debilitating hits. From a social aspect, the team is attempting to protect the health of the player as well as the liability of the team. Assume the player truly has a concussion and then returns to the field. Ten years later, the player begins to suffer the effects of the multiple concussions. It is likely the player will look for some remuneration or resolution from the team because of the impacts he suffered. This is an ever-increasing debate for the football world.

Michael Vick Dogfighting Scandal   Animal fighting was brought to the forefront by the highly publicized conviction of NFL star quarterback Michael Vick and three of his associates on federal and state charges for illegal dogfighting. Vick and his associates housed and trained over 50 pit bull dogs, staged dogfights, killed dogs, and ran a high-stakes gambling ring with purses up to $26,000. In 2007, after his three coconspirators pled guilty and began cooperating with authorities, Vick also pled guilty. He was sentenced to 23 months in prison; received three years supervised probation during which he could not buy, sell, or own dogs; and was fined $5,000 and ordered to pay $928,073 as restitution for the 53 dogs seized from his property. In addition, he was required to enter a drug and alcohol treatment program and pay for the cost of treatment.

In July 2009, NFL commissioner Roger Goodell reinstated Vick into the NFL with conditions. Vick was hired to play football for the Philadelphia Eagles with a base salary of $1.6 million for the first season. A court-mandated bankruptcy agreement that extended to 2015 required much of Vick's salary to go to paying off debts he accumulated prior to his incarceration. Vick agreed to speak to various community groups as part of an anti-dogfighting campaign organized by the Humane Society of the United States.

What are your thoughts about the ethical status of the decision of the NFL commissioner to allow Michael Vick back into the professional sports world? Assume someone in your town went to jail for dogfighting. How easy would it be for that person to resume a career once he had served his time? Yet, Michael Vick was able to return to the spotlight of football, making more money than many of us make in a single year.

Ray Rice Physical Abuse   In February 2014, Ray Rice of the Baltimore Ravens was suspended by the NFL commissioner after footage surfaced of Rice punching his fianceé in an elevator. In October 2015, the NFL supported Rice's attempt to return to the NFL. As of March 2016, no NFL team had chosen to pick up Ray Rice as a player.

Pete Rose Betting Scandal   Pete Rose has become infamous for sports betting. In August 1989, three years after he retired as an active player, he agreed to permanent ineligibility from baseball as accusations arose that he gambled on games while playing for and managing the Cincinnati Reds. He has also been banned from being voted into the Baseball Hall of Fame. The issue of Rose's possible reinstatement and election to the Hall of Fame remains a contentious one throughout baseball. In 2016, Rose was inducted into the Cincinnati Reds Hall of Fame.

Sports Scandal Analysis

These are just a sample of sports ethical issues. In previous chapters, we listed others. If you examine the various issues, when they occurred, and how the sports world and corporate world responded you will see the actions are broad and varied. Sports and the corporate world definitely do not have a clear black-and-white line.

Now, let's return to the concepts of the psychological mind and how various individuals process events. Staying with our sports theme, a good scenario to examine is the life and actions of Peyton Manning. As you read the following narrative, consider the various attributes which make up the personality, psychological traits, and talent of Peyton Manning.

At the writing of this manuscript, Super Bowl 50 was just completed. And the winner was—the Denver Broncos. Although I am from the Midwest, my team is the Kansas City Chiefs, who, needless to say, are fierce competitors of the Broncos. But, in Super Bowl 50, I found myself rooting for the Broncos. Why? Simply put, Peyton Manning is a brilliant person and an individual who exudes the persona of trust and ethics. Many reports are written about Peyton's kindness, generosity, integrity, truthfulness, and concern for fellow players.

Peyton's dedication to his profession, his endless hours of studying, and his ability to quickly assess a situation and see things that other quarterbacks may not recognize have the football world wanting to clone Peyton's thought processes. Columnists have reported that "Manning is arguably the NFL's most cerebral quarterback at the line of scrimmage. Manning, possesses one of the sharpest minds in the league for a player." His sharp mind comes from hours and hours of practice, repetition, inquisitiveness, and an eagerness for continuous improvement. To Peyton Manning, nothing is a given. Question everything, and then question it again. Then the answers will begin to come quicker and appear clearer.

Consider this trait when evaluating how individuals make various ethical decisions. Do they seriously consider what the consequences may be? Are they the type of person who can quickly assess a situation and arrive at the best answer? Just as Peyton Manning can instantaneously assess an opponent's defense, it would be ideal if all personnel could instantaneously arrive at the correct ethical decision. Possibly, some scientist will find a way to clone Peyton Manning's mind and use his quick analysis abilities to establish the proper ethical path for organizations. If only this was possible, the world itself could win a Super Bowl.

Section 2: Internal Auditors and Ethics

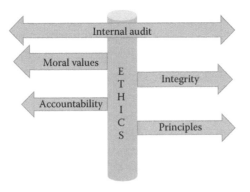

Introduction

Internal auditors face a difficult challenge when it comes to evaluating and handling ethical issues. There are many variables involved, and auditors must be able to accurately and timely assess a multitude of situations. Just as Peyton Manning assesses a defensive alignment using his experience and years of studying, internal auditors must assess potential incidents using past experiences, knowledge, and understanding of an issue. Football teams respect and trust Peyton Manning due to his many years of experience, knowledge, and abilities. Similarly, management will assess their perception of ethical interpretations by auditors based on their views of the auditors' experience, organizational standing, knowledge, trust, and honesty. This is one of the critical reasons why the internal audit profession must obtain a level of trust and respect in organizations. To accomplish this, CAEs must uphold the profession *Standards* and stand by the requirements of maintaining integrity and independence.

Internal Pressure

A report in the *Journal of Accountancy*, dated March 2015, indicated internal pressure is a pervasive threat to the objectivity inherent in internal audit. This places the internal auditor at a disadvantage when attempting to assess ethical issues. A separate report for the *Institute of Internal Auditors Research Foundation* was performed with 494 chief audit executives. More than one-half of North American CAEs surveyed indicated they had been directed to omit or modify an important audit finding at least once. Forty-nine percent said they had been directed not to perform audit work in high-risk areas. Would we assess this pressure as an ethical issue? The survey also found that 32% of respondents were asked to audit low-risk areas so that an executive could investigate or retaliate against another individual. Again, would an auditor assess this issue as pressure and unethical? Sometimes, the blame may fall to ineffective audit committees. Other times, audit executives face off with company lawyers who wanted to protect an executive. The research report indicated there was a sense of pressure not to communicate a finding with certain people so those people could have plausible deniability. Do you believe these survey results are a reflection of the ethical culture in organizations? There are specific lessons learned cited in the survey. They included:

- *Know Your Organization's Culture But Understand It Can Change*: An organization's culture and atmosphere can change quickly. A new set of executives may have different strategic objectives or focus on different goals. There could be changes in the board, executive positions, and even the external audit function. Internal auditors must be prepared to address these situations and build relationships that mitigate ethical concerns. Just because the composition of management has changed, does not mean proper ethical behavior should change.
- *Business Acumen Is Required*: Undeniably, to uphold integrity and ethics, internal audits must look to build credibility and demonstrate knowledge of the business and its strategies. But, this alone is not sufficient. The auditors must be able to apply that knowledge in assessing risks. Management often likes to assert—the internal auditors don't understand the business. Auditors must communicate effectively from a business point of view. They must be able to explain to management using the proper business acumen, risks addressed, findings, root causes of the issues, and potential mitigating actions. An effective CAE must be able to convey audit findings from management's perspective rather than from a sole internal audit perspective.
- *Anticipate Political Pressure*: CAEs and auditors must anticipate the potential for political pressure and be prepared to justify their reasoning and judgments on the significance of any issue. This stance becomes even more critical when the issue involves ethics. Often, management will test the auditor to see how resilient they are, in their opinion. The audit team must be able to come to an appropriate ethical decision and support that decision to management.

Section 3: Ethical Scenarios

What would you do?

Introduction

Now let's review a few ethical scenarios auditors may experience. The scenarios and alternative solutions can vary. The steps taken may depend on the auditors involved, their positioning in the organization, the trust or respect the audit team has within the organization, and even the generation, culture, or gender of the auditor versus that of the other individuals involved. In other words, there may not be one right answer to any scenario. Auditors must use their knowledge and ethical understanding to ensure they execute their ethical duty in the best possible manner.

Scenario One: The Audit Assignment Conflict of Interest   You are a senior auditor in a large publicly traded organization. Your department consists of 30 individuals. One of your coworkers has confided he is dating a director in another area of the company. Dating relationships are not prohibited by the company; however, the coworker indicates they are keeping the relationship quiet for personal reasons. He asks you not to say anything.

A few weeks later, the CAE assigns your coworker as the lead auditor on a review of the process area for which he is dating the director. The assigned auditor is considered one of the more senior professionals in the department, and the CAE feels his experience is essential for evaluation of issues within the project scope. Your coworker speaks to you about the dilemma. He realizes there may appear to be a potential conflict of interest. He informs you he attempted to convince the CAE to reassign the audit without relaying his personal relationship to the CAE. The CAE indicated the reasons he was assigned to the audit and felt his skills were essential to adequately review potential issues. Your coworker reconsiders the situation and decides he can adequately execute the audit without having his objectivity impaired. He again requests you not to say anything.

What would you do in this circumstance? Since the CAE is unaware of the relationship, he is obviously unaware of any perceived or actual conflict of interest. But your coworker has assured you he can execute the audit with adequate independence and objectivity. In addition, you do not want to cause any issues that may impact your friendship. When faced with this type of ethical question, what would you do?

Scenario One Alternatives: Viewing the situation from an independent manner, there appears to be a conflict of interest for the senior auditor. He should not be part of an audit where he is dating the director. Acknowledging the sensitivities of the situation, you may be able to understand why the auditor does not want to confide the relationship to the CAE. However, you are now aware of a conflict of interest that could ultimately impact the perception of your department. Regardless of personal friendships, you have a fiduciary duty to take action. Following are some alternatives.

- Speak to your coworker and outline how performing an audit of an area where he is dating the director could indeed present a conflict of interest. Even if the coworker believes he can act independently and objectively, if others become aware of the situation they may perceive a conflict. This would bring audit findings into question and may also question the integrity of the auditor. Encourage your coworker to confide in the CAE about the relationship and ask for the audit be reassigned.

- If your coworker still objects, you have another choice to make. You must determine how to alert the proper internal audit management that the assignment may have a potential conflict of interest. This does not mean you need to disclose the relationship between your coworker and the department director. However, you should speak to internal audit management and inform them you are aware of a potential conflict with the assignment. Internal audit management will likely ask you to relay the conflict. Initially, it would be best to ask management to speak directly to the assigned auditor. Management can let the auditor know it has come to their attention there may be an issue with the assignment. If the auditor still declines to be open about the relationship, you may need to let management know there is a personal connection you believe would be perceived as impairing independence.

Scenario Two: Management Pressure and Influence You are the CAE of a publicly traded company. Your department has performed a review of a large-scale project. Several findings were identified that indicate inappropriate handling of project work and expenditures. In addition, you have concerns over a potential conflict of interest between the project manager and the outside consultant engaged on the project. You have presented these findings to the senior executive responsible for the area being audited. Although the executive recognizes the issues appear questionable, he does not feel there are any intentional misappropriations. The executive indicates the problem may lie in the lack of proper administrative oversight of the project. He agrees to look into the issue and requests you to not release the audit report until he has reviewed the findings in detail.

After approximately three weeks and numerous calls to the executive, with no response, you set an appointment to meet face to face. At the meeting, the executive indicates he has been busy and has not evaluated the issues. You are concerned because the audit committee meeting is nearing, and the report should be issued. The executive promises he will review the issues in the next few days, which will then allow you to release the report on time.

Several days later, the executive calls and again indicates he has not had time to evaluate the issues. He requests further deferral of the report issuance. He also requests no mention of the audit be made to the audit committee. As the CAE, you are concerned about this request. You feel it is your fiduciary duty to inform the audit committee the audit has been completed, and you have specific findings and observations. You decide to discuss the issue with your direct supervisor, the chief financial officer. The CFO informs you the senior executive is very close to the CEO and explains it would be advisable not to issue the report or say anything to the audit committee without the executive's approval. You inform the CFO you have concerns about this request and believe the issues should be disclosed at the meeting. The CFO indicates he will not stand behind the report if it is issued without the final approval of the senior executive.

The following week at the audit committee meeting, the CFO pulls you aside prior to the meeting and reminds you not to provide any update on the audit in question. He cautions that if any questions are asked about the status of the audit, you should indicate the final report has not been completed.

Nothing is mentioned in the audit committee meeting; however, in private session, one of the members brings up the audit and asks about the status. What would you do?

Scenario Two Alternatives: Regardless of the severity of the audit issues you have identified, there are additional concerns. These include:

- Management's pressure to not disclose the information
- The lack of attention by the senior executive in evaluating the issues
- The CFO's nonsupport of the audit process

Each of these concepts is addressed in the *Standards* and would appear to be impacting your personal objectivity and independence. Assuming you have taken the proper actions toward informing management of the issues, and the information has been definitively confirmed, you have a fiduciary duty to raise the findings to the proper level. The scenario indicated you spoke to the executive over the project area as well as your direct reporting line (the CFO). Nothing has been said about speaking with the CEO. Possibly, this is an action you should have engaged in prior to the audit committee meeting.

Assuming you spoke to the CEO, or for some reason you were unable to reach him, you have a few issues important to speak to the audit committee about.

- The audit committee should be aware of the management pressure you have experienced. Ensure you have all facts and information correct, but at the very least they are the governing body and should be your advocate in this situation. For independence and objectivity purposes, you should find a method to communicate this concern to the audit committee chairman.
- You have to consider the issue of the project audit and whether it is something that should be disclosed to the audit committee, regardless of management's direction. If the issue falls in the tolerance range of the committee's expectation for communication, you have a responsibility to disclose the issues. You can indicate management is still researching the issue, but the committee should be made aware the audit has been in process and there are several issues identified. Again, you should ensure you have completed all relevant audit work and your findings are solid. If the issues are of significance, the audit committee should be aware.

- You must find a way to address the issue of the CFO's non-support of the internal audit process. You may want to visit with the CFO and inform him of your concerns related to independence and objectivity. You can review with the CFO the *Standards* and explain your fiduciary duty as a CAE. If these tactics are not successful, you must consider speaking to the audit committee.

Of course, these alternatives come with ramifications. This is where the auditor's ethical dilemma begins. Management obviously is not ready for the issues to be disclosed. However, it appears they have not taken the findings seriously, because the project executive has not set aside time to review the findings. As the CAE, you must be confident in the action you decide to take and be prepared for any political implications from your communications. In the end, ask, "If I do not inform the audit committee and the issues identified are over the tolerance of the board, am I fulfilling my role as CAE?"

Scenario Three: Revenue Recognition You have just accepted a position as the CAE for a publicly traded manufacturing company. The company has experienced exponential growth over the past two years. During the interview process, you speak with the CFO, audit committee chairman, CEO, and chief operating officer. The CAE position is open because the previous CAE, who had been with the company for seven years, has resigned to manage family issues.

You begin your new assignment after the company's fiscal year-end. The audit department is sparsely staffed. The audit plan at year-end primarily entails support of the external audit. During your first week, you speak with the external auditors. They inform you that one of the most important areas to focus on relates to revenue recognition. The external auditors feel some of management's tactics for revenue recognition are a bit aggressive. Past audits have required adjusting entries to the financial statements; however, to date, the entries have not been considered significant. With the growth the company has experienced, the external auditors want to ensure the revenue recognition process is appropriately managed.

Since the internal audit department is sparsely staffed, you decide it is appropriate to perform the revenue recognition testing yourself.

During your testing, you identify concerns related to several large contracts. You speak with the area manager of the department where the contracts have originated. You find he is not familiar with proper revenue recognition procedures. The manager informs you he followed the direction of the CFO on matters of revenue recognition. He indicates the previous CAE was well aware of the processes utilized and did not raise any questions.

Because of the dollar amount, you decide it is appropriate to speak to the CFO about the identified issues. During your conversation, the CFO becomes quite abrasive and upset at the potential implication of improper revenue recognition procedures. He steadfastly contends the external auditors and the past CAE were well aware of the procedures and agreed they are appropriate.

After your discussion, you contemplate what to do. You further research the issue and determine the procedures utilized are not correct. In addition, you have heard rumors the previous CAE left for reasons other than family issues. You are informed by some of your staff the previous CAE actually left because he was uncomfortable with revenue recognition processes, and he was fired by the CFO.

You decide to speak to the external auditors. You provide the auditors with detailed information about the contracts in question and the current revenue recognition processes. The auditors become disturbed and indicate they were not aware these contracts were being handled in such a manner. They inform you that your observations will certainly have revenue recognition implications. The external auditors decide they must speak to the CFO and the audit committee. Knowing that this will occur, you inform the CFO about your discussion with the external auditors. You relay to the CFO the external auditors agree there are discrepancies and adjustments will need to be made. The CFO becomes very upset and indicates you have stepped beyond your position, and he will have to "fix" things with the external auditors and the audit committee. He directs you not speak to the external auditors again without his permission. What would you do?

Scenario Three Alternatives: On the surface, it appears this activity had been going on for some time, and management was able to keep the external auditors from identifying the situation. In addition, the information regarding the former CAE's departure leaves room for concern, even though it is only a rumor.

From the perspective of your role as a CAE, it appears you followed appropriate protocol in reviewing the information and addressing the issue with the CFO. Admittedly, you are in a difficult position in determining what actions to take. You are ultimately responsible to the audit committee, so possibly it may have been appropriate to speak to the audit committee chairman prior to going to the external auditors. However, depending on how closely you have been working with the external auditors, your choice to speak with them about your findings may have been a logical step.

Another issue is the CFO's statement that "he will fix things with the external auditors and the audit committee." Since you have already reviewed the information with the external auditors, it would appear you have a solid case. The proper action in fulfilling your fiduciary duty would be to speak directly with the audit committee and inform them of your findings, observations, and past conversations. You may also want to alert them to other information you have observed during your time reviewing the contract information. Separately, you may want to discuss the issue with your company's corporate compliance officer or ethics office to evaluate if there are any potential ethical violations. This will definitely put you in a difficult position with the CFO and possibly impact your job role. However, the proper and ethical thing to do would be to disclose the information you have identified to the audit committee.

Scenario Four: Management Incentives You are the CAE of a large multinational company. The company is composed of eight separate business units. One business unit was acquired within the past year. Part of the acquisition deal included large incentives for management of the acquired business if certain sales goals were reached within the first year.

Throughout the year, the business unit did not meet their sales goals. Near fiscal year-end, you receive a call from the area controller for the business unit. He has concerns regarding the recording of sales at year-end and the amount of incentives which will be paid. He asks for your assistance in reviewing the recording of the sales to ensure the payout calculations are appropriate.

As the CAE, you report to the CFO of the company. The CFO has a very micromanaging approach to the audit plan. Your access to the audit committee is limited to quarterly meetings. Any changes to the audit plan must have the support of the CFO to be proposed to the audit committee.

Both you and the area controller speak to the CFO about the incentive issue and the request for internal audit to assist in the review. The CFO becomes upset and indicates the controller did not have the authority to request changes to the audit plan. He remarks there is not enough time allocated in the audit plan for internal audit to review the incentive issues. Furthermore, the CFO believes the issue is not within the purview of internal audit. He informs the controller that internal audit will not be involved with the review of the incentives, and he will assign someone from the finance area to examine the issue. The CFO informs you the issue is no longer your concern, and nothing is to be said to the audit committee. This statement concerns you, since the incentives are several million dollars, and there are concerns of potential manipulation of statistics to meet incentives. You are also concerned that you are being told you cannot inform the audit committee. You attempt to speak to the CFO further on the issue and assure him that a review of incentive calculations is one of your areas of expertise. With the incentive dollars in question, you feel the audit committee would agree to internal audit performing an independent review. The CFO disagrees and further instructs internal audit not to look at the issue or inform the audit committee. What would you do?

Scenario Four Alternatives: The scenario does not indicate how long you have held the CAE position with this organization or what your current relationship is with the audit committee. It indicates the CFO is very hands-on in relation to the audit plan. From comments made, it also appears you have limited access to the audit committee. These facts would infer your position may not be fully independent.

There are several additional facts we are not told within the scenario:

- Did the controller have concerns about potential manipulations of information, or did he simply feel there may have been information recorded incorrectly?
- Why does the CFO feel internal audit should not look at the issue? Does he feel they do not have the qualifications to

understand the computations, or is he more concerned that having internal audit involved would require reporting of information to the audit committee?

- How have you previously handled issues with the CFO regarding the audit plan? For instance, the scenario indicates he is very hands-on. Does this mean the CFO has full say and authority over which audits will be completed? If so, have you always agreed with the CFO when changes have arisen?
- Although you may not have frequent contact with the audit committee, have you ever taken it upon yourself to contact them outside regular meetings?

Ultimately, you must determine the significance of the incentives, not only to the financial statements but also to the ethical culture of the company. If you have any sense there could be inappropriate activity occurring, you have a fiduciary duty to bring the issue to the attention of the audit committee. This may not be the popular choice, but your stance on this issue will set a precedent for future issues.

Looking back, if other issues have arisen such as this, and you have relinquished your opinion to the CFO, you may have already lost your independent status.

Scenario Five: Audit Report Issuance　You have been a member of the internal audit department for your company for the past three years. The department has been cosourced during this time. The director position is held by the senior manager of the outsourced firm. Your company recently had a quality assurance review of internal audit. The review suggestions included a change in the structure of the department. This change involves fully insourcing the function.

As the organization begins to realign the structure of internal audit, you are promoted into the CAE position. In the past, all audit reports were independently released by the outsourced audit director after being internally reviewed. As the new CAE, you are assigned an internal reporting line to the chief legal officer (CLO).

The CLO informs you that all internal audit reports must be cleared by his office prior to issuance. You begin to work with the CLO on a new reporting format for the audit reports. The format will include a rating system for the audits. The rating system is a high/moderate/low rating assignment. A high rating indicates the company should implement remediating actions within the next 30 days. A moderate rating indicates remediating actions should be completed with 90 days, and a low rating indicates remediating actions are up to the judgment of management for timing of completion.

Within your first six months as CAE, you find the CLO takes a micromanaging approach to the audit reports. He often rewords the reports in a manner which takes issues out of context. In addition, the reports are beginning to read more like a legal document than an audit report. You also discover the CLO will not allow the auditors to rate any audit above a moderate rating.

You personally review each report with the CLO. You have noticed his changes are becoming numerous and are not representative of the issues identified. You attempt to speak with the CLO about his revisions and the impact on the reports. The CLO is a direct report and trusted advisor to the CEO. The CLO uses this fact to influence the reports and to intimidate you regarding his authority. After the meeting, the CLO informs you he will be taking over the responsibility of providing the audit reports and reviewing them with the audit committee. What would you do?

Scenario Five Alternatives: Since the internal audit function was previously cosourced, it is possible the audit committee and internal management do not have a clear understanding of the *Standards* and the CAE's responsibility for independence and objectivity. Although the department underwent a quality assurance review, depending on who performed the review, management may have misinterpreted some of the observations. Once the decision was made to insource the function, and you were promoted to the position of CAE, it would have been advisable to visit with the audit committee and management regarding your responsibilities as outlined by the *Standards*. This may have helped set the stage for a proper reporting protocol between your position and the CLO.

Assuming you did not have the opportunity to have this discussion, it is evident you must find a way to relay the information to the CLO as well as the audit committee. The first step may be to schedule a separate meeting with the CLO to review the department charter and compare it to the *Standards*. This would afford you the opportunity to point out discrepancies between the manner in which the department and its activities are currently managed and how the *Standards* suggest they be managed.

If this alternative does not work, you could attempt to reach out to the audit committee and ask for their time to review the role of the internal audit function and the information outlined in the *Standards*. Some individuals may suggest you reach out to the CEO first. This is a possibility, but you must remember information cited in the scenario. The CLO is considered a strong confidant of the CEO. If you choose to speak to the CEO, you may want to suggest a joint meeting with the CEO and CLO and use the time to review the internal audit charter as well as the *Standards*.

Another consideration is to outline various issues that have been changed within the audit reports by the CLO over the past several months. Outlining these issues and providing an explanation of how the changes impacted the overall intent of the findings may assist in demonstrating the impact the CLO's influence is having on the audits. By having the detail and facts handy, you may be able to get the CEO and CLO to acknowledge the changes have, indeed, impacted the reports.

Of course, each of these suggestions must be evaluated in relation to how your company's culture operates and how the organization's communication protocol is established. Although you may have been named the CAE, if your position is buried deep within the organization, management may not view it as having any semblance of authority. Many companies do not recognize the CAE position as a senior-level management position. Ultimately, you will need to make a decision regarding how ethically proper and independent the internal audit process is being executed. If you feel the process has stepped over your individual "black line," you may want to reconsider whether the position is one you wish to remain in.

Scenario Six: The Procurement Audit   You are the manager in your internal audit department. You have been assigned, along with two senior staff members, to perform an audit of your company's procurement process. The audit has been added to the audit plan due to concerns over potential conflict of interest incidents between procurement specialists and vendors.

The director of the procurement area has a strong and dominant personality. He is known to use intimidation as a technique to ensure outcomes are in his favor. He has expressed his disagreement with the addition of an audit within his area. Your team prepares carefully for the entrance meeting, ensuring you have the audit objectives well outlined. In addition, you have worked to anticipate any potential concerns that may be expressed during the meeting.

The audit entrance meeting is scheduled, and the procurement director and three of his senior staff are in attendance. On the date of the meeting, as expected, the procurement staff and director express strong disagreement for an internal audit. An audit of the procurement area was performed approximately 12 months ago, and no significant findings were identified. The audit team outlines the audit objectives carefully and explains the addition of the audit was at the request of the audit committee. They further explain the audit corresponds with a review of the company's conflict of interest process. The internal auditors ensure the procurement professionals that communication during the audit will be timely and open.

Post the entrance meeting, your team begins fieldwork. Within the first week of fieldwork, your CAE is asked to meet with the CEO. During the meeting, the CAE is presented with a tape recording made by one of the procurement professionals during the entrance meeting. The CEO expresses concern over several statements on the recording made by the internal auditors. Since the CAE was not part of the entrance meeting, he tells the CEO he will speak to the audit team.

The CAE calls a meeting of the audit team and presents the tape recording. The team are initially upset because they were unaware the meeting was being recorded. As they listen to the recording, they begin to notice several comments appear to have been edited out of context. As these concerns are expressed, the CAE decides it is important to speak individually to each member of the audit team to get individual and independent input.

The CAE meets with each team member and asks them to specifically identify what they believe was edited and their recollection of the conversation. The CAE finds the auditors' comments and recollections are consistent. With this information, he becomes concerned the internal auditors were being set up, and the recordings had been edited. Considering this information, what steps would you take as the CAE?

Scenario Six Alternatives: This scenario presents several challenges and potential ethical questions. Considering the audit was added by the audit committee due to concerns over potential conflicts of interest, it is reasonable for the auditors to be suspicious of what has occurred. The fact the procurement professionals recorded the entrance meeting without the knowledge of the internal auditors presents its own ethical issues. The complicating fact that it appears the recording was professionally edited to take specific comments made by the internal auditors out of context is even more concerning. Unfortunately, the facts of this situation may turn into a he said/she said issue. The procurement professionals will have their side of the story, and the internal auditors will have theirs. The internal auditors are at a disadvantage, because they do not have any formal tape recording of the meeting. They only have their personal notes and individual recollections. Each of these issues complicates the situation at hand.

The CAE could attempt to speak with the procurement director and obtain information regarding his side of the story. However, since the procurement director appears to have gone directly to the CEO, this meeting may not provide any benefit. The CAE could revisit with the CEO and provide the information he has obtained from his discussions with the internal auditors. He could also request a separate meeting with the audit committee expressing his concerns over the situation. Each of these alternatives is a possibility, and the determination as to whether either is appropriate may depend on the various relationships that exist with the CEO and the audit committee.

One aspect of the situation is clear; the internal auditors are at a disadvantage. The CAE must decide whether continuation of the internal audit by his audit team will be beneficial. With the issues that have transpired, it may be appropriate for the CAE to recommend to the CEO and audit committee for an outside independent party to be retained to complete the internal audit review. Of course, the CAE will need to address the issue of the tape-recorded entrance meeting and his concern over the editing of the tapes. It is uncertain how the CEO and audit committee will respond to the CAE on his interpretation of what has occurred. In any event, the committee and CEO should recognize the recording of the entrance meeting by the procurement professionals without the knowledge of the internal auditors is a questionable activity. Due to the sensitivities of the situation, the alternative of having an independent party perform the review may be the best solution to the challenge.

Scenario Seven: The Staff Auditor's Predicament   You are a third-year staff auditor and have been assigned to assist the external auditors with year-end testing for the financial statements and Sarbanes–Oxley purposes. You are asked to test and review a listing of purchase orders, validate the orders to receipting slips, and verify the items were properly recorded within the inventory system. Your selection population involves several different warehouses operated in various areas of the company's territory. Testing for warehouse A and warehouse C has several consistent discrepancies. You notice several instances of inappropriate segregation of duties. For several of the purchase orders, the authorization, receipting, and release from inventory are completed by the same employee. In some instances, you note the inventory appeared to be shipped to work sites which were not within the distribution territory for the warehouse. Warehouses A and C are managed by the same employee. The inconsistencies relate to his signature and authorizations.

You report the finding to your internal audit manager. The testing is close to the timing in which the external auditors must sign off on the financial statements. Your manager instructs you to inquire of the warehouse manager regarding the lack of segregation of duties. You speak to the warehouse manager, and he explains his assistant was unavailable on those days to provide the secondary sign-off. Since he needed to receipt in the inventory to ship it timely to the sites, he tells you one of the office managers watched him perform the transactions. You speak to the office manager who was purportedly the person who observed this activity. The manager indicates he does not recall observing warehouse receipting. You report back to your audit manager. He informs you the warehouse manager is a respected employee, and if he indicated someone observed the receipting, then that is what happened. The internal audit manager indicates it is too late to be bring these issues forward to the external auditors. You are instructed to get a signed confirmation from the warehouse manager affirming someone actually observed the process.

You are uncomfortable with this procedure and express to your manager there appears to be a controls concern related to inadequate segregation of duties. He responds the dollar values of the inventory in question are not material to the overall financials, and it is imperative the testing be completed without discrepancies. Your manager again tells you to obtain a signature from the warehouse manager. What do you do?

Scenario Seven Alternatives: This scenario is, unfortunately, one auditors frequently face. The audit manager may, indeed, not be concerned because of the immateriality. He may also feel there is a logical explanation. However, your audit work and documentation shows differently. Since you spoke to the office administrator whom the warehouse manager indicated observed the receipting process, you know any signed statement by the warehouse manager would be false.

In this case, the suggestion would be to bring the issue to the attention of your audit director or CAE. If there is not an audit director or a CAE, you may want to consider bringing the matter to the attention of the CFO. Finding an internal party to further vet the issue with is the first step to take prior to going to the external auditors.

If you continue to receive push-back from management, you must decide the significance of the exceptions and how they should be disclosed to the external auditors. This is obviously a control error. Being asked not to disclose the issue could be testing your ethical protocol. In addition, you have to consider the potential that fraud may have occurred in the process.

Scenario Eight: The Bank's Loan Review Audit   You are a senior auditor for a financial institution and have been assigned a review of loan files. During the review, you identify a group of loans approved by a specific loan officer that are consistently missing critical documentation. You speak to your manager and decide to expand the population of testing, especially as it relates to the loan officer in question.

As you continue your review, you come upon a specific loan file which raises your concern. The individual the loan was granted to is your relative. Within the loan file, your name is listed as a reference for the loan. There are notes on the file, written by the loan officer, which indicate he spoke directly to you about the creditworthiness of the applicant.

You become extremely concerned. You do not recall speaking to anyone about this particular application, but you know your relative has extreme financial difficulties and is about to file bankruptcy. You are aware he has defaulted on several loans. You begin to wonder how his credit was approved in the first place. By reviewing the date of the loan, you know the applicant did not have a job or steady source of income. You also note documentation is missing regarding his source of income.

You are extremely bothered by the situation; however, this is also a close relative, and you are concerned about blowing the whistle on his loan file. You contemplate whether to remove his file from the test sample. You know this action does not sound ethical, but you have family concerns and don't want to be seen as ratting on your relative. What action should you take as the auditor?

Scenario Eight Alternatives: The fact you are a relative of the loan applicant immediately puts you in a position of having a conflict of interest. Understanding you don't want to be seen as ratting on your relative, you still have a responsibility to speak with your audit management and indicate what you have identified. The audit management should remove you from the audit and allow another auditor to pursue the review. Also, remember this is a corporate issue, and it would not be appropriate to alert your relative about the loan review.

In addition, you should inform your audit management of the notes in the loan file that seem to indicate you were formally interviewed about the loan applicant. If this did not occur, the notes made by the loan officer are false and would lead to additional considerations of potential fraudulent behavior.

Scenario Nine: You Must Agree with Your Boss   You are the CAE and report functionally to the CFO. During a regular meeting with the CFO, you are discussing next year's audit plan. You present the internal audit group's risk assessment and outline the recommended audits for the audit plan.

The CFO reviews the listing and begins to question several audits under his direct reporting authority. You inform the CFO that based on a review of the audit files, two of the recommended audits have not been reviewed in the company's history. They are a review of payroll and accounts payable. In addition, you are aware of two separate frauds which have occurred in the payroll area in the past four years. You inform the CFO you believe these reviews are important and timely.

The company is a privately held company with an audit committee. They also have annual external audits due to banking requirements. The CFO directs you to exclude the audits of payroll and accounts payable from the audit plan. You again express your belief that these are areas which should be reviewed. The CFO informs you it is not acceptable for you to disagree with him and you will take the audits off the audit plan, explain to your department the audits are deemed low risk, and not mention anything to the external auditors or to the audit committee. What would you do?

Scenario Nine Alternatives: Two facts presented in this scenario put the CAE at a disadvantage. First, the company is privately held, and there are no requirements for an internal audit function. Depending on the history of the internal audit function and how it has been managed, the company may not recognize the need for independence of the group. Next, you administratively report to the CFO. It is interesting the scenario indicates there has never been an audit of the accounts payable or payroll area in the company's history (even considering the frauds identified). The scenario does not indicate whether there have been other audits performed under the responsibility area of the CFO. If there have not been, you should wonder why the CFO has not included audits under his area of authority. If you do not have any specific authority to speak to the audit committee confidentially, or possibly are not supported by an appropriate audit charter, you may be in a position where you are at the will of the CFO.

However, as a CAE, and in consideration of your ethical responsibilities, you should be concerned the CFO has instructed you to remove the audits from the plan and to inform your department the areas are deemed low risk. This appears to be a management intimidation method. You should also be concerned you have been instructed not to speak with the audit committee or the external auditors about the issue. You must consider whether this presents questionable behavior.

At a minimum, you should inform the CFO of your responsibility according to the Institute of Internal Auditors *Standards* and your responsibility for maintaining an independent and objective opinion. His directive that "you must agree with him" appears to be an intimidation factor. At the very least, you may need to make a decision as to whether this is the type of organization you wish to work for.

Scenario Ten: Is It Legal, or Is It Ethical? Your internal audit department is performing a review of the company's pension fund. During the review, you examine a listing of the top ten percent of investors who back the pension fund. You identify the name of one of the company's senior executives on the list. This executive is responsible for the area of the company which manages and directs the pension fund. You feel this is a conflict of interest. You examine the executive's personnel file and his conflict of interest statement. The executive has disclosed on the statement that he is a large investor in the pension fund. However, there are no notations this information has been seen by anyone outside of the human resource group. Based on the company's code of conduct, your assessment is this relationship represents a significant conflict of interest.

Since the issue involves a senior-level executive, you decide to consult with the company's legal counsel. The legal counsel reviews the information you have identified and tells you he needs to research the issue. A few days later, you are called to a meeting with the legal counsel and the CEO. You are informed since the senior executive disclosed his interest in the pension fund on the conflict of interest statement, the company would have a difficult time asserting any legal improprieties. You inform the CEO and legal counsel that, since the senior executive is responsible for the human resource function as well as the pension area, from an ethical perspective the relationship could be viewed as a conflict of interest. You recommend the company inform the audit committee to determine if a change in the investing of the pension fund should be made. The CEO and legal officer disagree. They contend there is nothing legally improper about what has occurred and instruct you not to include any of the information within the audit report. What would you do?

Scenario Ten Alternatives: Scenarios similar to this show the variance in legality versus ethics. According to the legal counsel, there is nothing illegal about what has transpired. However, just because it is legal does not mean it is ethical. When examining a conflict of interest issue, consider the definition of conflict of interest.

Conflict of interest—situation in which a person is in a position to derive personal benefit from actions or decisions made in their official capacity.

Since the executive is responsible for the area of the company which manages the pension plan, he would have the authority to direct the company to invest a larger percentage in the fund he holds an interest in. That directive could be viewed by individuals as a conflict of interest, because the executive may be profiting from the larger investment in the fund.

In this instance, you have taken the proper initial steps by bringing the issue to the attention of the legal counsel as well as the CEO. However, your dilemma is they do not agree with the assessment that this could be perceived as a conflict of interest. They have instructed the issue should not be mentioned in the report.

This is a difficult issue and one where you must again stand behind your own personal evaluations and assessments. Internal audit must remain objective, and this would appear to be an issue which should be brought to the attention of the audit committee. The proper and ethical action would be to inform the CEO and legal counsel that you respect their opinions, but you feel this is an issue which should be brought to the attention of the audit committee. You must then find a way to adequately communicate the issue to the audit committee or the audit committee chairman.

Summary

All scenarios we have visited are issues internal auditors may have to face. A recent study of CAEs released by the IIA indicated over 40% of CAEs have felt pressure from management in the past, either to not disclose an issue or to cover up the issue. The study also indicated many of the CAEs ended up resigning from their positions due to the issue.

Ethics and morality are very important in the role of internal auditing. If you feel unduly pressured or influenced to take an action that would not be appropriate, you should refer to the *Standards* and identify a way to communicate the undue pressure to the audit committee.

Until individuals performing the CAE role can fully and completely abide by the *Standards*, speak openly and transparently with management and the audit committee, and ignore management intimidation techniques, the profession will have trouble in advancing as one where the CAE is a person who is considered worthy of having a seat at the table within executive meetings. CAEs must be able to "stand the heat or get out of the kitchen."

6

REPORTING RESULTS OF ETHICAL EVALUATIONS

The Turning Point

Section 1: Dissecting Corporate Values

Introduction

If you were to visit the websites of the top 50 U.S. companies, what would you expect to see as their formally stated corporate values? Possibly they would list something like—integrity, honesty, social responsibility, loyalty, respect.

These are very honorable intentions and are linked to ethical conduct and behavior. But, how can stakeholders and society ensure corporations are executing these stated values in the manner the terms represent? Let's examine some of these principles and why corporate America may periodically question a company's true intentions behind these values.

Integrity

Merriam-Webster's definition of integrity is:

- Firm adherence to a code of especially moral or artistic values
- Incorruptibility
- An unimpaired condition, soundness
- The quality or state of being complete or undivided

In today's world of economic, social, and financial pressures, integrity can be a trait difficult to display. My personal definition of integrity is "doing the right thing when no one is looking." The fact federal regulators continue to legislate corporations and the way they conduct business might beg the question, "Is legislation required to

get corporations to do the right thing when no one is looking?" Let's consider some scenarios.

Scenario One: Integrity in Everyday Actions   We raise our children to do the right thing; however, we know there are many external influences that may tempt children to fudge when certain circumstances present themselves. To attempt to mitigate this risk, we put rules in place so children will know what the consequences are of not doing the right thing. That tactic may work well for young children, but as they mature we may not be present when they are faced with choices that may border the line of doing the right thing. We hope our lessons have taught the right values. Those values will, in turn, allow the child to make the proper and ethical choices. But, as we all know, sometimes the pressure and rewards of the moment will entice a wrong decision. Assume a child chooses *not* to do the right thing—and there are no consequences because no one knew. What is the probability he or she will be influenced the next time they are faced with a similar decision? Let's utilize this analogy in a business setting.

Scenario Two: Integrity in Business   Integrity in a business setting also equates to "professionals doing the right thing when no one is looking." So, why do we spend so much time setting up rules and guidelines in the form of policies and procedures? These procedures aren't necessarily established because we question the integrity of individuals in the organization. They are designed to help guide proper execution of responsibilities and attempt to ensure employees understand the expectations of the organization. In addition, most organizations are subject to some type of regulatory rules. Those rules may be in the form of financial reporting, taxation, labor laws, and environmental health and safety issues, as well as a host of other factors. These often require specific written procedures to ensure proper execution.

When it comes to the issue of integrity, does the establishment of procedures mean we question whether people will do the right thing when no one is looking? Not necessarily, especially in the case where the requirements may involve technical issues that aren't readily known by each professional. The concept of integrity is better cor-related to behavioral actions. It assumes individuals understand the proper course of action is (e.g., stated policies and procedures). The concept of integrity begins to focus on whether the individual chooses the right path, even when no one is looking. Policies and procedures assist in guiding the professional down the right path, but, because individual beliefs and behavior are involved when making decisions, there will still be an individual choice. A professional's individual choice and behavior cannot always be predicted or ensured. This is why we have checks and balances, laws and regulations, courts and the legal system.

In the corporate setting, compliance, internal audit, external audit, and other quality functions are established within processes to serve as checks and balances. These functions are put in place to hold individu-als and organizations accountable. Integrity in the workplace can also be translated to the manner in which organizations embrace and accept recommendations, improvement evaluations, and observations identi-fied. If the organization resists observations or recommendations, or attempts to provide reasoning and explanations why the observations are not important or relevant, they may be undermining the integrity of the organization and individuals within the organization. When evalu-ating this statement, ask yourself, "Were the policies and procedures put in place to guide behavior the organization deemed important? If so, why would compliance findings be minimized by management?"

Integrity incorporates every single person's actions in the organiza-tion. Management and professionals must display the proper behav-ioral characteristics of upholding the mantra of "doing the right thing." Management must ensure any policies and procedures established are those the company truly requires to be upheld. Any deviation from policy should be dealt with in an upfront and diligent manner. It is often the small observations that lead many down the path of larger long-term difficulties.

Corporate Social Responsibility

Corporate social responsibility (CSR) is often characterized in the public perception as a company's altruistic contributions. Yet, social responsibility steps far beyond being a good citizen and contributing to charitable causes. The term CSR became popular in the 1960s and 1970s, when multinational companies coined the term stakeholder.

The concept originated as a mechanism for organizations to display their accountability to shareholders and broader stakeholders. The term has grown in popularity post many of the corporate scandals. It is also attributable to the renewed emphasis on the environment and going-green concepts. There are criticisms of the CSR initiative. Some individuals believe the primary responsibility of business is to make a buck, and the social responsibility of government is to be sure corporate greed is channeled and constrained for the greater good of all. However, placing CSR solely in the hands of government regulators appears to be a reactive way of approaching the inherent issue of working toward a safer and better world.

So, what makes a company a good corporate citizen? Is it contributions to worthy causes? Creating employment opportunities for the community? Focusing on renewables and going-green concepts? Providing value to shareholders? Each item is important. In today's volatile economy, organizations must strive to examine their efforts in this arena and look toward a broader reach of social responsibility.

Let's examine a few examples, utilizing three very different business scenarios. We will examine positive traits as well as improvement opportunities.

Scenario one: The professional sports team
Scenario two: The multinational oil company
Scenario three: The multinational food manufacturing company

You may already be imagining scenarios of CSR in each of the examples, but can you identify where improvement opportunities may lie?

Scenario One: The Professional Sports Team   As we've discussed in earlier chapters, the ever-popular world of professional sports and the concept of social responsibility are strongly linked. Athletes are idolized for their unique physical abilities and accomplishments.

For instance, who comes to mind when you think of:

- The Chicago Bulls (Michael Jordan)
- The San Francisco 49ers (Steve Young and Joe Montana)
- The Green Bay Packers (Brett Favre)
- U.S. Olympic Ice Skater (Dorothy Hamill)
- Pro golf (Tom Watson, Tiger Woods)
- Hockey and the New York Rangers (Wayne Gretzky)

These individuals can represent the face of their organizations. Their behavior and actions reflect on the organization. On the positive side of social responsibility, these individuals, along with their organizations, contribute strongly to a multitude of efforts in the communities in which they exist.

Young children will often wish to be famous athletes when they grow up. However, we all know by watching athletic scandals over the past years that athletes are not perfect people, and they also have their ethical challenges.

In most professional sports teams, athletes are encouraged by their teams to form charitable organizations to contribute to their communities. Most people enjoy seeing the professional football player who travels miles to grant a sick child's wish of meeting their childhood hero. In a sense, this is showing corporate responsibility. These athletes don't have to do this, yet we see many who offer their time, talent, and money to these types of activities. In addition, their organizations are being socially responsible through fund-raising drives, continual improvement of their facilities to provide the ultimate fan experience, and focus on the safety and security of every single individual attending their events (to name only a few).

On the needs improvement front, when an athlete or professional sports organization is found to have done something wrong, the message quickly hits every type of social media that exists. Consider some of the more recent athletic "ethical" issues.

- Deflate Gate 2014 New England Patriots
- Tiger Woods scandal
- Lance Armstrong doping scandal
- Michael Vick dogfighting scandal

- Penn State child sex abuse incident
- Adrian Peterson child battery accusations

These are just a few recent ethical sports issues. Whether the issue concerns an incident with the questions surrounding steroid use by a baseball athlete, or the incarceration of an athlete for a crime, or even the Penn State incident, these issues may not provide the general public with the best representation of CSR. Could individuals associated with these instances claim their actions were in the best interests of the stakeholders? Also, linking CSR to integrity, could individuals associated with the incidents claim they did the right thing when no one was looking?

The answer seems obvious as we view these events in the rearview mirror. But where was the concept of social responsibility when the act occurred, and why didn't someone speak up about observed concerns? Or did someone speak up, only to have their concerns silenced due to the negative implications such an act may have for the organization?

The Penn State child sex abuse scandal was an incident in which a former assistant football coach was charged and convicted of multiple counts of sexual abuse of children. The actions of several Penn State University officials were questioned as to whether they met ethical, moral, and legal obligations in reporting.

With the Penn State incident, it appears information was available long before the issue broke into the media. Concerns were raised to certain levels of management. But, swift and effective actions were not taken to protect the interests of society as a whole. For whatever reason, judgments were made regarding the alleged events and the reputational impact that may occur. Was CSR appropriately represented here?

On a separate front, when the famous quarterback of the Pittsburgh Steelers was accused of sexual assault for a third time, the National Football League (NFL) chose to make a statement. Although the charges were eventually dropped, the NFL applied a several-game suspension for any inappropriate behavior on the athlete's part. This was their method of making a social statement that this type of behavior was not acceptable.

Scenario Two: The Oil Company   The Gulf oil spill is one incident highlighting the topic of CSR. In this instance, there were early indications certain oil rig components may not be manufactured to the quality specifications needed to withstand certain forces of deepwater drilling. Those concerns were silenced within the organization. The organization deemed there was a low likelihood an event would happen. They chose to accept the risk. Does this represent proper corporate responsibility?

Examining this issue further, British Petroleum (BP) had a strong CSR campaign in place at the time of the Gulf oil spill. In July 2000, it launched a high-profile $200 million advertising campaign to position the company as environmentally friendly. BP introduced a new slogan, and changed its 70-year-old logo to a green and yellow sunburst. This campaign was aimed at BP's smallest energy sector (renewable energy), while ignoring its investment in extractive oil operations.

In 1999, BP spent $45 million to buy a solar energy company. This investment is small compared to the $26.5 billion BP invested to buy the Atlantic Richfield Company (ARCO) to expand its oil-drilling portfolio. Some contend BP's public campaign was aimed at diverting the public's attention away from major environmental problems. Some of these problems included:

- In 2005, a major explosion destroyed a gasoline-filled tower at BP's Texas, refinery. Fifteen people were killed and 170 were injured. Investigation showed BP had ignored protocols for operating the tower. It had also disabled an early warning tower. BP pled guilty and paid more than $50 million in fines. However it didn't appear to impact the company's overall CSR culture.

- In 2006, BP was responsible for the leak of approximately 4800 barrels of oil into the snow around a pipeline in Alaska. BP had been warned by its own quality assurance specialists that they could expect a potential catastrophe from the corroded pipeline. The company ignored the reports until it was too late.

- In May 2008, BP was one of eight oil companies to settle a lawsuit brought by public water providers who charged that the companies' activities led to widespread contamination of public groundwater with a gasoline additive. The companies jointly paid $423 million in cash and agreed to pay 70% of future cleanup costs over the next 30 years.

What are the lessons learned from these real-life scenario? Some would contend that CSR and the organization's ultimate goal of financial earnings were not properly aligned. However, the concept can be debated regarding the sincerity of the organization's efforts toward CSR. The BP scenario is an obvious example of a company putting forth a positive reputational front yet not executing it in line with their stated CSR. Their CSR efforts were misguided by only focusing on a small segment of the business and not performing as an integral part of the actual operating culture. Looking in the rearview mirror, how ethical was this protocol?

The outcome of the Gulf incident points to the conflicting relationship between business and society. Charitable deeds performed by companies in their off hours should not be the focus of CSR. The focus should be whether they are doing their day jobs in ways that help or hurt the rest of the economy and world. In the instance of BP, a true indication of dedicated CSR would have been specific and definitive actions after the 2005 Texas explosion with publicized lessons learned and corporate responses. In other words, BP could take a few lessons from the Johnson & Johnson 1982 Tylenol scare and the manner in which they handled the contamination concerns.

Scenario Three: The Food Company In 2008, a milk scandal occurred in China involving the chemical melamine. This is an example of the delicate balance of power between social responsibility and corporate earnings. The melamine incident became public in September 2008. By November 2008, there were 300,000 victims reported. The chemical melamine was allegedly added to milk to make it appear to have higher protein content. Many looked at the incident as a large-scale intentional activity to deceive consumers for short-term profits. A Chinese company, Sanlu, was at the center of the incident. A New Zealand dairy cooperative, Fonterra, owned a 43% stake in Sanlu. Fonterra indicated local administrators refused a full recall of the milk.

In June 2008, the Administration of Quality Supervision, Inspection, and Quarantine (AQSIQ) indicated a rare occurrence of kidney stones in children was flagged by at least one member of the public and a urologist. These occurrences were causally linked to the Sanlu milk. Over the next three months, additional reports linking the milk to sick babies occurred.

The value of the company plunged from the scandal. Fonterra wrote down the carrying value of its investment by two-thirds, reflecting the costs of product recall and the impairment of the Sanlu brand because of the contamination of milk.

Again, where was true CSR? A conscientious and dedicated program would have taken a stronger hold on the issues and mitigated exposure at a much quicker rate. Considering this scenario, you can understand why many consumers question the concept of social responsibility as labeled by companies.

What are the lessons learned in these examples? If CSR is a stated value, companies should be prepared to back up their words with swift and dedicated actions when unforeseeable events occur.

Honesty

Do you believe in the saying "Honesty is the best policy?" There is another saying that "What the public doesn't know won't hurt them." Those statements seem to be controversial and opposite positions.

How often does management consider the thought process of what we don't know won't hurt us? Is this true, or is this a means the organization uses to protect its reputation? Years ago, I had a chief executive officer relay he felt many of his direct reports didn't always inform him about issues happening in the organization. They did this in an attempt to keep him from worrying about the issue, but, in essence, the CEO viewed it as a lack of honesty.

Consider this concept from a personal viewpoint. If you have teenagers, you may prefer not to know the specifics of something they are doing. This thought process may keep you from initial worry, but what precedent does it set for how your children should act?

Do we believe that honesty is truly in play at all levels of the organization, regardless of timing or positioning? If professionals feel this attribute is one which the corporation is providing lip service to, individuals may question the overall integrity of the organization. Honesty must be displayed and practiced in everyday settings and by each and every individual.

The old adage of "out of sight, out of mind" should not be present when dealing with true honesty in the workplace. If individuals feel they must make themselves invisible for certain reasons, or lay low due to issues that have surfaced, they will question management's true intentions related to honesty.

Loyalty and Respect

What comes first, loyalty or respect? The chicken or the egg? Loyalty can often breed respect, while respect can enhance loyalty. But, the culture and the atmosphere created must include other attributes which allow loyalty and respect to build among professionals and coworkers.

You may have been told when you were young to respect your elders. Like any other child, you may have thought, "Why do I need to do that?" Use this thought process in a professional setting. Early in our careers, it is much easier to accept the directive to respect those in higher positions or those who have been in the workforce longer. They have seen, experienced, and lived things we may not have yet encountered. But as we continue to mature in our professional experience, we start seeing the importance of receiving the appropriate level of respect from individuals for whom we work. Managers must not forget all professionals have individual skills, talents, and challenges. And in each case, they, too, deserve respect.

Scenario One: Personal Respect   Let's first consider an example on a personal level. Consider an instance where a high school freshman is asked to write a literary rebuttal to an article originally written by a senior in the high school newspaper. It was the first year for the school to include the freshman class as part of the high school setting. The original article focused on the senior's perception that freshmen were ruining the senior-year experience by being a part of the school. The article further declared freshmen had no respect for the seniors because they didn't follow the behavior expected by the seniors.

The freshman student given the assignment to rebut the article, was new to the school. She had been taught at home and at school that everyone required respect. The slant of her article was that although the seniors felt the freshmen were ruining their final high school year, had they considered how they may be making it difficult on the freshmen for their initial high school year?

The reaction of the senior class to the rebuttal article was alarming. They immediately took to the defense and an attitude of "How dare you talk to us like that!" The moral of the scenario is as a society, we begin to teach the pecking order at a very young age.

Summary

As the new generation of workers enter the business world, we will see additional shifts in the expectations of integrity, CSR, loyalty, and respect. Corporate values are important, but they must be more than just words. If organizations only focus on the words, how ethical would you assess this process to be? Corporate values must be displayed and acted on in everyday activities and practiced. They must be reinforced and encouraged, and they must be believed by all.

Section 2: Ethics and the Control Environment

Introduction

Prior to the corporate scandals of Enron, WorldCom, Tyco, and other organizations, the phrase control environment was a concept not often discussed in corporate settings or board discussions. The Sarbanes–Oxley legislation escalated the importance of the concept and the awareness of its implications on the internal dynamics of companies. Internal and external auditors began focusing on ways to evaluate the true meaning of control environment and experimenting with methods to effectively measure the existence of a proper control environment within corporate settings.

Evaluating the Control Environment

The phrases tone at the top, management philosophy and operating style, conflict of interest are well known. Each of these phrases contributes to the ethical control environment within a company. However, as previously discussed, organizations continually have difficulties identifying ways to accurately measure these attributes. Complicating this aspect are the political implications of attempting to communicate to management that their control environment may not be as effective and adequate as they believe. Have you ever tried to tell management that elements of their control environment may have design flaws or gaps which could result in unwanted behavior?

If so, what was the response you received from management or the board, or both? This is akin to telling someone to their face, "You are not ethical."

The control environment is a pervasive structure extending through the complete organization. It impacts many business process activities, and is the very foundation of proper ethical behavior. The control environment is an integral part of the internal control system and, therefore, must be understood, evaluated, and tested, first by management, and then by the external auditors. Anyone who has ever been involved in assessing the control environment of an organization will tell you it is easy to say but hard to do.

The subjective, non-transaction-oriented nature of the control environment creates many challenges. SOX requires evaluation of the control environment. Just because it may be a difficult thing to measure does not provide management with adequate rationale for noncompliance.

Let's consider a scenario outside the corporate realm that could be related to control environment. Take a minute to view the adorable picture of the golden retriever puppies. Now think:

> Control environment, what's the big deal? Could these cute pups possibly do anything their owner wouldn't want them to do? Look at those innocent faces!

Ok, you might think, come on now, this is quite a stretch! Well, not really. Those cute little puppies were born to my golden retriever on Super Bowl Sunday 2012. A litter of nine little pups, what could be more adorable? Here is how my scenario relates to the concept of control environment.

In the pups' first five weeks of life, their mother instinctively cared for her babies, making sure they were fed and cleaned. As the little pups started to learn to walk around and became a bit more active, momma backed off, and the requirements of feeding and cleaning up after them became quite overwhelming. In other words, the control environment shifted pretty quickly and dramatically. Within a few weeks, those adorable nine puppies became very active little rascals. Momma golden retriever decided it was no longer her role to always be around and clean up after their messes. We went from watching this adorable litter of pups stay close to their mom for protection and comfort to trying to figure out how to keep the pups contained within their whelping box while cleaning up after them and making sure mom was around when they got hungry. It was quite a job and, frankly, not one I was ready for.

I use this as an analogy because there are many similarities to what happens in our day-to-day business environment. Organizations start out by setting policies and processes to follow. In the early days, those policies and processes may work effectively and, possibly, don't require much monitoring. But, as the organization grows and changes, as people come and go, as the strategy of the organization shifts, those policies and processes established may not necessarily be as effective as they once were. The dynamics have changed, people have changed, the organization has grown or adjusted, so, logically, the control environment has changed. The organization must adjust its methods to ensure the intentions and strategies are effectively met. The question is, does this happen? How often do we see organizations attempt to get by with the methods they have previously used and justify it by saying that nothing has happened, so why should we change anything?

In earlier chapters, we provided some alternatives to evaluating control environment elements. These alternatives included surveys, interviews, and utilizing the maturity model approach. Let's take a few moments to further focus on the difficulties of an assessment and possible ways to overcome those difficulties. Each item covered won't necessarily work in every organization. It is incumbent on each organization to continually reassess specific capabilities and be open to suggestions and changes.

Measuring Tone at the Top

To adequately assess the control environment, you must be able to assess tone at the top. In most cases, individuals are evaluating the control environment of the whole organization, so tone at the top is interpreted to be tone as it relates to senior management and the board. We can easily see how any type of assessment of tone at the top can create challenges. If not effectively executed, assessments that relate to tone at the top may not provide sufficient insight into issues that should be further evaluated. If the assessment is being done by an internal group like compliance or internal audit, trying to adequately communicate to the CEO and board that certain actions may not be setting the right tone can be viewed as a pink slip waiting to be handed out.

Somehow, organizations must move past the simple check-the-box evaluation methods. These methods may help identify if certain elements exist such as board charters, codes of conduct, conflict of interest policies, authorization policies, and personnel evaluations. However, the existence of policies is only as good as the company's focus to ensure there are quality aspects embedded when executing each procedure. The procedures should not just exist because of some compliance requirement. Management must understand and buy into the concept that tone at the top means full support for procedures and evaluations. Recommendations must be readily evaluated for potential impact on the control environment. Consider the following example.

Scenario One: ABC Company Authorization Policy ABC Inc. has a written authorization policy for procurement professionals. On the surface, this process appears to contribute to a strong control environment. But let's look a bit deeper and evaluate a few more "qualitative" characteristics.

- What if the authorization policy does not cover strategic areas such as contract approvals, management overrides, bid tendering?
- Assume the policy was created solely by the finance organization without input from the procurement group or other areas of the company.
- What if the company does not have monitoring methods in place to identify when authorization procedures are bypassed?

All of these assumptions, taken together, could create issues with the control environment. Even one of these attributes could result in a design gap which may impact the organization's control environment and overall ethical atmosphere. We now have a dilemma. Consider the following factors.

- How does the evaluator communicate to management the potential risk of these control gaps?
- What if the issues are communicated, and management agrees to the findings. Later management decides the gaps are not of significant concern. This determination is because no significant issues have come to light regarding unauthorized payments being made.
- If an issue has not yet come to light or been identified, should this fact minimize the finding?
- What if the evaluator's opinion on how the identified gaps impact the control environment differs with management?

An obvious step may be to speak to the board or the audit committee. A challenge may be how the board views management's opinion versus the evaluator's opinion. If management has a more direct communication link than the evaluator, is the assessment criterion being communicated on an independent basis?

If you are waiting for a textbook answer to the aforementioned dilemma, you may be disappointed. All organizations are different, all relationships are different, all perceptions and evaluations are different, so the steps to take in resolving these dilemmas could all be different. Important criteria to consider include:

- The evaluator should have authority to analyze the situation beyond just the existence of policies.
- If the evaluator cannot identify specific quantative information related to how the issue may impact the control environment, they must be able to effectively communicate the qualitative factors that make the issue one that requires focus.
- Management must be able to understand the difference between a control gap and a control failure. Yes, it is important to know if the gap has created a failure; however, just because the auditors or compliance professionals cannot identify that

a failure has occurred should not minimize the potential impact of the gap on the control environment. Organizations must remember the fraud triangle and the risk control gaps have related to the opportunity portion of the triangle. Just because an issue has not occurred to date, doesn't make it any smaller of a gap.

• Organizations should ensure when assigning evaluators the responsibility of analyzing the effectiveness of control environment attributes that they are open to the issues that may be identified.

• Independent communication with senior management and the board is essential. If there is a disagreement related to the severity of the issue as perceived by management versus the evaluator, the board should have the ability to independently hear the view of both sides and not be influenced by the opinion of one side over the other.

Evaluating Management Philosophy and Operating Style

Let's take another example related to quarterly attestations by management for the control environment and internal controls. Most publicly traded companies have procedures in place for sign-off on internal control processes for SOX 302 processes. In this example, consider how this standard procedure may impact the organization's ethical environment.

Scenario One: SOX 302 Attestation   Organizations have established elaborate procedures to provide assurance to their CEOs and CFOs prior to final attestation for the Securities and Exchange Commission filings. These procedures involve requiring heads of major business units or subsidiaries to provide personal attestations on controls in their area of responsibility. With this in mind, many organizations view a strong control environment procedure is to require quarterly attestations by the heads of major business units or subsidiaries.

Now, let's assume the procedure utilized to obtain those quarterly attestations was established in 2004, the first year of SOX attestation. The procedure is a signature from each of the business unit leads that indicates:

To the best of my knowledge, internal control procedures within my area of responsibility as well as financial information provided to management is accurate and complete.

Those procedures may have been originally accompanied by specific training for the business unit leads related to SOX requirements. Fast-forward to present day; many of the personnel who are signing the attestations are individuals promoted or moved into a new position. What if the organization has not continued dedicated training on the purpose and importance of attestation sign-offs? The new personnel may look at the process as a "step" they must complete each quarter because of management requirements. They may not understand the implications of the attestation they are signing.

As an independent evaluator, consider the following questions when assessing the effectiveness and adequacy of this procedure.

- Do you believe management understands what they are attesting to?
- Since the attestation is a simple signature, do you believe business unit management would inherently know what types of control issues should be brought to senior management's attention?
- If you have questions related to these inquiries, would you be able to tell management the current control environment is working appropriately?
- If you relayed your control environment concerns to management, what would their response be?

Inherently, management may believe there is a procedure in place, appropriate personnel are required to sign the attestation, and, as a result, everything should be fine. Sounds good, right? On the surface, the assumption is logical but if management are looking for proper control procedures, they must be able to understand the potential ramifications of some of the qualitative control gaps identified. If they cannot and the control gaps are not addressed, deficiencies and control environment issues could occur that are unacceptable to management.

Where is the textbook answer for this dilemma? A suggestion would be to refer to the requirements of SOX and the associated liabilities of management if attestations are not adequately obtained. Outlining to the CEO and CFO the potential liabilities of simply relying on signatures for attestations, without understanding the complete process, may be sufficient to convince them to ensure attestations are obtained through full understanding and disclosure.

Evaluating Segregation of Duties

Segregation of duties can be difficult to adequately assess and evaluate for many companies, especially those with small or limited staff. However, it is an important component of the control environment and can directly link to ethical conduct and behavior. Segregation of duties is the concept of ensuring that more than one person has responsibility for completing a specific task. The intent is to ensure proper authorization, avoidance of error, and prevention of fraud. General categories of functions to be segregated include:

- Authorization
- Recording
- Custody of assets
- Reconciliation or audit

The reason that segregation of duties is critical to the control environment is because it involves how, when, and where job tasks are executed. It is critical that appropriate segregation of responsibilities be in place to minimize risk to the organization as well as protect individual employees from false allegations of wrongdoing.

The most prevalent difficulties for segregation of duty issues occur in smaller organizations where personnel sourcing is limited. In these cases, it is difficult for management to understand how and when segregation should be applied to various responsibilities.

As managers and executives, we believe we perform our due diligence to hire honest and trustworthy personnel. In times of resource constraint, organizations may place overreliance on critical personnel to perform duties which may put both the organization and the individual employee at risk. In these situations, the control environment is also at risk.

Regardless of the size of the operation and the availability of resources, organizations must do everything in their power to ensure appropriate checks and balances are in place for critical financial and operational activities. A strong control environment can only be supported through appropriate segregation of responsibilities and assignment of duties. In addition, employees must understand how these tasks relate to the control environment, control procedures, and ethical behavior. If the resources are not available to provide appropriate segregations, then management must assess the risk embedded in the processes and identify ways to appropriately monitor transactions and activity. In the end, the lack of appropriate segregation of duties will place liability on the CEO, CFO, and company board as it provides the opportunity for individuals to take advantage of control gaps and perform some activity that may be considered inappropriate, fraudulent or even unethical.

Summary

A company's control environment should be considered as the very foundation upon which the company can effectively execute its strategy and its ethical code. Gaps or flaws in the control environment must be fully assessed and regularly evaluated to provide adequate assurance regarding the sufficiency of controls. If management focuses only on the "check the box" activities for control environment attributes, they will miss critical attributes that may result in major breaks that ultimately impact the organization's viability.

Section 3: Corporate Director's Ethical Fiduciary Duty

Introduction

When considering the core of ethical conduct, contemplate the atmosphere set by a company's board of directors. Traditionally, being appointed to an organization's board of directors has been considered an indicator of reaching a level of expertise, professionalism, and recognition. In the pre-SOX days, presence on a board, regardless of whether it was private, public, or not-for-profit, was considered a résumé builder or a way of earning a bit of extra cash in your preretirement years.

Post the Enron incident and passing of Sarbanes-Oxley, the responsibilities and liabilities of individuals who serve as members of corporate boards have dramatically increased. Legislation holds directors accountable for their fiduciary duties and ethical responsibilities. Shareholders and stakeholders support this stand. To serve on a corporate board in today's economy, an individual must be ready to spend considerable time understanding and executing their fiduciary responsibilities to the organization. It is no longer acceptable to appear at the quarterly meetings, provide input, and collect your director fees. Now, directors are expected to be well prepared for meetings and be willing to step above and beyond traditional duties of quarterly meetings. You might say to yourself,

> Sure ... accountability for all positions in an organization is much stronger these days. It is only reasonable to ensure directors' responsibilities are following the same trends.

Most organizations have done a good job of ensuring that their boards have an updated charter and aligns with all regulatory requirements. They have also followed recommendations and mandates to ensure a certain level of financial expertise exists on audit committees. These are positive advancements in moving into the new arena of ethical responsibility. But, as in any case, there is much more to be focused on.

Evaluating Board Composition

Here are a few questions to consider when evaluating the composition and performance of boards and whether the composition truly sets the proper ethical tone.

How Were Board Members Selected? In years past, board seats were assigned by the CEO or executive team through personal appointments or recommendations by other executives for placement on the company's proxy. Often, these recommendations came with long-term relationships and ties to the company or members of the executive team. CEOs would surround themselves with individuals whose philosophy was much like their own. These situations made the concepts of fiduciary duty and independent thinking hard to execute.

In today's world, companies are encouraged to develop a robust process when selecting directors. Directors should be able to appropriately challenge management and ask the tough questions on issues such as strategy and budget. This requires the director to have a strong knowledge of the company's business model and to have a level of independence that will allow them to maintain an arm's-length relationship with the CEO.

Consider a few questions when evaluating the compostion of your board of directors.

- Do directors have a full understanding of all relevant governance requirements, including their implications to directors and to existing board structure and dynamics?
- When was the last time the board underwent a comprehensive training session executed by a third party or independent trainer?
- Does the board take their role of risk oversight seriously?
- Do they properly communicate with the internal audit function and take a strategic interest in compliance and enterprise risk processes?
- Is there a proper evaluation process in place to nominate or assign members to the board?
- Are there term limits on board positions?

If the answer to any of these questions is "no" or "I'm not sure," then consider executing an independent evaluation of board processes and board effectiveness. If boards are to be held accountable for responsibilities, as is appropriate, then companies must ensure they receive relevant, timely, and independent training on all areas of their fiduciary duty.

Have the Composition and Charters of Board Committees Been Compared to Exchange Listing Requirements? Legal requirements and personal liability are a concern for individuals who hold board seats. The organization, along with the directors, must ensure individuals serving on committees are sufficiently qualified to discharge their expanded responsibilities. Companies must find ways to adequately evaluate the true independence of board members. Independence can be hampered by more than just the obvious conflicts of interest. Long-term relationships or external interests can complicate board efficiency and effectiveness. If an independent director has served on the board for an extended period of time, companies should question whether the director's independence is impacted when attempting to execute responsibilities. The director may have unintended obligations or alliances to the CEO or other members of management that would inhibit fulfillment of responsibilities. Long-term relationships are difficult to sever; however, in the best interest of both the company and the director, sometimes the severance of those relationships will create a stronger independent culture.

What Is the Acceptable Practice of Board Communication with Individuals Outside Senior Management? One chief audit officer (CAE) relayed his organization prohibited anyone outside the senior leadership team from having independent communications with the board. Would you consider this an ethical process?

Companies must ask how often members of the board communicate with employees and management who hold positions outside the executive committee. Is this type of communication and interaction encouraged, discouraged, or ignored?

The practice of who can communicate with board members and when the communication can occur can take on many dynamics. Each organization will have its protocols. There may be no right or wrong answer, and it could depend on the organization as well as the individual director's time commitment. But, if the decision for limited communication is something championed by management, companies should evaluate their reasoning.

Truly independent directors should be able to communicate with whoever they believe necessary to understand the inner workings of the company. This should not be limited to the executive team or individuals "approved" by management. Management must also evaluate whether they are sending unintended messages regarding the access of the board to employees. Frequent and open communication should be encouraged between board members and the internal auditors, compliance professionals, and legal professionals. If communication is limited to quarterly meetings, board members themselves should be reaching out to these positions to gain clarity on issues.

Does the Board Have Input into Corporate Strategy? The Enron, WorldCom, and Tyco scandals all support reasons for the board to be actively engaged in the company's corporate strategy. Each of these scandals included many ethical violations. Pre-Sarbanes-Oxley, boards were often the "yes men" to management. They were only included in corporate strategy discussions at the back end when strategies were approved. By this time, management had developed the "company line" on the strategic direction. Boards were told what management felt they needed to hear to approve the corporate strategy.

New risk management procedures strongly suggest the board be integrally involved in the strategy discussions and decisions. This procedure is an attempt to maintain strong ethics within the organization. If the board has not been sufficiently exposed to strategy discussions and alternatives, they may not have the information needed to make informed decisions best for shareholders.

What Is the Board's Role in Understanding Fraud Investigations, Whistleblower Issues, and Corporate Misconduct? One of my favorite phrases is

> Sarbanes-Oxley was not put in place because someone forgot to document accounts payable from beginning to end.

Sounds simple, but we sometimes forget the importance of the concepts of tone at the top, culture, code of conduct, conflict of interest, and segregation of duties. Management can become so concerned about the tactics of conforming to SOX requirements that sometimes the forest gets lost in the trees!

If you don't agree, ask yourself what information is provided to your board on fraud investigations, whistleblower issues, or conflict of interest issues? Management will be quick to indicate "We report to our board on these issues quarterly!" But, is the reporting focusing on quantitative concepts only? Does the reporting lack the quality to allow the board to appropriately evaluate the issues and ask probing questions? Many companies report to their boards the number of calls coming through the whistleblower hotline. But, how often does the board hear the true details behind those numbers? Are the true details known? Have the complaints been adequately investigated by the appropriate independent parties?

If corporate misconduct has been identified within the organization, are assessments made as to what, when, and how the board will be informed? If so, do the procedures make sense? Of course you don't want to overload your board with insignificant issues, but who is making the determination of what is or isn't significant? If the concept of corporate tolerance has not been fully vetted, ask yourself and your organization why.

Does the Board Have Input into Performance Appraisals of Executives? The board is the ultimate governance oversight for the organization. They have a fiduciary responsibility to ensure individuals in critical organizational positions are fully and ethically fulfilling their responsibilities. It would then be a logical assumption to have board members involved in the personnel evaluations of critical organizational positions.

Can you ask this question of your management, or is it considered a political question that is only relevant to a few insiders? This may sound harsh, but part of tone at the top is the board assisting in the establishment of culture. What better way to have an impact on corporate culture than to have direct say on the performance evaluations of individuals who hold roles that have specific fiduciary duties to the company and shareholders?

A CAE relayed his recommendation to management that the audit committee have input into his own individual performance appraisal. The recommendation became a political career killer for the audit executive. Management viewed the recommendation as "inappropriate" and outside the audit executive's realm of authority. The recommendation came subsequent to a quality assurance review conducted by the Institute of Internal Auditors. The review was sanctioned by the audit committee and management. Of the handful of recommendations made by the reviewing body, the vast majority had to do with the internal audit department's independence and connection to the board and audit committee. One of the observations was for the audit committee to accept more ownership for the relationship with the audit executive. Management rejected the recommendations and the audit executive ended up leaving the company within the succeeding months. Regardless of any relationship between these events, the fact that quality improvement recommendations were ignored, and a long-term employee of the company (the CAE) left within months of the review, might beg questions around the independence of the internal audit department. The instance also questions the organization's overall tone and ethical atmosphere.

If there are certain roles within the organization that "by charter" and "by design" have responsibilities requiring direct access to the board or a committee, some level of input by that body to the lead executive's performance appraisal should be considered as a governance step. This input is not attempting to bypass management's authority over personnel evaluations; it is an important consideration of the true independence and ethical reporting relationship of individuals tasked with board reporting responsibility.

How Is the Evaluation of the Board of Directors Conducted? Adequate procedures for the evaluation of activities of the board are an important aspect of a company's ethical environment. The most important aspect of the exercise will tie to the intent of the evaluation. If the evaluation is to comply with SEC regulations or other charter requirements, the process employed may not always be the most effective. This is because management, legal, or the board may resort to a yes-or-no questionnaire process which does not provide strategic input into the internal workings of the board.

Board evaluation processes can be tricky. There is the need to truly evaluate the performance of the board and respective members while appropriately balancing legal concerns which could ultimately surface. Board evaluation processes are as varied as boards themselves. Consider the variance in the following methods.

Scenario One: Board Evaluation A high-level board survey questionnaire is provided separately for each board member to complete. The survey is a set of standard questions on fiduciary requirements, with a simple "yes" or "no" check-the-box response.

Scenario One: Benefits A high-level board survey will provide an overall evaluation of the performance of the board's fiduciary duties. If the survey is completed independently, each director will have the opportunity to answer the questions without immediate pressure from management or other board members. From a legal viewpoint, this method may be less controversial than open-ended questions.

Scenario One: Challenges As with any survey process, individuals may interpret questions in different ways. Lack of a consistent delivery method may result in inconsistencies with interpretations. A simple "yes" or "no" response does not provide a true evaluation of how effectively responsibilities were executed. A survey only provided to the board may not allow for a full 360-degree assessment of performance.

Scenario Two: Board Evaluations   A third-party independent review of board performance is performed. The review includes individual interviews, a facilitated board discussion, a review of charters and board minutes, and a complete independent assessment of effectiveness.

Scenario Two: Benefits   The ability to execute an independent third-party assessment may give the best insight into the company's governance process. An outside party assessing governance elements would not be encumbered by political ties or relationships that could make evaluation techniques difficult. The ability to separately interview board members and management utilizing open-ended questions may provide the best insight to process effectiveness. In addition, the ability to facilitate an interactive discussion with the board can provide valuable insight into how duties are being executed.

Scenario Two: Challenges   If proper due diligence is not performed when selecting the independent third party to facilitate the assessment, the organization may experience challenges. Also, if an assessment body is selected that utilizes very strict, standard evaluation attributes not in line with the objectives and processes of the organization, the evaluation assessment may not reflect organizational needs. On the other hand, if the assessment body selected has some connection to the company, either with past engagements or individual relationships, the assessment may not be as independent as expected.

The effective execution of a truly independent assessment, can bring with it many organizational and political challenges. This can often be a limiting factor in being able to execute such an assessment.

Scenario Three: Board Evaluations   An internal review is conducted by a professional within the legal, compliance, or internal audit group. The review includes individual interviews, a review of charters, discussion with management, and an overall assessment of effectiveness.

Scenario Three: Benefits   Utilizing an internal professional to perform the assessment can provide advantages. An internal evaluator may understand certain intricacies and aspects of how the board operates and is managed which may provide insight into board effectiveness. In addition, utilizing an internal resource may be more cost effective for the organization.

Scenario Three: Challenges This method may present the strongest political challenges and implications related to assessment accuracy. An internal resource may have pressures and expectations established for the manner in which they execute the assessment as well as the overall results.

Which alternative would provide the best assessment for your organization? There is no one correct answer. Whatever method is selected, the organization should understand both the benefits and the challenges of the assessment process.

How Does the Board Respond to Identification of Internal Control Issues? When considering an ethical environment and adequate tone at the top, the board's interest in understanding elements of internal control issues can set a strong precedent for the organization's ethical atmosphere. Some individuals believe the board has better things to do than to listen to control gap issues identified by internal audit, compliance, or the external auditors. But, part of their fiduciary duty is oversight of the audit process, as well as SOX compliance. As hard as it is to listen to what may be deemed as control issues the board must set the right tone and ethical stance and ensure they address issues brought to their attention.

It is helpful for the board to provide guidance related to their risk tolerance and risk appetite and when they expect issues to be brought to their attention. Ultimately, everyone wants to utilize the board's time wisely. Knowing their expectations of when they want to understand issues can be a very important attribute to achieving strong communication and an adequate ethical atmosphere. Ultimately, the board must remember that all groups who provide input on issues also have their own fiduciary duty. Sometimes, judgment and personal assessment drive the need to further discuss an issue with board members. If boards aren't willing to accept those occasional inputs, they may be sending a message to the organization that internal control issues are not of concern unless they meet the external auditors materiality threshold. This can be a troubling situation.

Accurately assessing board performance and effectiveness is a crucial aspect in today's corporate governance world. Boards and management must embrace their individual responsibilities related to the execution of duties and also be prepared for the challenges that may arise when assessing the execution of those responsibilities.

Section 4: Reporting Ethical Issues

Introduction

Reporting ethical issues to the board and audit committee can be filled with sensitivities. As a past CAE, I would attend audit committee meetings and listen to the corporate compliance officer report statistics of the whistleblower hotline or ethical complaints. Often, the committee would be provided simple statistics without any detail behind the complaints. I was always intrigued the audit committee did not seem to question the information or ask for more detail surrounding the particular complaints. The compliance officer would report the number of calls received on the hotline, and none was of significance. Never once did I hear an audit committee member or a senior management leader ask follow-up questions about the calls.

Employee Hotlines

When company hotlines receive only a handful of calls within a quarter, and the employee population is made up of a significant number of employees, could there be a possibility that employees don't trust the process? A low level of trust may result in the hotline being unused and thus being ineffective. In addition, who made the decision the issues reported were not important? In cases I observed, the audit committee didn't ask what the protocol was for evaluating the reported issues. In these cases, you could ask whether the audit committee was fulfilling their fiduciary duty in relation to the hotline process. Another question might be was the compliance officer providing the information necessary to allow the audit committee to understand issues being reported and whether the hotline was adequately communicated, understood, and trusted by employees? Ultimately, the audit committee and the board are responsible for ensuring the efficiency and effectiveness of the hotline. If the hotline is not being utilized, you have to question whether individuals truly understand or trust the process.

In another situation, I attended an audit committee meeting where the corporate compliance officer listed out each complaint, including the names of the callers. This situation became one of embarrassment, because a specific call came from the administrative assistant of the CEO. The hotline was supposed to be anonymous (even if the person disclosed their name). The fact that board materials listed the callers' names could be considered a breach of confidentiality. It was surprising this occurred, because the compliance officer was a lawyer. Most would expect a lawyer to understand the importance of confidentially. In this case, the issue resulted in extreme concern by the leadership team and the administrative assistant (she was the person who helped organize the board materials and noticed her name in the report). These are the types of mistakes that can quickly undermine your organization's confidentiality process. Although, as the CAE, I voiced my concerns about how the report was documented, it wasn't until an employee wrote an anonymous letter to the chief legal counsel that management decided they may not have handled the situation appropriately.

Lessons Learned

These examples are provided to stress the importance of how ethical issues are relayed to management, the board, and the audit committee. As we've discussed, ethics is an individual moral concept. In addition, it can be a politically charged organizational issue. Whenever questions arise regarding ethical instances, management and the organization may attempt to minimize the issues. After all, organizations believe they have hired qualified and ethical people. The last thing they expect to happen is for one of their employees to breach the organization's ethical conduct policy.

These factors contribute to the importance of ensuring there is a proper protocol for reporting, evaluating, and dealing with reported ethical issues. If employees feel the organization does not take complaints seriously, they will shy away from reporting their observations. This silence is a form of acceptance and does not help advance the ethical atmosphere of the organization.

Section 5: Protocols for Reporting Ethical Issues— The Whistleblower Hotline

Introduction

In days gone by, one way of stopping prank phone calls was to pick up the phone and immediately blow a whistle into the receiver. This was an effective technique when the phone rang in the middle of the night because young teenagers were playing phone pranks. Of course, this was before the prevalence of cell phones. But the action often accomplished its goal. Take this analogy and consider what could happen when protocols aren't in place to provide for whistleblower complaints to be made in a discreet and transparent manner. The whistle blow may get much louder than anyone in the company may have anticipated.

Whistleblower Procedures

Does your organization have a well-documented and well-outlined protocol for managing reported ethical issues? If your initial answer is yes, can you recite the procedures utilized when dealing with ethical reports? Do you know who within the organization receives the complaints and how they are vetted and evaluated?

Individuals often think the existence of a whistleblower hotline will provide the organization with adequate processes for reporting ethical issues. However, in order for the theory to be accurate, the organization must ensure the hotline is properly managed, monitored, and reported, and all issues are investigated by experienced individuals who understand the various concepts of ethical behavior.

The methods used by organizations to manage hotlines vary. They include methods such as outsourcing the hotline to a third party or allowing internal audit, legal, compliance, or even human resources to manage the hotline. There are advantages and disadvantages to each method. From the view of having an outsourced provider, employees may feel the hotline maintains an independent and confidential protocol. If the hotline is manned by an internal group, employees may have a concern the hotline is not completely confidential.

Few, if any, professionals enter a position within a company with the goal to be a whistleblower. But, in today's business world, things happen. When those incidents occur, if there isn't an appropriate outlet for reporting concerns or suspected wrongful behavior, and if the company has not instilled a culture of openness, transparency, and strong ethics, professionals can find themselves in a moral predicament. We know from studies of psychology and human behavior that concepts of right and wrong, good and bad, moral or immoral can relate strongly to an individual's upbringing, social or economic status, or even religious or personal beliefs. Most whistleblowers don't call a hotline because they are furious with a company or want to get back at a particular person; they have an intrinsic belief the observed behavior or actions were truly wrong. If the person has reached a point of feeling the need to call an anonymous hotline, then the potential issue may have already reached a peaking point higher than management may have anticipated.

Actual statistics of personal implications to whistleblowers can be daunting to anyone thinking of taking action. Information from a study of 233 whistleblowers revealed that:

- Ninety percent were later fired or demoted.
- Twenty-seven percent faced lawsuits.
- Twenty-six percent later sought psychiatric or physical care.
- Twenty-five percent suffered alcohol abuse.
- Seventeen percent lost their homes.
- Fifteen percent got divorced.
- Ten percent attempted suicide.
- Eight percent went bankrupt.

Despite all of these discouraging statistics, only 16% of the individuals in the study indicated they would *not* blow the whistle again. The reason is linked to their individual moral code or belief that what they were doing was the right thing to do. Ultimately, their sole purpose was not to rat on the company but to right some wrong.

Corporate Hotline History and Procedures   There has been so much written about the establishment of corporate hotlines. What more could possibly be added? Logically thinking, if what has already been outlined and written is strong and sound advice, would we continue to see corporate struggles and scandals? Would corporate struggles continue to lead to whistleblower complaints, along with the government's need to establish the Dodd–Frank law? Either the current processes are not good enough, or companies just aren't listening.

Let's start back at the beginning. Why should we pay attention to previously reported or high-profile whistleblower cases? In simplest terms, it is the same reason we have our school children study history. Whenever human behavior is involved, peering into past scenarios can teach us a great deal about which concepts work and which do not. Hopefully, we will learn from the mistakes of the past and take appropriate steps to prevent similar issues in the future. Well, as my third-grade teacher would say, "Someone isn't paying attention!" Preventing future issues requires understanding the reason why an issue occurred, how it occurred, and what could have been done to prevent it. Could it be possible there are short-cut steps being taken in today's fast-paced business environment?

Company Program Assessment   Before you dismiss this possibility, consider what you know about your own company's whistleblower process. Answer a few of the following questions to begin to assess your program.

How is the program communicated throughout the organization?

- Is communication primarily managed through the company's code of conduct? If so, how often are employees asked to affirm the code of conduct, and in what manner does the affirmation occur?
- Are there hotline posters throughout corporate headquarters? If so, where are they placed? Are they in strategic areas where employees would be able to quickly describe where they saw a poster? Or, are they in hallways, in corners, or behind doors?
- If the hotline process is posted on your internal website, is it in a place easily identified when signing on to your internal network?

How often does open communication occur by senior leaders regarding the hotline and its purpose?

- Do managers openly endorse the program or reluctantly comply?

- Is there an unwritten code regarding the hotline where employees may feel uncomfortable calling and reporting an issue?
- How does management communicate the protocol for investigating or following up on issues that come through the hotline?
- Would an employee be able to recite the protocol?

Who manages your hotline, and how?

- If it is internally managed, how does the company ensure employee confidentiality? Remember, it is not enough to state in a policy that the hotline is confidential; if actions are louder than words, policy statements alone will go untrusted by employees.
- If the hotline is externally managed, has the effectiveness of its operations been recently validated?
- If you were to call the hotline, how effective is the representative in understanding the issue being reported? If the caller is reporting a financial issue, does the call representative understand the concepts and terms being used?
- Do concerns have to be continually repeated to the call representative?
- Are you required to explain terminology and disclose names to the call representative?
- Is the phone call tape recorded, and, if so, is the caller informed they are being recorded?
- What type of facts and information does the representative ask for? Are they simply recording what you say, or are they receptive enough to ask questions to help better explain and understand the full scope of the issue?
- How quickly do calls get communicated to the proper individuals within the organization for investigation?

Are calls received through the hotline taken seriously or viewed by management as something that is an administrative nuisance?

- Would employees be able to relay positive outcomes of the hotline?

- If you are in a role where you participate in the compilation of hotline results, are the calls of the nature that reflect the true purpose of the hotline?
- How long does it take management to investigate or react to an issue?
- Are issues always resolved with no concerns? If so, do you have any concerns about how issues are investigated?
- Who decides an issue has been completely and thoroughly investigated? Is there a protocol for investigation?

How are the results of hotline issues reported to the board and audit committee?

- Does the board simply receive statistics of calls, or are members informed of the substance of the issues?
- Does the board ask difficult questions of management about reported issues?
- Does the board have input into the investigation process?

All of these questions are important when assessing the effectiveness or reliability of a whistleblower hotline. Be cautious of relying too heavily on statistics when assessing the effectiveness of the process. Statistics are only as good as the information collected and used to develop the statistics. If the hotline call is wrongly classified, improperly evaluated or assessed, or improperly handled and responded to, the statistics may have little or no meaning.

Board Program Assessment   If you are a member of a company's board, ask yourself the following questions:

- What information is provided regarding the content and resolution of calls coming through the hotline?
- Are you satisfied with the reporting of just numbers?
- How does the company classify complaints? Is there some measurement regarding whether an issue is high, moderate, or low risk?
- Are you aware of the facts behind more significant complaints?
- Are you satisfied with the investigative techniques? If not, ask yourself why.

Summary

Whistleblowers will continue to be a component of corporate America and part of the ongoing story of corporate governance practices. It is evident through recent legislation such as Dodd–Frank that regulators believe the existence of a whistleblower hotline is important. How effective these hotlines are will continue to be something to debate in the corporate world. Companies can make a difference within their own procedures. To do this, they must understand the reason and importance of the hotline process within their own governance procedures. Executives must set the right tone and be open to the communication protocols established to provide the proper outlet for the flow of information.

Section 6: Communicating with Management and the Audit Committee

Introduction

The previous sections of this chapter have covered elements about the board, management, and organization's fiduciary duty toward ethics. The fifth section outlined procedures management and the audit committee should consider when dealing with communications coming through the whistleblower hotline. However, not all ethical issues, complaints, or concerns will come through the hotline or be identified solely by internal audit, legal, or compliance.

Handling Everyday Ethical Issues Companies may sometimes fall into a false sense of security when they believe their whistleblower hotline is the "end all and be all" for reporting ethical issues. Organizations must recognize ethical issues may occur in everyday interactions and may be noticed by a variety of personnel. This requires the organization to have a defined protocol for communication procedures related to ethical issues. These protocols include defining:

- How individual employees should communicate ethical issues they observe or have concern with while performing their day-to-day responsibilities.

- What alternatives employees have for communicating ethical issues that may involve their own management. In these cases, the employees may not feel comfortable speaking to certain personnel and must know what alternatives they have in order to adequately relay their concerns.
- How employees or business process areas should communicate ethical issues identified during a review, day-to-day work, or a process evaluation.
- How communications will be collected, evaluated, and assessed and how the resulting evaluations will be communicated through the company as well as to management and the board.

Let's use a couple of scenarios to examine how the concept of communication of ethical issues can become difficult and encompass more than the whistleblower hotline.

Ethical Communication Scenario One   Internal audit is in the midst of a review of a business process area. During the review, they become concerned about communications observed between process area management and employees. The communication process is not officially part of the scope of the internal audit; however, the auditors are bothered by the manner in which communications impact the atmosphere of the work area. They observe the manager of the process area frequently going directly to the desks of employees and acting in a verbally abusive manner. In one instance, they observed the manager yelling very loudly at an employee because a journal entry calculation had been done improperly. The manager used inflammatory language and verbally threatened the person's job if they didn't "shape up." The issue occurred when most of the department was present. The employee being verbally abused became so upset they left the office for the day.

In another instance, an employee arrived late to work. The manager was in the work area when the employee arrived. He immediately called the employee out in front of the departmental employees and loudly proclaimed that "being late to work was unacceptable behavior and cause for termination." The manager also declared he didn't care to hear excuses and expected each employee contact him personally if they were going to be late for any reason. In this instance, the employee spoke up and mentioned he had tried several times to call the manager's cell and work phone but received no answer. The employee indicated he left a message on both lines explaining why he was running late. The manager reacted with anger and replied,

> "This is a perfect example of inappropriate behavior! I don't care that I didn't answer the phone. That is no excuse. You should have kept calling until you reached me personally."

What Should the Auditors Do? From the information we are given, it appears the manager of the process area is not setting a good example of tone at the top. A work culture of fear and repercussions may be created. However, the issues of work environment and management tone are not part of the internal audit. What should the auditors do?

This is an example of being in a politically sensitive position. The auditors are not present in the department's work environment every day. Possibly, their observations were due to some rare occurrence. However, it is obvious each occurrence mentioned displays aspects of management tone and operating style. The auditors have several options to consider. Prior to executing any action, the auditors must ensure internal audit management is aware of the observations and concerns. By discussing their observations with internal management, they can brainstorm methods to communicate the observations to the proper personnel.

Let's assume that there is a senior-level audit manager assigned to the project. The manager has personally observed scenarios as mentioned in the given example. In addition, he has heard other examples from his individual auditors. What would the next step be?

In today's world of understanding COSO and its implications on the company's control environment, when auditors observe these actions taking place, they must find a way to communicate the concerns and potential ramifications to the proper individuals. Without knowing all the specifics of the operating environment within this example, the auditors may consider several approaches to communication.

- Speak with the direct manager and communicate their personal observations of the harsh communication protocols and the potential impact on the department's work environment.

If the manager has a different view or does not agree with the auditors' observations, the auditors may want to suggest to the manager he or she independently speak to some of the personnel regarding the department's overall work environment. If the manager still objects, the auditors will need to surface the issue with their CAE, who may need to speak to the process area manager's supervisor.

- Separately, the auditors may feel there is a need to interview department personnel about the organization's work environment prior to speaking to the departmental manager. However, the auditors must keep in mind the department employees may have a concern about expressing their opinion to the auditors. This may be a difficult tactic to take without strong support from upper-level management or some assurance of confidentiality.

- The auditors could expand the scope of their review to include "management tone and operating style." However, if this is an option chosen, they will need to justify why the expanded scope is important to the previously identified risks.

- The auditors could report their observations anonymously to the whistleblower hotline; however, this is not a process that may be the most appropriate alterative. If the work environment is indeed impacted by the tone of management's operating methods, the auditors should consider pressures placed on how the personnel execute their everyday duties. By simply calling the whistleblower hotline, the auditors are deflecting the issue to someone else.

- The auditors could go directly to the operating manager's supervisor and report their observations. But again, this may not be the most transparent manner for communicating the issue. The manager may become defensive and contradict the auditors' observations with his rationale. If the employees fear repercussions from the manager, they may not support observations reported by the auditors.

- The auditors could wait until the end of the audit and mention their observations in the audit report. Again, this would not be a preferred method. Internal audit should proactively work to openly communicate with management and ensure they

are aware of the various risks and observations being identified. By waiting and including an observation in the final
report, the process area manager may feel the auditors are trying to "set him up."

As you can see, there are a multitude of alternatives the auditors
might take in this situation. As we have discussed there is no checklist
answer. The auditors must use professional judgment and understanding of the operating environment and management's expectations.
They should use this information to make an assessment on how their
observation may impact the department's work environment and the
risks being evaluated. The method used to execute any communication should be with the utmost dignity and transparency as well as
consideration of how the observation will be received and addressed
by management.

Ethical Communication Scenario One: The Reality   The scenario as outlined previously is true; in actuality, the actions of the manager were
much more egregious than mentioned. In the actual case, the actions
were witnessed by both the internal and external auditors. Neither
of the groups communicated their observations to management.
Approximately six months later, two of the employees filed grievance
lawsuits against the manager and the employer. The lawsuit mentioned the behavior was well known by management and observed
by the internal and external auditors. The lawsuit went to court, and
members of both the internal and external audit teams were called to
testify about their observations. This resulted in a significant finding
for the plaintiffs.

It was proved the employer knew or, at a minimum, should have
known about the manager's inappropriate behavior and should have
taken action. The auditors failure to communicate their observation
contributed not only to the continuance of an unacceptable work
atmosphere but also the exposure to an employee lawsuit.

Ethical Communication Scenario Two   Within the previous scenario, we dealt with a challenge faced by the internal audit group
during their observations while working on a particular audit.
However, as we have indicated, observations of improper behavior

and questionable ethical actions can come from many places and many people. Many of us can relate to being in a grocery store and watching a parent severely reprimand their child for what appeared to be a minor incident. Many take the observation further and alert store management or even the police. Others just walk away in disbelief that a parent would behave in such a manner. You may even start wondering what may be happening in the privacy of their own homes.

Let's take a different scenario, one that may be even more complicated. Assume you are a prospective job candidate interviewing at a well-known company with a strong reputation in your community. Your interview goes smoothly, and you do not experience any inappropriate questioning or behavior. However, as you are being shown around the corporate campus by an employee guide, you observe things that make you uncomfortable. You observe a staff meeting being held in an open forum within the cafeteria, and the speaker (or manager) is making inappropriate gestures, using profane language, and appears to be making inappropriate advances toward some of the young female employees. You ask your guide about the incident, and he quips:

"Oh that's normal for Joe. Everyone knows he's like that. We just ignore him."

Later on the tour, you observe an individual showing off his handgun within the company office. The state has a conceal-and-carry law; however, the company has a strict policy against firearms on the corporate presence. You again ask your guide, and he indicates:

"What management doesn't know won't hurt them. People feel they have a right to conceal and carry."

What would you do in these instances? Consider the following alternatives.

- At the conclusion of the interview, you speak with the human resource representative and relay your concerns and observations and inquire more about management operating philosophy.

- After your interview, you follow up with a personal phone call to the hiring manager, expressing your appreciation for his time. You take the opportunity to relay some of the observations you had while touring the facilities.
- You leave the interview knowing this is not a company you would choose to work for.
- You decide that if the employees are not verbalizing their concerns, who are you to bring the issue to the attention of in management?
- You leave the interview conflicted. The job is one you felt you were very interested in. However, your observations are concerning and appear to reflect on the overall tone of the company. You consider calling the company's human resources hotline to report your observations in a confidential manner.
- You happen to know a member of the company's independent board of directors and decide to report your observations to him directly.
- You previously worked for the company's external auditors. Since you still have a good relationship with the firm, you choose to tell the partner in charge of your observations.

Any of these actions could be taken. Some may result in political ramifications when being considered for the job. Some of the choices listed such as going to the external auditors or the board members may not be the best approach in this situation. However, as we have earlier covered, "silence" is a form of acceptance of behavior. If you choose to stay silent on your observations and choose to join the company, you are contributing to its overall atmosphere.

Summary

The critical point with any of these scenarios is professionals must be cognizant of how they communicate ethical observations in the workforce. This is an area where everyone has their own view on how the communication should occur. A potential alternative is to start at the lowest point on the chain of command that may be able to address the issue. If actions are not taken, then decide how to escalate concerns appropriately and with respect.

Section 7: Developing Action Plans to Address Identified Ethical Issue Gaps

Introduction

Previous sections discussed the process utilized when ethical issues are reported through the whistleblower hotline. In addition, we discussed how professionals may address issues when they surface during their everyday jobs. However, our discussions have focused primarily on how reported ethical issues should be communicated to management or the audit committee.

In order for an organization to maintain a strong ethical program, they must have established a strong methodology or framework for addressing issues reported or identified. Having a framework to follow will provide employees with assurances that management will adequately evaluate the issue and determine if remediating actions are needed.

Framework Action Plan

When referring to the existence of a framework, consider this terminology as a process the company follows to adequately evaluate, examine, investigate, report, and remediate. A methodology that is sound and consistently followed will provide employees and professionals with assurances the company takes ethical conduct seriously. With this definition in mind, would you be able to recite your organization's process for:

- Issue evaluation
- Issue examination
- Issue investigation
- Issue reporting
- Issue remediation

If your answer is no, or I'm not sure, you may want to relook at your communication protocols for this process. Using the given categories, we will outline a few questions that should be considered in each phase.

Issue Evaluation   Issue evaluation and the determination of credibility of the identified issue are precursors to issue investigation. Just because an issue has been reported through some avenue does not inherently give it credibility. The assessor must have a structured process to ascertain the facts and determine if the issue is one that should be further evaluated. Take, for example, an issue reported third hand to the internal audit department. If the department is unable to substantiate the information provided, a great deal of time and effort could be wasted in evaluating the issue. Although many companies have whistleblower hotlines or human resource hotlines, complaints and allegations can come through a myriad of situations. The organizations must have a structured process for where the reported issue will be taken and what that person will evaluate to ensure the issue is one deemed credible and appropriate to examine further. Some questions that should be considered include:

- How was the issue reported?
- Who was involved in the issue?
- Has it been reported to some level of management?
- Was any action taken if the issue was reported? If not, can you ascertain why?
- How long ago did the issue occur?
- Is there any corroborating evidence of the issue?
- Who else is aware of the issue? Can you speak with them?
- If there has been a time lapse in reporting the issue, can you determine why?

Examination and Investigation   Once the issue has been deemed credible and appropriate to take to the next step of examination, the organization must have a strong process in place to ensure the issue is given to the proper individuals for further evaluation. For instance, if the issue deals with an ethical concern, and the concern is related to a particular area of the company, is it appropriate for internal audit, legal, or maybe a representative from human resources to look at the issue? Who makes this determination, and who approves the determination? Each of these questions are important to consider. Individuals who are brave enough to bring an issue to the surface within an organization want to be sure the organization will handle it with the utmost care and respect for all involved.

Issue Reporting   Does your organization have a set protocol for how reported ethical issues will be handled regardless of how the issue is reported? If the organization only has a formal protocol for issues reported through the whistleblower hotlines, this may not be sufficient in establishing an open and transparent culture. If employees Feel that concerns they relay to their managers or human resources regarding ethical actions is not adequately Addressed, they will lose faith in the organizations stated "ethical tone". In other words, if the only way to get action is to call a hotline, employees may feel the organization does not care about behavior as a whole.

Organizations should have established protocols to ensure when ethical concerns are expressed by employees, in any venue, those concerns are appropriately evaluated and addressed. This requires adequate processes that are fully communicated and trained throughout the organization. Managers should understand alternatives for communicating issues that are brought to their attention. If the organization has an attitude of "leave it to manager discretion as to when, how and what will be communicated", it will create an atmosphere of inconsistent behavior that is left to the individual perceptions and morals of professionals. This may not establish the proper tone for creating an ethical culture.

Of course, managers will always need to apply their own professional judgment to issues that come to their attention, but if the issue reaches a certain tolerance level like sexual harassment, excessive and profane language or inappropriate gestures towards other employees, managers must understand the organization expects these issues to be communicated upward and there should be no "take care of our own" attitude.

This recommendation is not promulgating some elaborate communication process, it is indicating there should be some basic parameters around the need for communicating ethical issues forward.

Issue Remediation   The methods and level of issue remediation will be determined by each individual company. Unless the act is "illegal" or clearly against company policies, the manner in which any individual company may address the issue will vary. This concept is very similar to how parents may discipline children. Some parents have a very fine line when it comes to what they believe is proper or improper behavior for their child. Do you remember being young and involved in some teenage prank with your friends. Possibly your parents grounded you while other parents just gave their child a verbal warning.

When my boys were in their teenage years, one was part of a teenage prank involving tossing raw eggs at homes and parked cars on Halloween. Raw eggs are a mess to clean up and can actually damage paint. As parents, my husband and I took the issue a bit more seriously than other parents. We required our son to not only apologize to the homeowners but also clean up the mess created. In addition, we asked the homeowners to assign our son "chores" that he was required to complete over a weekend. Other parents let their children off with verbal warnings. You can imagine our son's displeasure with his punishment. Regardless as to whether we were right in our punishment or the other parents were right, we felt it was important for our child to take responsibility for what he had done. So in essence, our "tolerance" for this type of behavior was at a lower threshold than other parents. Similarly, companies will all have different tolerance thresholds for what they deem appropriate or inappropriate behavior. Their issue remediation or actions will also vary. The important concept is that whatever the level of remediation action is applied, it should be applied consistently for all employees involved.

Summary

This chapter dealt with evaluation of ethical issues, the corporate directors fiduciary duties, whistleblower hotlines and remediation actions. There are many considerations internal auditors should give to their involvement in these areas. To be effective, they must have the support and buy-in of management and the audit committee. Later in Chapter 8 we will discuss more about establishing adequate relationships with the audit committee that may facilitate internal audit's involvement with this process.

7

CORPORATE ETHICAL CULTURE IN THE FUTURE

Introduction

If there was a crystal ball to see into the future, what would be occurring with corporate ethical culture? First of all, I have to admit that if I had a crystal ball, I would use it for something other than seeing how corporate America was managing ethical culture. With that thought in mind, it may be interesting to peer into tomorrow's world and see the tools, techniques, and processes companies will use to manage and promote ethics and those attributes which contribute to an ethical culture.

In earlier chapters, we considered the potential that at some point, a software application might be developed to assist professionals in their ethical decision making. The person who develops the application will either be a millionaire for inventing such a tool or in a lot of trouble because they do not include certain elements and considerations within the application. In any case, we know ethics will continue to be one of those topics which has both successes and failures in the business world. Whenever individuals with multiple beliefs gather in one setting, the potential for ethical conflicts will always be a concern. This is what makes it difficult to forsee any type of ethical application to guide behavior as something that will be developed.

Understanding that ethics will evolve as businesses evolve, consider attributes that will impact how our ethical world will mature. In the following sections, we will make reference to the different generations currently in the workforce and how the various elements of technology and social media as well as the blending of generational cultures have impacted the ethical work environment.

Section 1: Social Media and Technology Advances

Many view social media as a platform which began with applications like Facebook or LinkedIn. Actually, social media started as far back as 1969 with CompuServe, the first major commercial online service in the United States. It wasn't until the 2000s that the platforms went viral and became an increasing part of everyday life and business.

Social media is considered any form of electronic communication where users create online communities to share information, ideas, messages, and other content. Social media includes social blogs, wikis, Twitter, Internet forums, social networks (Facebook), Pinterest, Snapchat, and many others. Individuals from the Baby Boomer generation (individuals born between 1946 and 1965) may have never envisioned telling people good night on a social forum or announcing they were leaving for a beautiful one-week vacation in Hawaii. In a way, these statements are like telling the world, "OK I'm away so you can come rob me!"

Social media has truly changed the face of the world and with it, the aspects of how ethics is applied in personal and professional life. It has certainly changed how the millennial generation and Gen Z have matured. My three children would be considered millennials. The oldest was entering middle school when Facebook arrived on the scene. I recall, at first, not understanding what the platform was for or about. At one time, I even thought it was like old school annuals that existed when I was a child. Then, parents began talking about cyberbullying and monitoring their children's Facebook accounts. I tried that—but kids are smarter than we think, and they would develop avatar personalities difficult to identify and trace. If you demanded the child "friend" you, they would just tweak their profile to ensure certain things were not visible to the parent. The world continued to change with new social forums and teenagers became glued to their smart devices. It was no longer parental guidancerated movies that needed to be monitored; you had to understand all the new platforms children and teenagers could take part in. Then Twitter arrived, and teenagers developed a new language code of their own. I remember asking my son's girlfriend what LOL meant. I had no idea it was being used as "laugh out loud." It was as if the teenage generation developed a secret code in a short period of a couple of years. But more than just using code words and posting unthinkable comments on Facebook, the advent of these social forums helped shape the millennial generation's own thought processes and moral code. Anything and everything went on social media, and it was as if they didn't care who saw what. Cyberbullying, sexting, online dating—the list continues. The computer age became more advanced than the old *Jetsons* cartoon could have ever envisioned.

Individuals seem to be more open with comments on social media. The forum allows individuals to sit behind a computer or smartphone and send out comments or thoughts with little to no accountability for their words. Remember the days of company meetings, where the organizer would ask if there were any questions or comments and no one would raise their hand? Then organizations tried the comment cards, but still, employees would not fill them out. Next came the secret comment box. The list continues. Now employees can post comments and complaints about their employer or some aspect of their job on social forums.

In the past several years, as social media and the millennial generation have become a larger factor in the workforce, organizations have begun including information in their codes of conduct regarding the company's expectations of employees when engaging on social media. These policies often address expected behavior both within and outside the workforce. Social media has stretched the legal boundaries of free speech in America. Shortly, we will discuss concepts related to how organizations should posture their social media policies to be legally and ethically proper.

Regardless of the type of social media, some employees will use the platform as a vetting tool about employers. Comments are made about issues occurring at work, a person's employment status (or lack thereof), and workplace culture. There are even platforms like Glassdoor that allow individuals to rate employers and make comments anonymously.

With this new infusion of social media conduct in the working world, employers are struggling to determine the proper way to balance the individual employee's personal rights and ensure confidentiality of company information. Along with this effort, many employers have also begun to use social media to keep tabs on employees or to vet prospective employees. A 2007 survey by the American Management

Association about how employers were utilizing social media provided some interesting information.

- Twenty-eight percent of employers have fired employees for misuse of e-mails.
- Thirty percent have fired employees for misuse of the Internet.
- One-half of all employers surveyed said they were concerned about their employees browsing social networking sites while at work.
- In some instances, employees have been terminated due to their comments and posts on social media websites.
- Other employers admitted to using social media to conduct background checks on potential hires.

Each of these actions brings with it ethical questions.

- How acceptable is it for employees to use social media to speak about their employers? What about discussing concerns of culture in the workforce?
- Should employees be allowed to access social media websites on company time if it is not an integral part of their job responsibilities?
- If the employee is utilizing his or her own smartphone device to access social media sites, how would the employer know, unless the employee is posting comments during work hours?
- Is it ethical for employers to visit the social sites of prospective employees to assess whether they are a fit for the corporate culture?
- What information can employers utilize from social sites to screen prospective employees?
- What information can employers utilize from social sites to reprimand employees?
- What happens when certain smart devices are company paid but are also allowed to be used for personal purposes?
- What happens when the employee leaves the company and returns the smart device? Is it ethical for the employer to access personal text messaging or e-mail from the employee's archived files?

These are just a few questions that come with the increased usage of social media in today's business world.

A young professional who attended an ethics course I taught relayed an experience he faced when searching for employment. He had interviewed several times with a particular company and was given a job offer pending a background check. After the background check, he was told by the human resource professional the offer was being rescinded. Since he did not have any type of criminal record or credit history issue, he did not understand why the offer had been rescinded. He called the employer to ask. The human resource professional informed him that they regularly do a search of prospective employees' social media sites. They had viewed several of his sites and looked at postings that extended back into his high school days. They did not feel his postings were reflective of their corporate culture. The young man was astonished. The company was viewing postings he had recorded at the age of 17.

Should those have reflected on the person he was at 24? Remember the discussion in earlier chapters about the brain not fully maturing until the age of approximately 24? Was it proper or ethical for the company to utilize the information as a decision factor for employment of this young man? The scenario does point to the fact that individuals need to be cognizant of how they use social media, even for personal purposes.

Ethics and Social Media Policies

At a professional conference, a labor lawyer presented on concepts employers should understand when developing social media policies. She discussed how the concept of free speech came into play. The lawyer relayed the era of social media is bringing a whole new set of issues to the legal world. The legal system now has a whole new aspect of free speech and employee/employer rights to consider.

A recent article on Monster.com cited a case involving a company's social media policy. The National Labor Relations Board (NLRB) filed a complaint against an employer who terminated a staff member for making inappropriate comments about a supervisor on Facebook. The case was eventually settled out of court. However, the company was reprimanded by the court, with several rulings related to how they were allowed to discipline employees who were making comments on social media. They also had to revise their employee handbook policy around workers discussing work conditions with coworkers.

In another incident, an employer was found to have violated a National Labor Relationship Act (NLRA) section when he fired an employee for venting frustration with a manager on Facebook. The employee used profanity-filled language in the post and ended with "Vote YES for the UNION!!!!!" The post was visible to his Facebook friends, including coworkers. The employee posted the comments during working hours but while on break; however, there was no evidence the activity interrupted the work environment or relationship with customers. The comments were found to be in agreement with other employees' complaints about disrespectful treatment by management and their desire to join a union. Yet despite the employee venting and profanity, the company was still viewed as violating the NLRA.

The issue to note with each of these scenarios is rules and laws of social media are evolving, and the concepts around ethical and proper use of social media in the workforce will continue to evolve. Courts are beginning to develop precedent as more and more legal cases are filed. Laws, including long-standing communication laws on trade secrets, labor relations, First Amendment rights, discrimination laws, and more, are being tested.

Recent NLRA statements have indicated certain social media comments can be what is referred to as *protected concerted activity* or union activity. *Concerted activity* is a legal term used in labor policy. It is meant to define employee protection against employer retaliation in the United States. The principle defines the activities workers can partake in without fear of employer retaliation.

The 2010 NLRB fact sheet explains the board began receiving charges in regional offices about employer social media policies and discipline for posting on social media sites. In some cases, the agency found the communications were protected, and there was reasonable cause to believe an employer's policies or disciplinary actions violated federal law.

Employers must stay informed of the rulings associated with social media policies and how they may impact the ability to constrain free speech of employees. Private employers do not have First Amendment concerns. There is no constitutional duty to allow or tolerate free speech. However, they must consider the NLRA and various state laws that prohibit employers from disciplining employees for off-duty conduct.

In an article on Monster.com regarding social media policies and free speech, two labor and employment lawyers were interviewed about social media discussion and how it is interpreted by the courts. It was mentioned that many online activities are considered a form of concerted activity. This extends to Facebook posts on wages or working conditions shared with coworkers. This type of discussion is considered protected under the law until it reaches the point of being disloyal to the employer. However, it is complicated to define the term *disloyal*. The courts must distinguish comments that are complaining about work from other comments which actively seek to reduce business by driving customers away. These concepts begin stretching the corporate boundaries on setting ethical policies.

Internet Usage Policies

From a legal viewpoint, labor lawyers may suggest that employers put in place Internet usage policies as well as social media policies. But employers must be cautious about wording used in those policies that may appear to infringe on an individual's constitutional rights. The policies should carefully outline and clarify information such as:

- The company's expectations regarding infringement of confidential information.
- Use of statements which could be considered slanderous or libelous toward the employer, especially those resulting in a detrimental impact on the business.

Some lawyers suggest companies inform employees that when posting thoughts or comments on social sites about employers, the employee should clarify the comments are personal opinion and not made on behalf of the company.

This is similar to what individuals may refer to as the safe harbor policy. If you have ever been to a conference and heard Federal Bureau of Investigation (FBI) agents speak, they typically begin the presentation with the agents stating the information about to relay is their own personal insights and do not represent the formal stance or opinion of the FBI.

Social Media Sites and the Hiring Process

Individuals in job search mode know when going online to apply for a job, there will be an option to link the application to a social website such as LinkedIn. LinkedIn and other professional social websites encourage users to have a complete profile. This complete profile will often include a photo. Other personal social networking sites such as Facebook ask for information such as birth date, religion, affiliations, or other personal information that, if utilized by an employer in the prescreening process, could be construed as prejudice.

Posting a photo on LinkedIn provides prospective employers a sense of the applicants ethnicity, gender, and even age. Each of these factors, if utilized by an employer in the preemployment screening process could be potential for an applicant to claim discrimination. If the photo or birth date clearly identifies the applicant as an individual whose age is over 55, and all individuals selected for interview are under 40, this could be a cause to claim age discrimination. If the photo identifies the applicant as a certain ethnicity, and the employer has a preconceived perception of the ethnicity, this could also be grounds for discrimination in the hiring process. Of course, if the applicant receives a face-to-face interview, the employer will most likely be able to identify many of these attributes at that time. However, it might be harder to claim discrimination on the part of the employer, because they have had the opportunity to speak to the applicant in person and can claim the selection process was solely based on skills.

This can be a dilemma for the prospective employee but also for the prospective employer. When open access is provided to a LinkedIn profile, viewers can see a good deal of personal demographic information. The catch is, can the employer utilize personal facts they find on these forums to exclude you from the interview process? Most professionals think of LinkedIn as a second form of a résumé. There are firms who instruct individuals how to optimize profiles to obtain more views from potential employers. These firms encourage individuals to insert in their titles "actively seeking new opportunities," "open to all new connections," or "open networker." Each of these phrases may identify the applicant as a person out of work. Examine the "who's viewed my profile" option on LinkedIn, it is evident recruiters use the tool to view information of prospective employees.

Those who have been in the job search mode know it is easier to find a job when you currently have a job. Employers do not like to see long periods of unemployment on a prospective employee's résumé. Some individuals attempt to mask the unemployment period by listing "self-employed"; however, unless some activity or accomplishments can be cited during the self-employment period, employers may eliminate a candidate from the prescreening process because of the length of unemployment or the desire to have someone with a consistent employment history. Is this ethical and legal?

Since it is logical to assume employers will utilize social networking sites to vet and view potential employees in one manner or another, professionals must understand this dynamic and be cognizant when posting information to personal sites. Posting on social sites indicates you have willingly and openly put your information in the public domain. It is similar to company websites. Prospective employees will view those websites to learn more about prospective employers. Although it may seem unethical for recruiters to utilize information on social networking sites to understand the profile of candidates, it is logical to assume this will happen in one form or another. Employers must train recruiters that personal information viewed on social sites should not be utilized in the prescreening process to automatically deny someone an interview. Whether it is ethical or not for an employer to use the information within the hiring process is a good question, but it may be difficult to prove inappropriate intent.

Using Information on Social Media

What does an employer have the right to use and not to use on social media in relation to employees? In general, an employer has the right to discipline employees for inappropriate online behavior during working hours. Assume an employee is spending significant time posting on Facebook or Twitter, browsing shopping sites, or even engaging on gambling sites. This would not be considered work for the benefit of the company. But, like other employment issues, employers must ensure they are consistent when enforcing social media policies. If challenged in a court of law, the employer would be at a disadvantage if found to have disciplined some employees while knowingly allowing others to engage in the same behavior.

Ethical or not, social media will continue to influence individuals' opinions about a person's skills, character, and personality. This influence may stretch to hiring managers or human resource personnel. When participating in any type of blogging forum, understand not everyone will agree with your opinion or the manner in which you express an opinion. The caution for employees and prospective employees is to be cognizant of what you write in the public domain. Understand that a verbal comment may be heard by only a few individuals, whereas a written comment may be placed on a social site for anyone and everyone to see.

Section 2: Ethics and the Generations

Introduction

We would be remiss in not discussing the impact of the generational variances on organizational ethical culture. Each generation has matured with its unique experiences, and those experiences impact the generation's work morals and overall ethical expectations. The morals and values of the varied generations are impacted by events of the period. Briefly, let's discuss some of the social and moral aspects that formed the ethical beliefs of each generation.

As you review this information, understand the attributes listed are those identified by psychologists and researchers of generational values and norms. The attributes are listed as generic in nature and may not reflect the actual behavior of any one specific person.

Baby Boomer I

Born between 1946 and 1954, these individuals entered the workforce between 1963 and 1972. As of 2016, this generation would be between 62 and 74 years in age. There is a strong possibility some of the Baby Boomer I generation is still in the workforce. Life experiences, society, and behaviors were very different during this time. The period is bounded by the Kennedy and Martin Luther King assassinations, the civil rights movement, and the Vietnam War. In general, Boomers I had good economic opportunities and were fairly optimistic about their own lives. Of course, it goes without saying that this generation came up during a period of no computers and few technology inventions and, as a result, have a strong work ethic towards manual processes.

Baby Boomers II

Born between 1955 and 1965, these individuals came into the workforce between 1973 and 1983. This generation is the first post-Watergate generation. Baby Boomers II lost trust in governments and the optimistic view Boomers I may have had. Boomers II had AIDS as part of society. They were also just beginning to see the advent of technology as they entered the college environment. That technology encompassed large mainframe computers stored in huge computer rooms which were kept cool for environmental conditions. Studying information technology in those days was akin to learning the old COBAL programming. Cell phones were not invented during the early Baby Boomer II years. Most Baby Boomers expect some degree of opposition to their opinions. They tend to be workaholics with a belief they can be whatever they want to be.

The Baby Boomer generation entered the workforce in an era where computers didn't exist, workstations were actually closed offices, there were no smartphones and no texting, and there was no caller ID on desk phones. This generation was brought into the workforce with the assumption of hierarchy, boundaries, and being at work by 8 a.m. and not leaving until 5 p.m. or after. Showing respect to superiors was not an option; it was expected. Taking personal time off was viewed differently, and many managers would brag about the fact they had carry-over vacation. This was a period where professionals actually talked to coworkers during the day when questions arose rather than texting or sending a picture. In addition, workers were conditioned that the supervisor was always right. An atmosphere of open and transparent communication was not necessarily in existence. Many managers would view an employee's act of questioning as insubordination. This generation saw the infusion of women into the work culture and grappled with the many dynamics this caused.

As a member of the Baby Boomer II generation, I recall many of the challenges experienced during the interview process and my initial working years. Balancing events that would now be considered potential sexual harassment as well as supervisor intimidation and unethical behavior by superiors was difficult but something expected at that period of time. In the 1980s, many of these concepts were accepted, or heads were turned. If you spoke up, you had to accept the ramifications.

One specific instance I recall occurred during a time when I was with my second employer. It was the mid-1980s, when the environmental issue of asbestos was a strong concern. My employer was doing renovations in our building. Asbestos was found in the rafters in certain areas of the building. Construction workers taped and placed plastic over the entryways of the areas being remediated. However, many workers remained concerned with environmental exposures.

At the time there were five women on my floor who were pregnant. They came to work every day, assured by supervisors that the company was taking adequate precautions. Once the children were born, all five suffered from some health ailment that extended from bronchial problems to other issues. Two of the children died. At the time, no one linked the cause of the children's illnesses to the potential asbestos remediation.

Shortly after these children were born, I became pregnant with my first child. Prior to announcing my pregnancy, I came into the office to find construction in the ceiling rafters directly above my work area. My first concern was breathing in whatever dust was in the air. By mid-morning, I was so nauseous that I had no alternative but to inform my supervisor what was happening. I also mentioned that I was concerned about the potential that the work area had asbestos and wondered how the company was sure there wasn't any risk. My supervisor was very understanding and had me leave for the day. He indicated he would discuss the issue with his superiors. I later found out management was not happy that I had even insinuated there could be a health issue. Luckily, my supervisor was very supportive and actually brought up the recent occurrences of sick babies to women pregnant while the construction was taking place. Whatever he said convinced management they should not take a chance. I was allowed to work from home for about two weeks until the construction was finished. Keep in mind, this was in the mid-1980s, when working from home was not something professionals were able to do. Also, management demeanor at this time was that they were right, and employees were expected to do whatever told. I was fortunate to have an understanding supervisor who spoke up for my cause. Otherwise, I may have been out of a job, or worse.

Oddly enough, my pregnancy met with some complications. My son was born four weeks early with respiratory problems. I returned to work when he was seven weeks old. In his first week at day care, he developed severe pneumonia and was hospitalized for over two weeks. He was very ill, and although he recovered, he continued to have many respiratory issues through his teenage years. Although there is no proof, I wonder whether the workplace construction had something to do with the sick children born to my coworkers as well as myself. What did management know and not know, and how many other individuals from that time period were affected?

Generation X

These individuals were born between 1966 and 1976 and entered the workforce in 1988–1994. This was the first generation of the latchkey kids (whose parents were most likely in the Baby Boomer II generation). Gen X is often characterized by high levels of skepticism, "what's in it for me," and a reputation for some of the worst music ever to gain popularity. Moving into adulthood, the aspect of parental divorce during the childhood of many Gen Xers is one of the most decisive experiences impacting how this generation feels about the family unit. Gen Xers are among the best-educated generations, with 29% gaining their bachelor or higher degree. The Gen Xers became even more accustomed to technology. By the time they entered the workforce in the late 1980s, the prevalence of personal computers and e-mail was beginning to enter the corporate structure. Gen Xers with their better education caught on quickly.

Although this generation may not have grown up with social media, as soon as they entered the workforce, the beginning of social media and the Internet came upon the scene. Companies were beginning to move the large computer mainframe to the personal desktop applications. Technology was still new, and many individuals had to learn the DOS application and understand the aspect of floppy disks. Gen Xers began to quickly adapt to these new forms of communication and work processes. Technology had a significant impact on the workforce during this period. This generation has a sense of entitlement, partly because of how they were raised by their Baby Boomer parents. Gen X workers saw the hard labor put in by Baby Boomers and searched for easier ways to make their living. Gen Xers are generally comfortable with authority; they want to be listened to and will work as hard as is needed. They have an attitude of "take care of yourself." They put a strong emphasis on work–life balance.

Gen Y (millennials)

This generation, born between 1977 and 1994, entered the workforce between 1998 and 2006. This generation, due to their latchkey exposure, is very much the entitled generation. They were beginning to be exposed to the new technology and "new math."

The millennial generation is a whole new breed. They have grown up with computers and smart devices. The generation is much more tech savvy and comfortable with the slang language used in communication. They have been brought up through an educational system that promoted and encouraged teamwork, online studying, and open questioning of team members. Their preference for work environments is open office space rather than closed-in offices. The era of telecommuting and working from home has replaced being at the office 12 hours a day. They also expect and demand more flexibility between their personal life and their professional obligations.

Gen Z

These individuals were born between 1995 and 2012, entering the workforce in 2013–2020. Not much is known about Gen Z yet. We do know a lot about the environment they are being raised in and the educational tools they are exposed to. Gen Z kids will grow up highly sophisticated in media and information technology and tech savvy techniques.

Combination of Generations

With the economic slump of the 2000s, many Baby Boomers are working further into what previously was considered retirement years.

In addition, there is the influx of new millennials into the workforce. This combination of generations has created an additional dynamic. For older baby boomers in their late 50s and early 60s, the topic of ethics and ethical behavior may have a different meaning than it does to the millennial generation.

Consider these stark comparatives, and now envision a workforce made up of baby boomers, Gen X, and Gen Y. The dynamics of what is said, how it is said, what is done, how it is done, and where it is done become more difficult to gain consensus. Now, throw another twist into the mixture. Consider that the Gen Xer is now the supervisor of the Baby Boomer. Each of these scenarios by themselves can create ethical issues. Combined, it is like a EF-four tornado waiting to hit. In some ways, it is similar to when women entered the professional workforce. That time period created many issues such as identifying the boundaries of sexual harassment, diversity in the workforce, equal pay for equal work, and identifying candidates for promotion.

As the mixture of the workforce changes, ethical culture will change. This isn't to say organizations have to change their ethics code, but they will have to recognize the variance in learning and communication styles. They also must recognize the differences in the generations, their work style and work expectations, and how these can impact work atmosphere. Let's consider a couple of scenarios.

Scenario One: Work Atmosphere Your company is a new entrepreneurial venture selling leading-edge health and cosmetic products. At the corporate headquarters, scientists, chemists, sales personnel, and back-office personnel maintain their home base. The company was founded by a group of latestage millennials with a strong interest in the health and wellness markets. The target audience for the product is the collegeage and new millennial worker. As the product has grown in popularity, the founders have employed skilled chemists to enhance the formulation and increase market share. Your workforce employs a diverse range of generational workers.

Following are specific facts about the workforce:

- The founders are late-stage millennials with innovative, aggressive, entrepreneurial, and individualistic goals for the company. Their philosophy for the corporate work environment is an open atmosphere with minimal physical barriers and offices.

- Sales management is primarily Gen Xers with a background in sales. They maintain offices at the headquarters. These managers are expressing concern regarding the open work environment. They feel a need for privacy in order to effectively conduct discussions with customers and staff. In addition, you notice these managers are flexing their work schedules due to family obligations. They feel they can more effectively speak to staff and customers in an atmosphere where there is minimal background noise and the discussions can be confidential.

- The sales force is composed primarily of young millennials and some late-stage Gen Xers. The millennial owners have a theory about how sales should be approached.

- The Gen Xers are primarily assigned to corporate health and wellness accounts. Their maturity allows them to better apply sales techniques in the corporate setting. However, with this division of responsibility comes a variation in how the individuals align their schedules.

  The millennial salesperson is assigned to the college market. They often staff the sales booths at university gatherings and speak to students regarding the product. They also work to find contacts within fraternity and sorority settings to provide product demonstrations. The company has noticed that the millennial workforce is taking advantage of the college setting and adjusting their work schedules to meet their personal preferences. They often attend sorority or fraternity functions on company time (saying that they are there to try to promote the product). This makes it difficult to conduct staff sales meetings.

- The chemists are typically late-term Gen Xers and Baby Boomers who are physically located in a laboratory setting at headquarters. The chemists are disgruntled because, due to the nature of their work, they are required to be in the office on very set and rigid schedules. They often work an abundance of overtime to meet the requirements set by the Gen X sales management on new product rollouts. In addition, the chemists are often excluded from corporate update meetings because millennial management views chemists as having a set role, which is to develop and enhance product. The millennial founders and management do not see a benefit in having chemists involved in corporate meetings which discuss sales and marketing strategy. The chemists disagree, because the sales and marketing strategy directly impacts their work schedule.

- The back-office personnel are typically late-stage Gen Xers and some Baby Boomers, who have experience in the specialty accounting required for the business. These individuals also maintain standard work hours at the corporate headquarters. The back-office personnel are typically excluded from many of the corporate functions. Since the company was started by late-stage millennials, their philosophy is that "it's all about the sale," and they see the back-office function as a needed evil. They do not see how the connection of the two could enhance the value of the company.
- The company has invested technology to allow the sales force to work remotely but has not invested in technology to allow the back-office personnel who manage payroll, accounts payable, and other necessary accounting and financial functions to work remotely.

Since staffing has grown tremendously in the last six months, your company has a need to establish standard human resource guidelines along with a code of conduct. Because of the mixture of work philosophies and requirements of the workforce, the company is having a difficult time getting workers to accept and agree to standard guidelines. What would you do in this circumstance to ensure all employees are treated equitably, ethically, and fairly?

Scenario Alternatives Since the company has a diverse mix of generational workers, you must obtain a strong understanding of the various traits, beliefs, and attitudes important to each group. There is a theory that leaders don't need to develop generation-specific skills; rather, they should be able to adjust leadership styles to suit the individual. In this case, it appears the leaders are millennial workers who may not have as much experience in the corporate world. There is a potential that Gen Xers and millennial workers would benefit from leadership training specifically focused on traits of the various generational workers. This may assist in adapting communications and processes to effectively reach each generational worker. The fact the company is owned by millennial workers, and they have chosen to invest in technology for the sales force and not for other working groups, may appear to other workers as favoritism for those individuals who are closest to the age group of the owners. The owners may not understand the importance of ensuring proper financial reporting or how improving technology processes for the back office and chemists could also improve overall efficiency in the workplace.

The issues noted have created a tense atmosphere between the working groups. This has resulted in questionable comments and representations of the employer by employees on social media sites. In addition, management is concerned the comments on social media, as well as the general employee atmosphere, are beginning to impact the effectiveness of the workforce.

From the perspective of human resource policies, management must ensure they understand the various concerns of each of the employee workgroups, as well as the various generational workers. A policy should consider the various unique traits of each area's job responsibilities, how they must execute those responsibilities, and the requirements for maintaining a fair and equitable work atmosphere. For example, the millennial salesperson is responsible for meeting with college-age students. The scenario indicated the salespeople attend fraternity and sorority outings on company time. Would this be considered ethically correct? The human resource policies should clarify aspects of gifts and entertainments as well as acceptable behavior when conducting company business or representing the company on business time.

If a policy is established to allow professionals to work remotely, it should be equitably applied across all work functions. The scenario stated the back-office professionals and chemists do not have the information technology infrastructure to allow remote working situations. Technology has been provided for sales personnel to effectively work remotely. The company may have to reevaluate their capital investment strategy to determine where advanced technology is most needed to meet the strategies of the company, as well as workers' needs.

From a code of conduct perspective, a company should develop a code which represents the overall philosophy of the business. The code should not be developed for specific categories of generational workers but should be one that is fair to all. It should be one which demonstrates the values and objectives of the organization. Some of the issues the organization will want to address include:

- Expectations for maintaining company information private.
- Expectations for behavior by employees when representing the company.
- Clarification of the concepts of integrity, respect, and honesty. This may mean different things to different generational workers. The concept should not change based on the generation workforce but, potentially, the communication method to ensure that each worker fully understands the expectations may change.
- Expectations surrounding acceptance of gifts by salespersons.

Summary

This is certainly a new age, and companies must be ready, willing, and able to adjust processes to appropriately manage ethics and conduct in the workplace. Management must understand the dynamics of today's workforce and how those dynamics might manifest in their own work environments.

Section 3: Ethics and Business Globalization

The evolution of technology and work processes, combined with the limitless workforce boundaries, creates new and unique challenges to enabling ethical culture in business. We previously analyzed how combining various factions of workers with varying beliefs under one corporate entity can create varying opinions and observations on what is proper and what is not. Now we add the additional complexity of companies that operate in various areas of the world. Corporate culture may be different from one country to another. It becomes harder to develop holistic policies that can effectively translate multiple boundaries.

In the United States, we have the Foreign Corrupt Practices Act (FCPA), which, among other activities, makes facilitating payments a criminal offense. In many countries, what may be defined by the United States as facilitating payments may be looked at as a way of doing business. It becomes difficult for workers to apply U.S. requirements and laws in these foreign territories. Yet, compliance with these laws is a critical aspect of doing business for U.S. companies. Organizations spend a significant amount of time and training to communicate the rules and laws around this issue to their employees. Let's consider a couple of scenarios.

Scenario One: Globalization of Business and Ethics

A construction company is building a large facility for a customer in Vietnam. The construction of the facility is projected to take at least two years. Due to the skills required to construct the facility, a large number of engineers and construction professionals have been assigned as expatriates for the project and have been moved from the U.S. to Vietnam.

The project manager has been given very strict time lines for the project, based on the needs of the customer. If a time line is missed, it could result in delay of the finalization of the project, which could significantly impact the country as well as the success of the project.

In Vietnam, there are numerous procedures and significant paperwork required for various types of work such as permitting, obtaining new equipment, bringing new workers on site, hiring local workers, and others. Within the first three months of the project, the on-site manager begins to identify significant issues with obtaining the proper government approvals and sign-offs on a multitude of items. The government officials who come to the site to provide the approvals often allude to the fact that the approval process can take many months unless the company is willing to expedite the process by paying a special surcharge on the permit fee. The operations manager realizes the government official is actually referring to cash payments that would be made to the official directly so he will expedite the request. The operations manager knows this practice is against U.S. FCPA laws. He reports the concern to his supervisor at the corporate headquarters in the United States. The supervisor encourages the operations manager to continue to work with the government official, because it is critical the process not be delayed, especially due to paperwork issues. As the operations manager, you continue to work with the government official and explain to him that these types of payments are not allowed according to U.S. law. The government official provides a method by which the payments can be made without appearing to be facilitating payments from your organization. You again consult with your supervisor back in the United States. His comment is, "You know the project time line. You need to work with the government official to ensure you obtain the required authorization in line with the project schedule." What should you do?

Scenario One: Alternatives   Although the answer seems straightforward given the description of the scenario, the operations manager is in a very difficult situation. The supervisor's comments are stressing that the project must stay on schedule; however, the supervisor has not specifically told the employee to make the facilitating payments. His response could be considered an intimidation factor. The operations manager has relocated to Vietnam for two years. It is only three months into the assignment, and he could fear for his job. He has clearly heard the supervisor's statements of "work with the government official" but also "the project must stay on schedule." The operations manager could take a few different actions:

- Speak to the supervisor again, and let him know the government official will not provide the requisite approvals without the under-the-table payment. Tell the supervisor that based on company policy, these payments would not be appropriate and a discussion needs to occur regarding the impact the nonpayment of these fees will have on the construction schedule. This will require the operations manager to stand his ground and ensure the supervisor knows that if he is unable to take the issue up the chain, the operations manager will alert the senior manager on the project.
- Report the issue to the senior manager whom the supervisor reports to. Explain what the predicament is and that he has consulted with his supervisor. Let the senior manager know his concerns regarding the potential for facilitating payments.

Make it clear the government officials are putting pressure on him related to project delays if the payments are not made. Possibly, the senior manager has stronger connections within the country who can work through the issues with the government officials.

- If neither of these options works, and the senior manager and supervisor still require the operations manager to do what is needed to work with the government official, the operations manager must be prepared to blow the whistle on his employer. This is easier said than done. The operations manager is putting his job at risk. However, the alternative is being charged with a criminal offense under the FCPA.

Section 4: Internal Audit's Ethical Role in the Future

So, what is internal audit's role in the ethical evaluations and culture of organizations in the future? Again, we need a crystal ball. Since organizations all take a different approach to internal audit's role within the organization for ethics, predicting a future role is difficult. However, following the guidelines outlined by the *Standards*, internal audit would benefit by assuming an ongoing education and evaluation role in company procedures which define and evaluate ethical behavior. Some of the tactics outlined in this book could be utilized by the auditor in the future. Of course, we don't know what technology will bring us in the next 20 years, and the evolution of job roles, the workforce, and business in general will have a strong influence on what the internal auditor will be able to do. In addition, the manner in which the global economy continues to evolve will most definitely have an impact on how organizations establish, manage, and monitor their ethical behavior.

From an internal audit viewpoint, the best advice is to stay vigilant to the *Standards* and understand the profession's code of conduct. Ensure your organization understands the potential role of the internal auditor in evaluating corporate governance issues. Provide them with insight into how this can provide overall organizational value. From a profession viewpoint, for internal auditors to continue to advance in the business world, organizations must see value in the CAE position and the inclusion of that role as part of the leadership team and strategy-making decisions. This will provide auditors with a direct link to corporate strategy issues and potential insights into issues that may result in ethical dilemmas down the road.

The Final Word

By considering the concepts covered within this book, the internal auditor can obtain new insights into evaluating and managing ethical issues. In today's age, it is difficult to predict if there will be a simplistic answer to the ethical issues faced in the corporate world. However, by understanding the dynamics and psychology behind ethics as well as how individual morals and traits impact individual perceptions, auditors can move forward and advance their knowledge of ethics and its impact on the workforce. Remember the acronym used in Chapter 3 to describe ethics.

E —Everyone is responsible.
T —Tone at the top is essential.
H —Honesty is the best policy.
I —Integrity is a measure of ethics.
C —Corporate social responsibility is expected.
S —Silence is not acceptable.

Index

A

ABC Inc., 212
Action plans, for ethics, 240–243
    examination and
        investigation, 241
    framework, 240
    issue evaluation, 240–241
    issue remediation, 242–243
    issue reporting, 242
Administration of Quality
    Supervision, Inspection,
    and Quarantine
    (AQSIQ), 206
AIDS, 255
American Management Association,
    247–248
Applied ethics, 66
AQSIQ, *see* Administration of
    Quality Supervision,
    Inspection, and Quarantine
    (AQSIQ)
ARCO, *see* Atlantic Richfield
    Company (ARCO)
Atlantic Richfield Company
    (ARCO), 205
Auditing Standard 5, 32

B

Baby Boomer I, 254–255
Baby Boomers II, 255–257
Behavior curriculum, 68–72
Board program assessment,
    232–233
BP, *see* British Petroleum (BP)
British Petroleum (BP), 205
Business consequentialist theories,
    60–66
Business deontology ethics, 59–60
Business globalization, and ethics,
    263–266
Business virtue ethics, 57–59

C

CAE, *see* Chief audit executive
    (CAE)

CFO, *see* Chief financial officer (CFO)

Chief audit executive (CAE), 4, 70, 108, 158, 177

Chief financial officer (CFO), 4, 100, 109, 181

Chief legal officer (CLO), 47, 85, 109, 187

CLO, *see* Chief legal officer (CLO)

COBAL programming, 255

Code of Ethics, internal auditors

and corporate values, 90–92

global, diverse, and expanding workforce, 92–99

and internal auditing, 73–74, 76

objectivity, independence, and assurance, 73

overview, 72–73

principles, 76–82

competency, 77, 81–82

confidentiality, 77, 80–81

integrity, 76–79

objectivity, 77, 79–80

professional skepticism, 74–75

Rules of Conduct, 82–90

Committee of Sponsoring Organizations (COSO), 70

commitment to competence, 114–116

dissecting ethics, 132–136

implications of

challenges, 127–128

overview, 126–127

internal audit's role, 128–131

internal control responsibilities, 116–123

organizational requirements

considerations when examining, 125–126

overview, 123

principle mapping process, 124–125

and organizational structure, 113–114

overview, 103–105

role of board of directors, 107–113

updated framework, 105–107

Communication, ethical, 233–239

Company program assessment, 230–232

CompuServe, 246

Concerted activity, 250

Consequentialism, 57

business consequentialist theories, 60–66

Control environment, and ethics, 209–214

evaluation of, 209–211

measuring, 212–214

overview, 209

Corporate director's ethical fiduciary duty

evaluating board composition, 218–226

overview, 217–218

Corporate hotline history, 229–230

Corporate scandals, 8–22. *see also specific types*

Corporate social responsibility (CSR), 135–136, 202–207

Corporate values, 90–92

corporate social responsibility (CSR), 135–136, 202–207

honesty, 133–134, 207–208

integrity, 134–135, 199–201

loyalty and respect, 208–209

overview, 199

COSO, *see* Committee of Sponsoring Organizations (COSO)

CSR, *see* Corporate social responsibility (CSR)

D

Deontology ethics, 56–57
  business, 59–60
Dodd–Frank law, 230, 233

E

Employee hotlines, 226–227
Enron, 7–9, 26, 28, 36, 46, 57, 104,
      105, 136, 139, 147, 209,
      217, 220
Ethical communication, 233–239
Ethical/moral judgments, 66–68
Ethics
  action plans for, 240–243
    examination and
      investigation, 241
    framework, 240
    issue evaluation, 240–241
    issue remediation, 242–243
    issue reporting, 242
  and business globalization,
      263–266
  challenges to, 27–33
  communicating with
      management and audit
      committee, 233–239
  and control environment,
      209–214
    evaluation of, 209–211
    measuring, 212–214
    overview, 209
  and corporate scandals, 8–22
  corporate values, 90–92
  and generations, 254–263
    Baby Boomer I, 254–255
    Baby Boomers II, 255–257
    combination of, 258–263
    Gen Y (millennials), 258
    Gen Z, 258
    Generation X, 257–258
    overview, 254

  and high profile cases analysis,
      22–27
  internal audit's role in, 266–267
  and internal auditors
    Code of Ethics, 72–99
    internal pressure, 177–178
    international professional
      practices framework
      standards for, 38–48
    overview, 177
    scenarios, 178–198
    working with diverse cultures
      and beliefs, 99–102
  learning, 1–5
  management and board
      acceptance of, 157–159
  and maturity model approach
    and assessment process,
      166–169
    developing, 160–161
    identifying attributes, 161
    matrix customization, 162–163
    naming convention for stages,
      163–166
    overview, 159–160
    stage definitions, 162
    subject matter experts, 162
    utilizing output, 169
  and moral compass, 33–38
  and perception, 156–157
  psychology of, 49–51
  and questionnaires
    to evaluate ethical culture, 146
    overview, 137–139
    process of, 139–145
  reporting ethical issues
    employee hotlines, 226–227
    importance of, 227
    overview, 226
    protocols for, 228–233
  and social media policies,
      249–251
  and sports

overview, 171–173
scandals, 173–176
and surveys
analyzing results, 152–153
and company's code of
conduct, 146–147
distribution, 151–152
effectiveness of, 145–148
logistical information, 150
objectives of, 148–149
one-on-one, 152
online, 151
overview, 137–139
process of, 139–145
purpose of, 150
requirement for anonymity,
150–151
testing, 152
theories and principles
applied ethics, 66
description, 52–53
everyday moral/ethical
judgments, 66–68
meta-ethics, 54–55
normative ethics, 55–66
overview, 51–52
university organizational theory
and behavior curriculum,
68–72
Everyday moral/ethical judgments,
66–68

F

Facebook, 140, 246, 247, 249–253
Facilitation, 167–168
FBI, *see* Federal Bureau of
Investigation (FBI)
FCPA, *see* Foreign Corrupt Practices
Act (FCPA)
Federal Bureau of Investigation
(FBI), 251
First Amendment, 250

Foreign Corrupt Practices Act
(FCPA), 85, 264
Framework action plan, 240

G

Gen Y (millennials), 258
Gen Z, 258
General Audit Management
conference, 139
Generation X, 257–258
Generations, and ethics, 254–263
Baby Boomer I, 254–255
Baby Boomers II, 255–257
combination of, 258–263
Gen Y (millennials), 258
Gen Z, 258
Generation X, 257–258
overview, 254
Global and diverse workforce, 92–99
Goodell, Roger, 174
Gulf oil spill, 205

H

Honesty, 133–134, 207–208

I

IIA, *see* Institute of Internal
Auditors (IIA)
Information usage, and social media,
253–254
Institute of Internal Auditors
(IIA), 72
Integrity, 39–40, 42–43, 76, 83–85,
134–135, 199–201
illegal actions, 86
legitimate and ethical
objectives, 86
Internal auditors, and ethics
Code of Ethics
competency, 41–42

confidentiality, 41
and corporate values, 90–92
global, diverse, and expanding
  workforce, 92–99
independence and
  assurance, 73
integrity, 39–40
and internal auditing,
  73–74, 76
international professional
  practices framework
  standards for, 38–48
objectivity, 40, 73
overview, 72–73
principles, 76–82
professional skepticism, 74–75
Rules of Conduct, 82–90
internal pressure, 177–178
overview, 177
questionnaires
  to evaluate ethical culture, 146
  overview, 137–139
  process of, 139–145
scenarios, 178–198
and surveys
  analyzing results, 152–153
  and company's code of
    conduct, 146–147
  distribution, 151–152
  effectiveness of, 145–148
  logistical information, 150
  objectives of, 148–149
  one-on-one, 152
  online, 151
  overview, 137–139
  process of, 139–145
  purpose of, 150
  requirement for anonymity,
    150–151
  testing, 152
Internet
  forums, 246
  usage policies, 251

Interviews
  and company's code of conduct,
    146–147
  effectiveness of, 145–148
  overview, 137–139
  process of, 139–145
  techniques
    building rapport, 154
    controlling, 154–155
    listening, 155
    and overanalysis, 155
    planning, 154
Issue evaluation, ethical, 240–241
Issue remediation, ethical, 242–243
Issue reporting, ethical, 242

K

King, Martin Luther, 254

L

LinkedIn, 129, 140, 246, 252
Loyalty, and respect, 208–209

M

Management philosophy, and
    operating style, 214–217
Maturity model approach, and
    ethics
  and assessment process,
    166–169
  developing, 160–161
  identifying attributes, 161
  matrix customization, 162–163
  naming convention for stages,
    163–166
  overview, 159–160
  stage definitions, 162
  subject matter experts, 162
  utilizing output, 169
Meta-ethics, 54–55

Michael Vick dogfighting scandal, 174–175
Millennial generation, *see* Gen Y (millennials)
Monster.com, 249, 251
Moral compass, and ethics, 33–38
Moral/ethical judgments, 66–68

N

National Commission on Fraudulent Financial Reporting, *see* Treadway Commission
National Football League (NFL), 173–175, 204
National Labor Relations Board (NLRB), 249
National Labor Relationship Act (NLRA), 250
New Orleans Saints "Bounty" scandal, 173–174
NFL, *see* National Football League (NFL)
NLRA, *see* National Labor Relationship Act (NLRA)
NLRB, *see* National Labor Relations Board (NLRB)
Normative ethics, 55
consequentialism, 57, 60–66
deontology, 56–57, 59–60
virtue, 55–59

O

One-on-one surveys, 152
Online surveys, 151

P

PCAOB, *see* Public Companies Accounting and Oversight Board (PCAOB)

Penn State child sex abuse scandal, 204
Perception, and ethics, 156–157
Pete Rose betting scandal, 175
Pinterest, 246
Principle mapping process, 124–125
Professional skepticism, 74–75
Protected concerted activity, 250
Psychology, of ethics, 49–51
Public Companies Accounting and Oversight Board (PCAOB), 32, 104

Q

Questionnaires
to evaluate ethical culture, 146
overview, 137–139
process of, 139–145

R

Ray Rice physical abuse, 175
Respect, and loyalty, 208–209
Rules of Conduct, 82–90
competency, 45–46, 89–90
confidentiality, 44–45, 89
integrity, 42–43, 83–85
illegal actions, 86
legitimate and ethical objectives, 86
objectivity, 43–44, 86–88

S

Sarbanes–Oxley (SOX) legislation, 7, 8, 10, 13, 24, 28–31, 46, 103, 104–105, 107–108, 117, 123, 128, 138, 146, 192, 209, 210, 214–215, 217, 220, 221, 225
SEC, *see* Securities and Exchange Commission (SEC)

Securities and Exchange
      Commission (SEC), 104
Silence, 136
Snapchat, 246
Social media and technology,
      246–254
   ethics and policies, 249–251
   and information usage, 253–254
   Internet usage policies, 251
   sites and hiring process, 252–253
SOX, *see* Sarbanes–Oxley (SOX)
      legislation
Sports, and ethics
   overview, 171–173
   scandals, 173–176
      Michael Vick dogfighting,
         174–175
      New Orleans Saints "Bounty,"
         173–174
      Pete Rose betting, 175
      Ray Rice physical abuse, 175
Super Bowl, 176, 210
Surveys
   analyzing results, 152–153
   and company's code of conduct,
      146–147
   distribution, 151–152
   effectiveness of, 145–148
   logistical information, 150
   objectives of, 148–149
   one-on-one, 152
   online, 151

   overview, 137–139
   process of, 139–145
   purpose of, 150
   requirement for anonymity,
      150–151
   testing, 152

T

Time magazine, 49
Treadway Commission, 103
Twitter, 129, 246, 253
Tyco, 10–11, 28, 209, 220

U

University organizational theory,
      68–72

V

Vick, Michael, 174–175
Vietnam War, 254
Virtue ethics, 55–56
   business, 57–59

W

Whistleblower procedures, 228–229
Wikis, 246
WorldCom, 9–10, 28, 209, 220